THE POWER OF PERSONAL INFLUENCE

THE POWER OF PERSONAL INFLUENCE

Richard Hale
Peter Whitlam

McGRAW-HILL BOOK COMPANY

London · New York · St Louis · San Francisco · Auckland · Bogotá
Caracas · Lisbon · Madrid · Mexico · Milan · Montreal · New Delhi
Panama · Paris · San Juan · São Paulo · Singapore · Sydney · Tokyo · Toronto

Published by
McGraw-Hill Book Company Europe
Shoppenhangers Road, Maidenhead, Berkshire, SL6 2QL, England
Telephone 01628 23432
Fax 01628 770224

British Library Cataloguing in Publication Data

Hale, Richard
    Power of Personal Influence
    I. Title II. Whitlam, Peter
    158.1

    ISBN 0–07-709131–0

Library of Congress Cataloging-in-Publication Data

The cataloging-in-publication data of this title is available
from the Library of Congress, Washington DC, USA

12345   98765

Typeset by Nick Allen Editorial Services, Oxford
and printed and bound in Great Britain by the University Press, Cambridge.

Printed on permanent paper in compliance with ISO Standard 9706.

This book is dedicated to
Shan and Madeleine
whose commitment and patience
led us to realize our vision of
'the power of personal influence'

Contents

Foreword

The idea of power is central to management, business, politics, and just about any sphere in which people play a part. But there were periods in the last couple of decades when people—at least ordinary people—seemed to be secondary. Real power, it seemed, lay with inanimate multinational corporations, wielding enormous influence not just over nameless cogs in an institutional machine, but over whole societies. During these times the 'search for excellence' was a search for excellent companies, not excellent people. And the panacea was more likely to be a seven-point model or new structure than any change that Joe or Mary might bring about at a personal level. As has often turned out to be the case, the management flavour of the decade and the unquestioned wisdom of the gurus flew in the face of common sense. The excellent companies, it turned out, owed their success largely to an individual leader who provided the vision and determination that no articles of association could provide. But more than that, these apparently special people relied on veritable armies of ordinary folk—people who got the ideas, made the mistakes and learned the lessons, went the extra mile, and wielded the kind of power that changed whole business landscapes. Nor, it seems, were the top people so special in any event. They followed—mostly unknowingly—the very principles of personal power and influence that are available to every one of us. These principles—principles that we see at work in those we admire all around us, and the learnable skills that accompany them—are explained clearly in *The Power of Personal Influence*.

The current vogue of empowerment, in its many varieties, recognizes this dimension of real people power. And, whatever the lip-service paid in many companies, real leaders repeatedly identify their number one challenge as releasing the full potential of all their people. They know where the answer lies—and they know the impact. This devolving of power, when it happens, is accompanied by quantum and sometimes dramatic change. There is no limit to what people can achieve—and it starts at a personal level.

With the increasing availability of technology, and the removal of whole layers of management, the people factor has become critical for competitiveness and survival. *The Power of Personal Influence* makes an important contribution to this sea-change, which I think will turn out to be one of the most significant factors associated with the heralding of the new millennium. The individual—at every level in the organization—takes on a very special significance. And we do not have to wait for the power mantle to fall on us, or a memo that says we are empowered. Personal power is within personal control. It is largely a DIY matter.

There are signs galore of this 'people' phenomenon. By courtesy of the ubiquitous personal computer and information superhighway, ordinary people in even the smallest companies have virtually unlimited access to the world of information, and the power this brings—another inroad into the old power of the large organization.

Yet with all our new-found resources, the gross inequality of power and achievement seems set to continue. One person, with no great hereditary advantage, wields enormous power, while another, blessed with a more-than-adequate brain and natural talents, achieves so little. *The Power of Personal Influence* recognizes the potential of every one of us to achieve much more, and make an impact in whatever sphere we choose. But, more than that, it gives all the practical, commonsense help we need to release that power.

Some important research has gone into this book, which offers the right balance between what we *do* and how we *think* in interpersonal situations. Richard Hale and Peter Whitlam have vast experience in applying the skills described, and this comes across in the many illustrations based on lives cases taken from business and personal life, which have a true and familiar ring. The result is a comprehensive and very accessible self-coaching manual for influencing others—and understanding yourself better in the process. Some of the techniques outlined are extraordinarily effective, and the results might almost sound magical. Some of the skills may involve important questions about ourselves and our attitudes. But in this book any mystique is stripped bare, jargon is either clearly explained or eliminated, and you are left with simple, effective, win–win ways to achieve what you want. Enjoy a journey of learning and step-by-step improvement that will translate into a whole new world of personal power and confidence.

Dr Harry Alder*

---

* Author of *The Right Brain Manager, NLP: The New Art and Science of Getting What You Want, Think Like a Leader, NLP for Trainers,* and *The Right Brain Time Manager.*

Acknowledgements

Many people helped us in the research, design, and development of this book, and it would be impossible to acknowledge everyone individually.

However, we would like to acknowledge the special support and contributions received from the following people and organizations in helping us to produce *The Power of Personal Influence*:

Dr Harry Alder

Management Centre Europe

and all those who have contributed ideas through our research, our seminars and consulting assignments.

FOR FURTHER INFORMATION

The authors would be pleased to hear from you if you would like to discuss the subject of influencing skills further or if you are interested in training courses or seminars on 'The Power of Personal Influence'. They can be contacted in the following ways:

Mr Richard Hale
Asset
'The Birches'
2 The Dingle
Coombe Dingle
Bristol BS9 2PA
United Kingdom
Tel: + 44 117 9682 299
Fax: + 44 117 9682 299
e-mail: rhale@asset.co.uk

Dr Peter Whitlam
Asset
'Broomhill'
21 Cliff Drive
Cromer
Norfolk NR27 0AW
United Kingdom
Tel: +0 44 1263 515 150
Fax: +0 44 1263 515 150
e-mail: whitlam@asset.co.uk

Background

1 The background

Chapter objectives

- To explain the background to the book and our motivation for writing it.
- To introduce our recent research both into the identification of the competencies as well as the use of mental imagery in goal achievement.
- To discuss the nature of power and why personal power is becoming increasingly important in organizations.
- To look at some of the significant business trends affecting the individual skills required for success.
- To discuss the steps of influencing as shown in the 'EDICT' model of the influencing process, and introduce the identified primary and secondary competencies.
- To explain how to get the most out of this book.

AN HISTORICAL PERSPECTIVE

The Power of Personal Influence was born out of two aspects of our work with international managers. Firstly since 1988 we have delivered a successful management development programme of the same name to hundreds of managers each year.

What these managers have in common is a desire for self-insight and exposure to a range of techniques and behaviours that will improve their ability to make an impact and raise their influencing skills. While this programme is focused primarily on the context of the managers' organization, we inevitably pursue the subject of influencing in everyday situations. Arguably most human encounters provide the opportunity to influence others, and we strongly believe that the behaviours and skills we address are transferable from one context to another. In a similar way our work across Europe, as well as in the United States and Japan, tends to suggest that the findings of our research and the subsequent principles of our teachings hold good in different multicultural environments. Much of the material presented in this book is drawn from our experience of the 'Power of Personal Influence' Programme; in fact as a reader you are encouraged to use the book in a very practical way to stimulate ideas, to help you to practise techniques and to provide an opportunity for focused reflection.

A major drive behind the book stems from our desire to share our research into two very different, yet related areas.

Firstly a critical, yet often neglected, dimension of the influencing process is that of the mental or psychological approach taken by successful people.

Traditionally skills training programmes and books have tended to focus mainly on the visible or audible techniques of influencing and negotiation. In other words it has been possible to identify the right words to say and how to say them, and these are the skills which are learnt and practised. There is very little evidence, however, of an equally practical approach being taken to addressing the internal or psychological techniques which we have found to be just as important.

Our studies clearly demonstrate that such techniques are frequently used either consciously or intuitively by many successful leaders in organizations. We have also found that where training addresses only the development of behavioural skills, without exploring the appropriate mental processes, then there is a decreased likelihood of the successful transfer of such training.

Our interviews with chairmen and chief executives of multinational organizations identified a number of specific common characteristics these people displayed in relation to their internal thought processes. These included the effective use of inner dialogues or 'background conversations', as well as recognizing the importance of their own perceptual or mental processes. We found that such individuals tended to make explicit use of both mental practice and imagery/visualization to improve all aspects of their current and future performance.

Sports psychologists have known for some time that mental practice can improve actual physical performance. There is also evidence of the successful application of imagery in the sphere of medicine to assist the healing process, as well as enabling psychologists to help individuals who may experience a number of issues like fears and phobias. Until now, however, research into the application of such techniques in the teaching and business field has been primarily anecdotal in nature.

This study, combined with the simultaneous evolution of the influencing skills development programme, led to the realization that such mental processes could in fact be learnt, and that such learning would significantly improve the likelihood of new skills becoming 'lasting' or embedded in the behaviour of the learner. We will therefore be looking at how to use such techniques in order to improve your chances of success.

The second area of our research was aimed at identifying the skills or competencies of successful influencing. To do this we involved over 1000 individuals over a period of three years and identified that those that were perceived by others as being strong influencers— those who appeared to share a series of key skills or competencies.

These competencies were later accurately defined, and as a result of further analysis we were able to recognize that some of these behaviours could be classified as primary, or of critical importance, while the others were secondary or of slightly lesser value. With this latter group of competencies, an overriding consideration was the application of the competence only in specific situations. For example, listening was seen as a primary competence, needing to be employed in all influencing situations, whereas *controlled demeanour* was seen as being important only in a number of specific situations.

UNDERSTANDING POWER, INFLUENCE, AND AUTHORITY

Influencing may be defined in many different ways; however, for the purposes of our book we have defined it as follows:

> Influencing is the process of getting other people to accept our view(s) and feel happy about it; and for them to remain persuaded and enthusiastic enough to positively influence other people.

Our definition aims to show how influence should not be seen as either a coercive or manipulative process. By including a reference to remaining persuaded, we exclude the notion of using heavy selling techniques. Likewise the ultimate sign of success in any person who has been influenced is the way that person may positively influence other people.

Power might be seen as the opportunity to exercise influence on another person's actions. The power to influence is central to many human endeavours. We see various types of power being used in different ways to influence other people's actions. The following sections give various categories of power.

Position or legitimate power

This is the power which comes from the position that one person holds relative to the next person. In a military context this about who has the most stripes on their arm, and in an organizational sense it is related to the job role and its position in the hierarchy. In extreme cases people using or abusing this source of power will use brute force in order to achieve results through others. As organizations are downsizing, delayering and reorganizing, the use of position power is clearly diminishing.

As an influencing strategy the use of this sort of power might achieve results in the short term, but it is likely to cause resentment if it is abused.

6 The power of personal influence

Coercive power

Coercion is about force. In today's organizations such coercive power can mainly be seen in some organizational systems. Because of changing social values, the use of any coercive actions has come to be viewed in a very negative light. Consequently where coercion is used by individuals, it will tend to be covertly masked or hidden.

Coercion is often a more subtle type of power and is frequently used by people who have some seniority in terms of position. The use of coercive power is also forceful but the use of such force is not always overtly declared. A good example of this is the manager who wants to force co-operation of a peer, but instead of being direct makes a comment such as 'I am sure you will want to go along with this, it would be awful if we had to go to your boss to get this resolved.' Similarly there is the example of the bank manager who, in forcing the sale of an insurance policy to a customer, says 'We are keen to maintain our good relationship particularly as we are supporting your overdraft.'

As an approach to influencing others, coercion might be effective in the short term but frequently the consequence is that the other person will feel resentful and in the long term may fail to comply. Alternatively if the balance of power between the two parties shifts, then it is possible the person who has been coerced in the past will seek to 'pay back' the coercer at a later date. So in the examples above the coerced manager might ultimately get promoted to another department and could then be obstructive in his or her dealings with the old colleague, and the bank customer might move his or her account to another bank.

Information power

This is the power which stems from knowledge and is a category which should not be underestimated. Increasingly organizations are recognizing the power of information, and knowledge workers are selling their intelligence at a premium. In order to protect their organizational knowledge power, employers draw up contracts which specify that employees cannot take their corporate knowledge with them when they move to a new employer.

On an individual level one only has to demonstrate slightly more knowledge than the other person in order to hold the balance of power. For example, the employee who is in the personnel director's office and happens to see a memo regarding an imminent internal reorganization may then hold great information power. This could be used in a number of ways: the information could be traded with others for more information; it could be used to build an impression of being 'on the inside track'; or even used to intimidate others.

Resource or reward power

Resource power stems from the possession or control of valued resources.

These valued resources could be material or non-material—anything that other people want or value highly. So the manager who controls the headcount, the budget, and overtime allocation has a great deal of resource power. However, resource power is not necessarily related to position: the secretary who controls office layout, allocation of equipment, and access to conference rooms may also hold a great deal of resource power.

Referent power

This is the power that an individual gets from their formal position and relationship with others. A typical example of this might be a secretary who acts in the same distant or formal way that they feel their boss might behave in dealing with junior managers. In this case they assume that the junior manager will assume that they hold the power that is normally afforded to their boss.

This power may or may not be given to the individual. Where this power is abused it stems from the individual acting as if they are able to control and influence the other person. Like most issues of power, it can only be successfully used where the person being influenced allows it to take place.

Dynastic power

This power is similar to referent power in as much as it is the power that comes not from what you know or what you have, but from who you know. Unlike referent power, the relationships will probably not be formalized and as such will cross all formal boundaries. An example of this might be a junior member of staff who derives dynastic power from a social relationship with the chairman. In this example there is no formal relationship, any relationship that does exist might be based on some shared past common experience such as knowing the chairman socially through membership of some club or society.

A frequently used dynastic influencing strategy is to associate with someone who is respected by the other party. Consider the following interaction between a supplier of consultancy services and the manager he works for in the client organization:

> *Supplier* It's good to see you again. It was only last week I was talking about some of the changes taking place in your department.
> *Client* Oh, were you . . . ?
> *Supplier* Yes I was at the golf club with your chief executive; there are some interesting ideas being discussed at board level currently.
> *Client* Mmm . . . I have heard a few rumours about changes.
> *Supplier* Well it seems there is no organization that can avoid change; I was talking with your main competitor recently and they have some really innovative approaches.

What is important here is not so much what the supplier says but what is not said. The supplier actually has no position power over the client, but is making good use of dynastic power by inferring close relationships with key people such as the chief executive and the main competitor. What the client does not know is that the supplier was actually carrying the chief executive's golf clubs, and in the discussion with the competitor was bidding for business rather than giving consultancy advice.

Consider the recruitment interview situation where the job hunter is keen to make a good impression. The more influential interviewees are likely to focus not only on impressing the interviewer, but will also make an effort to create a good impression with the secretary. What they have realized is that the secretary actually holds both referent and dynastic power because he or she works closely with the interviewer who is the decision maker.

Expertise

As the role of experts becomes more important in organizations, so the power base is shifting from those who have traditionally held power due to their position, to those who might actually hold more junior positions. Indeed the consultant in the example above only really holds power due to expertise but is making use of dynastic power in order to influence the client.

It is surprising how often when someone only has expertise power, that others will assume they hold position power. Again some people will make good use of perceived expertise to build a power base for influencing others. Techniques that capitalize on the use of expertise power, often with powerful results are:

- Deliberately using jargon which the other person does not understand.
- Overtly assuming the other party will understand while actually knowing they will not.
- Quoting facts or figures.
- Referring to research and third parties.

We each use all of the above sources of power at different times, many of the changes of our sources are contextual; however, each of us will have our primary and secondary power sources, and these will in effect provide a hierarchy of our personal preferences. Despite this, we should now consider a source of power that is available to us all, and in addition is capable of being dramatically improved as a way of influencing others.

Personal or charismatic power

Personal power is easier to recognize than analyse. When asked to describe some of the characteristics of the most powerful influencers they know, people will frequently make comments such as:

'They just seem to have some quality I cannot describe . . .'
'She is really strong in dealing with people but I do not know specifically what it is she does or how she does it.'
'He has got charisma—when he walks into the room people know it.'
'She seems to get people on her side.'

While such personal power is often considered to be indefinable, we have studied, using powerful analytical behavioural techniques, the particular characteristics and skills which such people demonstrate, and as a result of this we have been able to develop the 'EDICT' model of influencing shown in Fig. 1.1.

This model forms the basic structure for the book. We believe that successful influencing involves five key steps: gaining *entry* to the influencing situation; *diagnosis* of the actual problem or situation; effective *influence* skills; *confrontation* of difficult issues with the person or people you are attempting to influence; and finally ensuring there is a lasting *transition* in the person you have influenced from the pre-influence situation to the new situation. *Transition* also applies to how you personally make the transition from your current level of influencing skill to the new level after you have been exposed to the techniques discussed in this book.

It is in fact possible to describe and define the specific competencies which are required at each step of the influencing process as defined by the EDICT model. We refer to these as being either the primary or secondary competencies for successful influencing and they are shown alongside the relevant EDICT step in Fig. 1.1.

Parts 2–6 of the book address each step of the EDICT model in turn and you will find that we tackle each of the competencies within the relevant chapters. In Chapter 3 we discuss the EDICT model in more depth and provide detailed descriptions of the competencies. You will find in Appendix 3, a questionnaire called the EDICT Inventory which you are encouraged to complete in order to profile yourself against the specific competencies; this will then enable you to focus in particular on the relevant chapters in the book according to your own influencing profile.

By focusing on these specific competencies of influencing, managers we have worked with have proven that personal power is not simply an innate strength. It is something that can be developed with practice and the appropriate mental attitude, both of which we will be discussing in detail later in the book.

THE CASE FOR INCREASED INFLUENCING

A major reason why personal influencing has surfaced as the key competence for managers of the future is due to the massive change taking place in the structure and *modus operandi* of organizations, or at least those that will thrive into the twenty-first century. Organizations are shrinking, the theme is 'small is

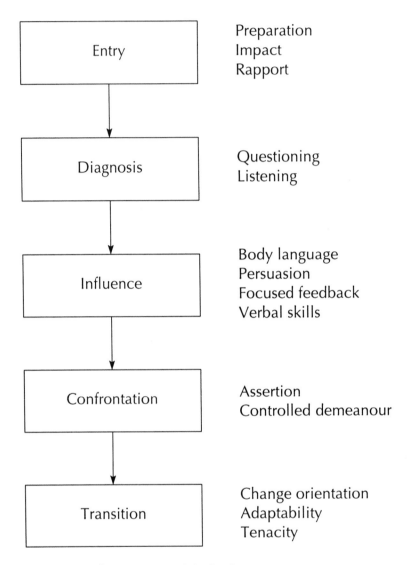

Figure 1.1   The EDICT model of influencing

beautiful' as opposed to the 'big is beautiful' mentality of the mid to late twentieth century.

Charles Handy in his book *The Empty Raincoat* (1994) refers to the chairman of a company who said that his policy is to have half the number of people, pay them twice as much so that they produce three times as much, which will result in productivity and profit ($1/2 \times 2 \times 3 = P$). Handy argues that in the future this means organizations will consist of a core of permanent workers with temporary labour and specialists being bought in as and when needed. He also presents a strong case for the 'federalist' idea, whereby organizations will adopt a structure and style of reverse delegation; the role of the centre will be to orchestrate the decentralized units which actually hold power based on their expertise. Clearly there is evidence that this scenario is slowly evolving; consequently there are implications for developing personal influencing skills.

Similarly John Naisbitt in *Global Paradox* (1994) identifies some interesting trends and makes some predictions regarding the future which are already ringing true in a number of cases. In summary he identifies the following:

- Big organizations are deconstructing and reconstructing as networks of autonomous units.
- Networking and entrepreneurial skills are coming to the fore.
- Strategic alliances are replacing mergers and takeovers.
- Co-operation is required even with your strongest competitors.
- Everyone will need to become a politician.

And in an article published over a decade ago in the *Journal of Management Development* (Helius, 1984) a number of emerging social trends were identified which we are now seeing in reality. In summary some of these were:

- An emphasis on personal growth and self-realization.
- Variable loyalties and unclear responsibilities.
- Growing disrespect for authority of position and government, and growing respect for demonstrative expertise.
- Acceptance of dissent, tolerance to non-conformity, innovation, change, and flexibility.

What we are concerned with here is the impact such changes will have on the behaviour and skill set of the manager in the future. In fact the title 'manager' is being used less and less in organizations as the whole nature of organizational roles is changing. As the key players in organizations have fewer people to manage directly and have less position power, they are having to rely on the more subtle use of interpersonal skills to achieve results through others. And the 'others' are not just those inside the organization; increasingly the lines between the organization, its customers, competitors, suppliers, and stakeholders are becoming blurred.

Clearly such changes have been a driving force behind a number of organizational change initiatives. However, what we are concerned with in this book is not total quality management, quality circles, business process re-engineering, performance management, or whatever the latest management trend is, but more importantly the personal attributes required to survive in this exciting and dynamic, if frightening, environment. The requirement is for strong personal skills and the ability to achieve results in situations where simply telling the other party what you want does not guarantee co-operation.

As the number of managers in the traditional sense is decreasing, so the number and range of specialists is increasing. A critical success factor for specialists in a leadership role is the ability to communicate effectively and to influence the non-specialist. Service functions are being set up within organizations as businesses which have to sell their services internally in order to justify their existence; this again calls for strong persuasive and influencing skills.

HOW TO GET THE BEST FROM THIS BOOK

Well-developed influencing ability demands a broad repertoire of skills, a number of 'clubs in the kit bag' which need to be selected judiciously depending on the situation and the nature of the personalities involved. This calls for an understanding of behaviour from two perspectives: firstly an insight into one's own behaviour, and secondly an understanding of the behaviour of others. As you read the book and work through the exercises it will help to think of both your own personality and style and that of the person you need to influence; indeed some of the exercises will assist this process of self-reflection and will enable you to see how you measure up in comparison to other managers.

The book is meant to be written in a very practical and 'user-friendly' format; learning is more powerful if you are able to interact, and so you are encouraged at various stages to reflect on and actually answer questions which are posed. Think of real influencing situations that you find yourself in and how you handle them—and how you might handle them having been exposed to the material in the book.

There are many checklists and summaries, as well as case studies based on real situations and people which we call 'storyboards'. Occasionally we will ask you to 'pause for thought' by presenting provocative questions. There are diagnostic instruments and questionnaires which enable you to see how you measure up against other managers and successful influencers. At the end of each part of the book there are question and answer sections. This is a way of dealing with some of the questions that frequently arise on our programmes; you may find some of your questions answered in these sections.

There are references to our research throughout the book; however, some of the detailed findings are presented in the appendices and are for reference purposes only; these deal with questions from readers with an interest in the theoretical and academic grounding of our work.

UNDERSTANDING OUR APPROACH

The approach taken to the subject of influencing is very much an analytical one. The specific competencies that need to be practised in order to influence effectively are identified, carefully defined, and discussed. This competency approach is important because it ensures that there is a clear focus on what you need to do and how to do it; to develop influencing skills it is vital be able to distinguish clearly between and describe the various components of effective influencing. It is important to know 'what it looks like' so that particular competencies can be practised. As a discipline, this approach will also help you to identify the specific strengths and weaknesses in others as well as yourself, and provide an additional opportunity for learning.

Naturally we tend to learn and develop our skills by modelling or copying the behaviour of others; by considering how others measure up against the specific competencies it will be possible to maximize the benefits of this natural process of learning in a focused way. It is worth considering that most people have certain strengths when it comes to influencing; what makes the subject so interesting is that one person's strength may be another person's weakness.

We have also frequently found that the weaknesses and strengths of individual managers are more closely related than might normally be assumed. For instance, if a manager's strength is defined in terms of ability to achieve results and get things done, then in terms of influencing skills there may be a tendency to 'steamroller' decisions and be insensitive to the needs of others. The implication of this might be that other people will respond as though they are persuaded; however, such persuasion is likely to be only temporary in nature. This relationship between strengths and weaknesses is a helpful way of looking at influencing styles and it is a concept we will be referring to throughout the book.

As mentioned above, we have categorized the competencies of influencing into the five broad headings of the EDICT model which reflect the normal sequence of the process:

*E*ntry	The early stage of influencing which includes the primary competencies of 'impact' and 'rapport', with *preparation* being a secondary competence.
*D*iagnosis	The use of 'questioning' and 'listening' are seen as critical competencies in order to ensure a good understanding of the information and perspectives of different parties.
*I*nfluence	'Body language' and 'persuasion' are seen as primary competencies, while the importance of *verbal skills* and *focused feedback* are seen as being of secondary importance.
*C*onfrontation	Using the primary competency of 'assertion'; *controlled demeanour* is also identified as being of secondary value.
*T*ransition	Having influenced, the secondary competencies are *change orientation*, or being aware of the process by which people change, and *adaptability*, being concerned

with personal flexibility rather than rigid or polarized ways of thinking. *Tenacity* is also recognized as a secondary competence which contributes to making things happen.

We have found that by concentrating on these competencies in a very specific way, there is more likelihood of bringing about significant and lasting changes in the skills of managers. Clearly this is a very analytical approach that takes the subject of influencing and carefully dismantles it into its component parts.

In applying and refining the skills of influencing, in practice it is necessary to synthesize these competencies, i.e. to reassemble them and to try to integrate them in a manner that does not appear too rehearsed. At first this may seem like a mechanistic approach; however, with practice and by combining the techniques with appropriate thought processes and attitudes, you will be able to effect real change.

While we have taken a systematic and scientific approach to defining what makes for an effective influencer, one of the most interesting and dynamic characteristics of human behaviour is that it is extremely complex, situational, and sometimes even unpredictable. We are frequently asked by managers for definitive answers to given or hypothetical situations. Often it is not possible to offer one solution to a problem. There may be many possible solutions or approaches and these may depend on a number of variables such as the personality traits of the different parties, their relative authority, political positions, and the context of the situation. What we do provide here is a range of approaches, models, and techniques; the ultimate skill of the individual is to be able to judge which to use when.

Another central factor determining the success or otherwise of different influencing techniques and styles is that of culture. As managers are increasingly expected to operate in multicultural and cross-cultural environments, there is much to be gained from developing an awareness of what are often subtle and unwritten cultural differences. These differences are too important to ignore when it comes to influencing. While it is dangerous to stereotype people based on their culture or nationality—because we can so easily make false assumptions—having an awareness of attitudinal issues related to culture is arguably just as important as understanding customs and mores. So, for instance, being aware of cultural communication styles and attitudes to relationships can provide distinct advantages when trying to influence others in a cross-cultural environment. We will be addressing the subject of cultural differences throughout the book.

Pause for thought

What are the sources of your power? Try to allocate percentages to the categories described in this chapter (coercive, information, resource, refer-

ent, dynastic, expertise, personal) and consider examples of situations where you have exercised such power.

What changes are taking place in your organization which suggest that personal influencing skills are becoming more important?

Think about individuals that you believe are successful influencers. In what way are their behaviours similar to the competencies that have been described?

On a scale of 0–10, how committed are you to improving your personal influencing skills?

REFERENCES

Handy, C. (1994) *The Empty Raincoat*, Hutchinson, London.

Helius, P. (1994) Developing Managers For Social Change, *Journal of Management Development*, vol. 3, no. 1.

Naisbitt, J. (1994) *Global Paradox*, Nicholas Brealey, London.

2 The EDICT model of influencing

Chapter objectives

- To continue to explore the unique research on which this book is based in order to satisfy the reader as to the validity of our approach.
- To explore the process of the EDICT model of influencing, explaining the different steps and to familiarize the reader with the notion of primary and secondary competencies of successful influencing.
- To provide the definitions of the primary competencies as well as starting to explore how these behaviours may be demonstrated. Also we introduce an understanding of the secondary competencies and how they relate to the total picture.
- To offer the EDICT Inventory as a questionnaire which you can use to profile your own behaviour against the EDICT model.

OUR UNIQUE RESEARCH

There are numerous books and training programmes on the subject of influencing skills, but it is our contention that many of these books or programmes are primarily anecdotal in nature. This book is different because it is based on solid research, yet we have deliberately written it to enable it to be of immediate value to the reader.

The research comprised two separate yet linked study projects which were conducted by the authors between 1989 and1994.

The first project involved the detailed study of successful influencers, and by the use of powerful interview techniques it became possible to identify the competencies of successful influencing performance. This resulted in fourteen specific competencies being identified; these in turn were ranked and rated as either being of primary or secondary importance. The study included over 1000 participants over a three-year period, and the findings were consequently examined for reliability and validity during the actual provision of The Power of Personal Influence programme provided by the American Management Association in Brussels. It was this initial study that indirectly led to the second research project.

During the course of the validation studies it became clear that we seemed unable to achieve the levels of success in transferring the skills that we assumed we were going to be able to achieve. Initial investigations suggested that this difficulty was inextricably linked to the individuals' mental or thinking processes. This, we recognized, was an area of development that would not usually be undertaken in such traditional skill development programmes. Despite this we decided to investigate the matter further.

An additional period of two years elapsed. First we studied all the literature that had been published on the subject of mental processes linked to learning, change, and personal achievement. Next we explored the area of sports psychology and the way sportsmen and sportswomen used mental processes to improve their actual performance. Finally we worked with successful chief executives and chairman of multinational organizations. This enabled us to contrast individuals who were using their thinking skills to a greater or lesser extent and thereby helped us to identify the really critical mental skills.

The findings from this latter study were quite dramatic, so as a result of this research we were able to integrate the findings of the two research projects and significantly improve the number of individuals that were able to apply successfully the skills they had learned.

At this point that is probably enough about the research. Let us now move on to consider the model that we are using to explore the steps in the influencing process

A MODEL OF INFLUENCE

The EDICT model provides a framework for considering the key steps that we need to progress through. These are as follows:

- *Entry*, including how we prepare mentally and physically for the process of persuasion.
- *Diagnosis*, which is about how to explore issues and ensure a clear understanding of the current and desired situation.
- *Influence*, which includes a structured approach to influencing and the application of specific techniques which raise demand in the mind of the person you are trying to influence.
- *Confrontation* in order to ensure that there are no significant differences of either fact or opinion.
- *Transition*, which looks at how as an individual you can ensure that your attempts to influence others result in a lasting and meaningful change.

As previously described, we have taken the key steps of the EDICT model and identified fourteen competencies which are regularly demonstrated by strong influencers. These behaviours have been further defined in order to identify which of these competencies would be considered as primary or critical, and which would be seen to less important or secondary .

These competencies are outlined below by way of introduction to the overall framework of the influencing process. The following chapters are based around all the competencies and provide detailed discussion of the competencies, taking care to describe specifically 'what effective performance looks like'.

First we will consider the definitions of the five steps within the framework of the EDICT model in a little more detail. In each step we will focus on the primary competence with a brief reference being made to the secondary competencies.

ENTRY

This first step of the influencing process is about gaining effective entry to the discussion or situation through our ability to make a positive 'impact' in the first few minutes of an interaction and then going on to develop the relationship. This step is seen as critical, not least because individuals often make an immediate judgement and once this has been made they will only seek evidence to support their initial opinion. Effectively we never get a second chance to make a first impression. The second key competency associated with entry is 'rapport'. Lets us now consider these two competencies in more detail.

Impact

Impact focuses on the first few minutes of an interaction; this is the critical period where first impressions are formed and frequently this is where the opportunity to influence the other person is inadvertently lost.

'Impact' is defined as creating a positive first impression and establishing credibility during the first four minutes of the interaction. This means use of appropriate social skills like smiling, making the appropriate greeting, using the other person's name, and generally demonstrating confidence.

In some ways you might argue there is an overlap between being prepared and impact, and indeed we would agree that it is possible to make a positive impact by demonstrating that you are prepared. But we make a distinction here because impact really relates specifically to the very early stage of the interaction. Impact might come from the things you say or do as well as the way you say or do them. The way we dress is likely to have an impact, as is using open gestures and demonstrating a reasonable level of confidence. Some people are very skilled in taking advantage of the first impressions phenomenon, recognizing that the opportunity to influence can be made or broken at this stage.

Conversely some people, who may often have the stronger message, fail to influence because of their lack of ability to make impact. They will often be at a gathering with others without people even knowing they are there. Such negative examples of impact are sometimes due to a lack of social presence, which when you study the skills in detail could mean: lack of contribution to the discussion, low volume of speech or monotonous tone of voice, or even a tendency to undervalue one's own contribution with comments such as 'I do not know much about this but . . .'

Rapport

Rapport is the ability to build the trust and confidence of others, often when there is little time available. Building rapport is critical in terms of establishing a good psychological climate for discussing the real issues. Without investing time in building rapport, it is unlikely that an open and relaxed discussion will ensue.

> 'Rapport' is continuing impact by displaying genuine warmth, concern, and interpersonal sensitivity. This includes the use of social small talk as well as other techniques aimed at putting the other person at ease. It frequently involves the use of self-disclosure and demonstrating levels of integrity.

Can you think of any people you know who manage to put you at ease very effectively even though they may be much more senior or potentially imposing due their position of status? If you were to analyse their skills in some detail you would find that they demonstrate good rapport-building ability; you are made to feel equally important and they will tend to show a genuine interest in you. This could mean engaging in 'small talk' about social matters, or talking about a subject that is of real interest to you. Rapport building is basically about identifying with the other person. Some people seem able to do this relatively quickly, whereas with others it is possible to be in close contact for a long period without really ever feeling there is any common bond. Sometimes rapport is accelerated by disclosing a little bit of personal information; by practising a little self-disclosure the message is 'I am human too' and 'I am like you'.

Some people demonstrate negative rapport skills. You often hear these people referred to by others as 'abrupt', 'severe', or 'intense'—the implication being that they would do well to relax a little more and take a more natural approach. With all of these competencies in the influencing process it can be instructive to look at the specific behaviours of those demonstrating good skills and equally those who show lack of the appropriate skills. By looking at both sides of the coin in this way it is possible to gain a clear picture of what 'a good one looks like'.

A secondary skill in this first step of entry is that of *preparation*. The importance of preparing for the influencing process cannot be overestimated. Clearly this competency will be situational, i.e. opportunities for influencing often arise without a great deal of warning, e.g. the chance meeting with the chief executive in the lift or the potential client in the next seat on the aircraft. However, the principles of good preparation are still valid .

DIAGNOSIS

The diagnostic stage may begin before the actual meeting as part of the process of planning. However, once engaged in a discussion and having effectively made impact and created rapport, it is necessary to spend some time trying to understand where the other person is coming from before presenting your own views or proposing specific solutions.

You can not influence what you do not understand, consequently the key competencies in this step of the model are those of 'questioning' and 'listening'.

Questioning

Questioning in an influencing context is to do with attempting to understand the perspective of the other person so that effective and appropriate persuasive techniques can be used.

'Questioning' is the application of a range of different questioning styles focused on gaining critical information. It includes the use of a broad range of different types of questions as well as using a hierarchy of questioning in order to identify core values as a basis for influencing.

Questions can take many forms. There are diagnostic or open type questions, usually starting with words such as 'Why . . .' and 'How . . .', which are useful for drawing the other person out and identifying their perspective. Then there are probing questions, which seek to really explore a viewpoint in some depth, and behavioural questions, which ask about how a person behaved in a specific situation. Probing questions and behavioural questions are very effective in helping to understand the other person better, which is the main objective at the diagnosis stage of influencing.

We also look at particular types of question we refer to as pinpoint questions, which are useful for seeking specific information or facts, or indeed to pick the other person up on throwaway comments they might make in order to make sure that potentially useful information is not lost.

Just knowing about the different types of question is not sufficient in terms of influencing skills. It is important to be able to use the full range of different types of question and to be able to judge which are appropriate when. One particularly powerful way of diagnosing the other person's views is to adopt what we refer to in Chapter 7 as three-level questioning, which starts by asking for factual information about the person and then progressively probes in order to identify that person's underlying motives and values. It is only when we are in receipt of such understanding that we are able to influence effectively.

Of course there are some traps that we can fall into in developing a line of questioning. A common one is the use of the multiple question; this is where one question is asked, but before the respondent has a chance to reply they have been hit with a further two or three questions. Apart from confusing the other person, it provides them with an opportunity to pick and choose which question they would like to answer.

Listening

Listening as a competence is often mistaken for hearing; it is, however, a skill that may be both passive and active. It is the latter that we are particularly concerned with using in the influencing process, and as such it should include a demonstration to the other party that there is a common understanding.

> 'Listening' can be defined as using a hierarchy of both passive and active listening behaviours aimed at identifying key information and underlying attitudes and beliefs. It means showing the other person in a convincing way that you are both listening and understanding what they are expressing, whether these are words or feelings.

People who listen effectively tend to give all sorts of appropriate messages, which suggest they are listening, through their body language and verbal behaviour. This could range from nodding the head to maintaining a reasonable level of eye contact. But listening can also be demonstrated by what the listener actually says. Summarizing the other person's views and replaying them back in order to check you have understood the message as it was meant to be communicated is also a good sign of active listening.

Often people say that they are listening, and indeed they may be, but the fact that they are looking out of the window or continuing to type on the keyboard of their computer as they listen does nothing to help the speaker. At an advanced level, listening means showing understanding of the underlying feelings which the other person is experiencing; showing empathy is a skill which can accelerate the rapport-building process.

Listening, however, is not only about maintaining harmony and building relationships. It may be necessary to pick the other person up on inconsistencies or to challenge them on their statements; it might be considered that in doing so one is showing strong listening skills. The difficulty arises when you hold opposite views compared to the person you are attempting to influence. It can then be very difficult to resist the temptation to present your own view instead of listening properly.

INFLUENCE

This is where, having built the solid foundations of a relationship by positive impact and rapport, then having explored the situation from the perspective of the other person, specific influencing techniques are used.

This means reinforcing our verbal messages by the appropriate use of body language, as well as interpreting the behavioural communication of the other party. Key competencies here are 'body language' and 'persuasion'.

Body language

Body language can be viewed from two perspectives. First we consciously or unconsciously convey messages through, for instance, our facial expression and our gestures. Secondly the person we are trying to influence will constantly be giving non-verbal messages which need to be interpreted in conjunction with the verbal communication.

> 'Body language' is the use of proximity, posture, expressions, gestures, and other non-verbal behaviours aimed at supporting the verbal message in an influencing situation. This means being positive and direct, and reinforcing words with actions and expression.

This is one of the most fascinating aspects of human interaction and the fascination no doubt stems from the inquisitive nature of people who want to find out what the next person is really thinking and feeling. Of all the competencies we address, body language is the most difficult one to fake; this is because we can attempt to mask our own feelings by saying what we think are the right words, but it is often the facial expressions, hand and body gestures, and tone of voice that give away our real feelings.

From an influencing point of view it is advantageous to be able to interpret the body language of the person we are attempting to influence. Interpretation of body language could help in recognition of the fact that the other person does not really understand although they say they do; and knowing when the other person is giving the signs of wanting to 'buy' or accept your proposal, or equally that they have certain hesitations and you need to spend some more time convincing them.

In order to recognize such signals, the skill is in looking for clusters or groups of behaviour which are consistent; this could come from eye contact, hand gestures, sitting position, or even tone of voice.

Equally, in order to increase the chances of success in convincing the other person to do something or to accept your proposals it is essential to ensure that your body language is consistent with your spoken words. One should be aware of mannerisms or habits which could be distracting or could even be misinterpreted.

All of the communication process has implications for significant cultural differences. This is particularly true in relationship to non-verbal aspects of how we communicate. For the international traveller this can present specific difficulties and it is easy to see how a misinterpretation of a signal can lead to disastrous results. For example, the informality of using the first name of someone in the United States, might well be found offensive in Germany where formality is much more the norm. We will be exploring this issue of cultural implications of body language in more depth in Chapter 8.

Persuasion

Persuasion is about using a systematic structure to move the other person towards a mutually acceptable solution to which both parties remain committed. There are a number of specific techniques which effective influencers use in order to achieve this.

> 'Persuasion' can be defined as the use of appropriate verbal and non-verbal behaviours, together with the use of a systematic process which results in the other person making a commitment to a decision or course of action.

In order to persuade effectively it is helpful to consider the process from the perspective of the person you are attempting to influence:

- Do you share a common understanding of the current situation and the outcome you are looking to achieve?
- Have you anticipated the objections or questions which are likely to be raised?
- What is the style of the other person and what style are they likely to respond to best?
- Do you have a range of proposals to suggest with one or two preferred options?

These are all important questions which can both help with preparation and might serve as a checklist when proceeding through the persuasive discussion.

We have observed the behaviours and techniques used by successful public figures and those engaged in influencing others, and have identified a number of regularly used techniques. These range from saying things in threes, to ending and then starting their sentences with the same words in order to emphasize a point. People who are less well known and whose reputation does not go before them tend to use other methods such as building their own credibility slowly and steadily, often with passing side comments which demonstrate or infer they have expertise.

No longer are the hard-sell techniques of the past sufficient in order to influence others; there is a need to build a broad repertoire of skills and techniques and to be able to exercise discretion in their application. It is only through the use of such flexible techniques that we can expect that the person who has been persuaded will stay persuaded, and equally importantly may well influence others.

Two secondary competencies are related to the step of influencing: *verbal skills* and *focused feedback.*

Verbal skills are related to the way in which we as individuals use words, construct sentences, and use the range of our voice. There is no doubt that those people who are effective in influencing others make optimal use of this skill—arguably they are subscribing to the maxim 'It's not what you say but the way that you say it.'

Focused feedback is one of the most powerful influencing skills; this is the skill of providing information for the receiver regarding observations of behaviour and how it might be modified in the future. If the receiver of focused feedback is willing to make changes to his or her behaviour as a result of the feedback, then influencing will have taken place. As with the competence of *preparation,* this will tend to be highly situational.

CONFRONTATION

This is the step that is often neglected in the influencing process, probably as a result of our innate concern that to disagree with someone may adversely effect our relationship. This is almost certainly true where the individual lacks the necessary skill to confront in a win–win manner. Consequently in order to confront effectively, it is important to have strategies for dealing with differences of opinion and managing conflict. The key competency of 'assertion' is now described in more detail.

Assertion

The key to reconciling differences between two parties is to recognize when it is appropriate to confront the other person and to do so in an appropriate style. We will look at the different options available regarding the management of conflict and provide the opportunity for self-reflection on the style which you tend to prefer.

> 'Assertion' can be defined as the ability to show understanding and to state clearly what is thought, felt, and wanted and to express the outcome that is desired. It includes the ability to seek a workable compromise or find win–win solutions.

We all learn from a very early age to behave in a certain way, and our predominant style of achieving things becomes established during our childhood.

Consider the child who gets things by shouting, screaming, and taking things from other people. The chances are that if this strategy works for the child it will be reinforced and replicated, albeit sometimes in a more subtle way, as an adult. So the manager will achieve results by taking and ordering without asking or supporting. Equally, if the child's way of achieving things is to cry, sulk, and invoke the sympathy of others and this approach works, then it should be no surprise that this behaviour and style recurs throughout adulthood.

What we are describing here is the way we learn to be aggressive or passive—of course there is a middle ground which we explore in more depth in Chapter 11 under the heading of assertiveness. On a percentage basis the assertive approach is likely to yield better results and there are a number of assertive techniques which can be learned as well as recognized steps of assertiveness when responding to a provocative comment or situation. Assertiveness is really a philosophy which emphasizes respect for oneself and others and seeks to achieve successful outcomes for both parties rather than insisting that there always needs to be a winner and a loser.

Of course there may be occasions where a more aggressive, passive, or even avoiding approach may be more appropriate, and again the skill of the successful influencer is first of all to develop the whole range of skills and styles and then to be able to apply good judgement in their application.

A secondary competence of this step is *controlled demeanour*. This competence is about how in the influencing process we are able to stay cool and calm when we are dealing with others who may be either emotional or even directly aggressive. As a skill it has two components: our ability to deal with other people's anger, as well as our ability to manage our own feelings. Clearly both of these will be closely linked. It is about the ability to stay controlled when faced with either personal or professional attacks. This means not reacting to provocation, but responding in a stable and disciplined manner. Rather than behaving aggressively or passively, it is about behaving in an assertive way.

TRANSITION

This final step of the EDICT model of influencing focuses on how one ensures that the verbal commitment of an influenced individual is translated into actions. It also addresses the issue of how, in developing your personal influencing skills, you can bring about a lasting change in your own behaviour.

Transition involves three secondary competencies. Firstly there is *change orientation*. This can be defined as the process which brings about lasting changes in behaviour. It focuses on the ability to understand the process of change and to accept change as a constant.

Secondly there is *adaptability*, which is about having a favourable disposition towards change and being able to utilize a range of styles and behaviours. We have identified that the most successful influencers seem to possess what we refer to as chameleon-like qualities. This is often demonstrated through an ability to recognize the styles of other people or organizations and then to blend into them so that they do not seem out of place.

Finally there is the competence of *tenacity*, which is essentially about our ability to keep at something when it might be easier to concede or give up. Undoubtedly this competence is linked to our skills of judgement, for with tenacity it is also recognized that there is strength in knowing when to give up.

It is interesting to note that these last two competencies are strongly linked to our personality and are developed early on in our lives; consequently they probably present the least opportunity for development.

SUMMARY

Having taken an overview of the key skills of successful influencing, you may now wish to see how you currently measure up against the competencies described.

We have developed a diagnostic exercise (Appendix 3) entitled the EDICT Inventory. This is a questionnaire with twenty-eight questions based around aspects of the primary competencies of influencing. You should answer the questions as candidly as possible as you reflect on your own approach to influencing.

We would encourage you to complete this exercise so that when you consider the interpretation of the results you will be able to identify, in a focused way, the aspects of influencing which you wish to address.

The structure of the remainder of the book follows the EDICT model and you may wish to pay special attention to the steps of influencing in the model which relate to your personal needs.

Pause for thought

Why do you feel background research might be important?

How do you feel you currently perform in respect of the primary competencies of influencing?

Can you think of ways in which you can improve your adaptability and tenacity?

Question time

HOW DO I INCREASE MY POWER?

In effect, other people give us power. Like beauty it is in the eye of the beholder. If we want to increase our power we should first consider the sources of power that we are drawing on; the reason for doing this is to recognize that some sources of power are more potent than others. For example, information power will tend by nature to be more limited by time, whereas expertise power would normally be more enduring.

If a person wanted to increase another person's perception of the extent of their expertise, then they need to let the other person know the depth of their knowledge, skills and experience. There is evidence to suggest that the more slowly and subtly this evolves, then the more powerful the impact. Consequently we should aim to build our personal credibility slowly, always making sure to reinforce that which is already known.

Developing our other sources of power should follow similar principles, i.e. the initial question should be `How do I raise awareness of this with the other person without being obvious?'

WHY IS CHANGE TAKING PLACE SO FAST?

Change has always been with us, indeed it is mankind's ability successfully to manage such change that differentiates us from many others in the animal kingdom.

Undoubtedly the rate of change is accelerating. In simple terms it can be assumed that this is being driven by technological progress; however, this only explains part of the situation. In order to understand more fully the nature of this change we would need to explore wider issues of the economy, political factors, and social changes.

WHY IS THE BACKGROUND RESEARCH IMPORTANT?

Primarily because it provides the reader with a measure of confidence that the areas that they are studying are in fact the areas on which to focus. Without such reassurance it is understandable that the reader may be somewhat uncertain as to value of the data. There is much anecdotal information on the achievement of human potential and the development of influencing skills; however, our techniques have been developed following extensive research.

CAN I REALLY DEVELOP THE PERSONAL COMPETENCIES OF INFLUENCING?

The simple answer is 'Yes'. Most of the fourteen competencies are skill based and as such provide ample opportunity for real development; however, behaviours like *adaptability* and *tenacity* are probably more difficult to address.

In order to address these characteristics you will need to consider several other issues including aspects of your self-image. This subject is discussed in more detail in the next section.

Part 1

Entry

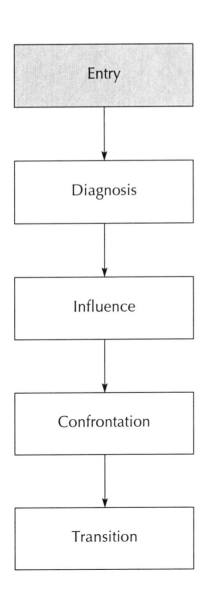

Preparation
Impact
Rapport

3 The importance of preparation

Chapter objectives

- To consider the importance of preparation in anticipation of influencing.
- To examine the 'push' and the 'pull' style of influencing and explain the importance of trying to understand the other person's perspective.
- To show how to draw up a perspective specification which is a key tool to help with preparation, while at the same time examining the importance of managing information.
- To discuss the importance of understanding the other person's values as a prerequisite to achieving lasting change.
- To look at how to influence people more effectively by anticipating their style.
- To discuss the importance of controlling inner dialogues when preparing for important influencing situations.

In the opening section we have looked at the EDICT model of influencing in which we have described five key steps through which successful influencers appear to pass in the process of influencing others.

We have looked at these five steps and have shown that each step consists of either or both primary and secondary competencies. It is focusing on these competencies or behaviours that seems to provide the best opportunity for improving our skills.

In this part of the book we will now turn our attention in detail to the step of *entry*; this will allow us to consider the primary competencies of 'impact' and 'rapport', and the secondary competence of *preparation*.

This latter competence will include practical issues of preparation as well as the important psychological aspects of preparing mentally to influence.

Entry is about how we gain effective entry to the influencing process; if the entry stage is managed effectively, then it is more likely that the opportunities for influencing at a later stage will be increased. By contrast, there is evidence to suggest that if this step of entry is mismanaged, then the chances of success are considerably reduced.

Although entry involves preparation, impact, and rapport, in this chapter we will focus particularly on the natural first stage of entry: *preparation*.

> *Preparation* as can be defined actions which indicate a degree of mental and physical readiness for a particular influencing situation. This includes recognizing the information needs and perspectives of the other parties; it includes being able to demonstrate preparation to the other person by our words or actions.

So good preparation for an influencing situation could mean thinking through in advance what the other person is likely to be thinking. It is also advantageous actually to discuss with the other person what you are looking to achieve from the interaction. But preparation is not just about knowing you have prepared effectively; like so many of the influencing skills it is about showing, through your behaviour, that you are prepared. How, for instance, might you demonstrate that you are prepared for an important presentation? You might show your preparation by arriving in good time, setting the furniture out in a particular way, having materials laid out on the table, having an introductory slide showing on the screen, and approaching the guests as they enter to introduce yourself. All of these actions actively demonstrate preparation. Equally, preparation could be shown simply through demonstration that you know your subject. How often have you been in a meeting where you have reached a stalemate because the other person did not have to hand all the information or detail that was required?

It could be argued that preparation is not always possible because we cannot always anticipate what to expect of the person we are trying to influence or because there is simply very little time to prepare. In part we would agree with this line of thought, and consequently we have classified this as a secondary competence.

Assuming that we do know that we are going to try to influence someone, however, we will look at a practical technique for preparation, known as the perspective specification. This technique can help with the common problem of not being able to predict the approach of the other person.

In a similar way we will make reference to the importance of managing data in the preparation phase. This we will show can be managed by the use of an information specification.

Returning to the argument that there is little time for preparation it is true that influencing opportunities often arise unplanned and in these situations it is important to be able to 'think on one's feet'; however, it is still possible to apply some of the same disciplines of preparation, albeit in a less formal way.

The key principle of successful influencing which is relevant to every stage of the EDICT model is:

You cannot influence what you do not understand.

With the competence of preparation this means that before engaging in the influencing process it is critical, in order to maximize the chances of success, to be able to understand issues such as the other person's background, values, motivation, experiences, and objectives.

It is equally important to understand the style of the person so as to be able to adopt a suitable style of influence yourself. This also means being aware of significant cultural differences, particularly if working in a multinational environment.

UNDERSTANDING THE STYLE OF OTHERS

A common trap that people fall into when attempting to influence others is to work from their own frame of reference or value set rather that of the other party. This usually leads to what might be described as a push rather than a pull style of influence (see Fig. 3.1). With a push style of influence the strategy adopted is to be clear about your own argument and then to aim to impose your views on the other person. This is clearly a forceful or even aggressive stance; if the other person disagrees or holds a different opinion to your own, then you will block it with the same degree of force that they present it. Arguably there may be some situations where this approach is appropriate, such as

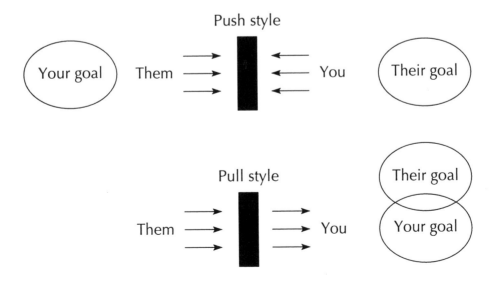

Figure 3.1 Push and pull styles of influencing

when:

- There is no time to use a more persuasive approach and fast decision making is needed. For instance, on matters of safety or security where you are absolutely sure that you are correct.
- Where unpopular decisions need to be taken such as cost cutting or the implementation of unpopular rules. Even in this situation it is important to consider carefully the style of influencing and the requirement to listen to the views of the other party.
- Where the other party is using an aggressive or forceful approach with no effort being made to listen. Even in this situation it may be possible to adopt more of a pull approach rather than having to push against the other person's arguments, but sometimes the only way to hold back the force of the other person is to start with an equally forceful stance.

The analogy of American football fits well with the push type approach. Frequently we see the footballer running directly at the other team and being met by the opposition player running equally fast, heading for a direct collision. Often it is brute force that will win the day, which is fine if you are bigger and stronger than the other person. It is hardly surprising that the players need the help of substantial padding and painkillers!

In the influencing situation the football approach is about meeting the other person head on, presenting your argument as forcefully as they do, and emphasizing the differences.

The pull approach, however, can best be likened to the sport of judo. Judo relies on skill, guile, and when appropriate the use of force. Most important of all, judo relies on being able to sense the movements, actions, force, and direction of the other person. Interestingly this is the reason that visually impaired judo players often make such good contestants; they compensate for their inability to see their opponent visually by focusing on feeling their actions and intentions. The loser is thrown or beaten by their own strength and force, which is used against them by the winner pulling the opponent in the direction they were already travelling and applying often subtle techniques and twists.

In an influencing context the pulling approach means sensing and trying to understand where the other person is coming from, seeing things through their eyes, and then deciding on the tactics for influencing them; often, as in the judo analogy, it is an effective strategy to use their own arguments and values to persuade them.

EXPLORING PERSPECTIVES

Understanding the perspective of the other person can be especially difficult if you happen to hold strong and opposing views. The instinctive reaction is to

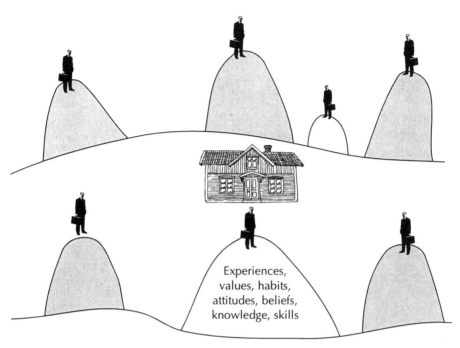

Figure 3.2 Perspectives

meet force with force; however, attempting to understand the other person's perspective can be very revealing. Frequently different people will look at the very same subject or situation from quite different perspectives. A helpful analogy is used by Calvert *et al.* in the book *First Find your Hilltop* (1990) where it is suggested that each of us views a situation from our own unique perspective or 'hilltop'. This perspective is based on our own experiences, motives, values, opinions attitudes, and more. So in Fig. 3.2 each person, if asked to describe the building shown, would give a slightly or even significantly different description based on their position or unique hilltop. The important skill is to be able to identify the nature of the other person's hilltop. Arguably what we need to do is to come down off our own hilltop and go up onto the hilltop of the other person. It is only by doing this that we would really be aware of how they see things. This is, of course, not actually possible; however, a useful questioning technique for helping us understand the other person's perspective is three-level questioning. This approach is discussed further in Chapter 8.

Three-level questioning is a diagnostic technique and is particularly useful when we have contact with the other person. If we do not have contact with the other person, however, it becomes important to attempt to anticipate the perspective or view of the other person or indeed various persons. A practical technique which can be used at this stage of early preparation is the perspective specification.

THE PERSPECTIVE SPECIFICATION

To draw up a perspective specification you first need to be able to identify the different parties involved. This may sound obvious, but it is frequently the case that there is more than one person to influence, and politically it is crucial to recognize who the key decision-makers are. Take, for example, a selling situation where a salesperson is attempting to secure a commitment for further orders from an existing customer. While the salesperson might deal with the buyer from the customer organization, other key players in the decision to purchase might be the purchasing manager and the manager of the department which is the end-user.

On a similar note, take the case of the university lecturer speaking at a careers convention. The lecturer, who is in the influencing role, may be trying to persuade a number of quite different potential customers of the strengths of his or her university: the potential students, the school teachers, and the parents of potential students. A worked example of a perspective using this situation is provided in Fig. 3.3.

The different parties are named at the head of the columns of the perspective specification form. Then the different sections of each column are completed by trying to see the situation from the different perspectives of each person. Not all of the headings in the columns will necessarily be appropriate for every influencing situation, and there may be additional headings you want to use as appropriate to the situation. In this case simply make the changes you feel are relevant; the important matter is the discipline of attempting to see things through the other person's eyes.

Clearly at this stage it is not possible to predict with pinpoint accuracy the position of the other person; however, by using the discipline of a perspective specification you are likely to reduce the number of unexpected surprises and awkward questions once the influencing discussion has started.

UNDERSTANDING AND MANAGING INFORMATION

Understanding the other person's perspective is a critical preparatory activity prior to the process of influencing. In a similar way it might be beneficial to consider the information that you are using as the basis of your approach to influencing. This is particularly important where the issues or situations that we may be influencing are complex.

In these circumstances it can be helpful to structure the preparatory analysis by the use of an information specification. With this technique we first ask ourselves 'what do we really know for sure?' about the person or situation, then by contrast we ask ourselves what we do not know, and 'what we need to find out'. This structured approach can be further enhanced by superimposing the 7Ms over the initial framework. This allows us to consider and identify both known and unknown facts against the criteria of money, market, man-

LECTURER	STUDENTS	SCHOOL TEACHERS	PARENTS
Knowledge	**Knowledge**	**Knowledge**	**Knowledge**
Own subject known well Local knowledge	Some course details	Of their own specialist subjects	Will range from good knowledge of the university/courses/system to no knowledge at all
Gaps in knowledge	**Gaps in knowledge**	**Gaps in knowledge**	**Gaps in knowledge**
Future changes—some information known, but knowledge is limited	Some new course information Recent changes to courses Local factors	May be unaware of some of the more academic research being conducted	
Attitude/beliefs	**Attitude/beliefs**	**Attitude/beliefs**	**Attitude/beliefs**
Education standards are important Breadth of education is important, students should not specialize too soon	Whole person education is important Seeking independence with security Some fear/trepidation	Education standards are important, strong commonality with own perspective here	Want the best for their children Will want to know their children will be safe and secure May be anxious about becoming 'distanced' from their children
History	**History**	**History**	**History**
Long history of traditional teaching	Mainly high school educated Some mature students		May have followed similar courses of education in the past
Motivators	**Motivators**	**Motivators**	**Motivators**
Rewards associated with seeing students achieve personal growth	Keen to make their way in the world but want some protection, security	May be interested in strategic links between schools and the university	Security, standards of education
Objections	**Objections**	**Objections**	**Objections**
	May be critical of the fact that the campus is more dispersed than in other institutions	Likely to question the standards and grades achieved by past students.	Where have previous students ended up? Funding arrangements & sources How does it compare to other universities?

Figure 3.3 Worked example of a perspective specification for a lecturer speaking at a careers convention

power, methods, machines, materials, and minutes. Of course not all these criteria may be appropriate or necessary; however, they are helpful in structuring our thinking in complex situations.

RECOGNIZING CRITICAL VALUES

It is certainly a distinct advantage to try to identify the underlying motives of the people you are attempting to influence and actually to consider their basic values or driving forces. We all are driven by a hard core of values, probably numbering no more than a handful. These values then fuel in us things like our beliefs and ultimately our attitudes.

While it is helpful to be able to identify and anticipate the behaviours and actions of the other person, it can be even more advantageous to be able to identify fundamental values. This is because most of our behaviours tend to be driven by our core values. For example, if the person you are trying to influence is a person who holds a core value of independence, i.e. they believe it is important for the individual to retain independence, then this should affect your influencing strategy. Supposing you were trying to persuade this person to take on a task which you want to delegate. You will need to emphasize the fact that the task is one they will be able to tackle with a strong level of individual choice regarding how it is done.

Examples of fundamental values might include the following:

- The importance of education
- Family values
- The profit motive
- Belief in a god or an overall power
- Personal responsibility
- Fairness and equality
- Work ethic

Each of our core values may in themselves consist of numerous related beliefs. For example, we could have a value in the importance of education; this may mean that we could have a belief in the notion of an individual's potential to achieve, or that education is a about wealth creation or physical or mental well-being. In turn we may have hundreds, if not thousands of attitudes related to these beliefs. Using the same example of value of education, I may well have an attitude towards higher education; I could also have attitudes towards the use of technology in education or access to kindergarten education for all those who want it.

Interestingly organizations also have values, and frequently they are considering what these values should be and overtly stating them. Often they can be identified from written sources such as the mission statement or vision statement. For example, Steve Jobs of Apple Computers states:

Our goal has always been to create the world's friendliest, most under-standable, most usable computers—computers that empower the individual. (quoted in Weyer, 1994)

McDonald's are well known for their key values of quality, service, cleanliness, and value, and they clearly attempt to work to these values consistently across locations. Hewlett-Packard commit their values to writing in 'The HP Way', a document available to all employees.

A more accurate judgement of organizational values might be drawn from discussion with employees at various levels. These values are essentially about the culture of the organization or 'the way we do things around here' and even if they are not openly stated, then there is no doubt that they will exist. Organizational values might include, for example, the following:

- Dignity for the individual
- Integrity
- Loyalty
- Innovation
- The profit motive
- Contribution to society

From an influencing point of view there is a lot to gain by successfully identifying the core values of the individual and the organization. The primary benefit is that you will be able to use the values of the other person or organization as part of the influencing process. You are likely to be significantly more persuasive by using arguments that use the other person's value system rather than trying to impose your own values on them. Let us consider some examples which highlight this principle.

STORYBOARD   USING WHAT IS IMPORTANT TO OTHER PEOPLE

Susan is a new recruit to a conservative consumer products organization and has considerable experience of working in a fast-moving American high-technology corporation. She has joined in a corporate role as product manager to try and bring about significant product changes and to enhance the image of brands in the marketplace. She is currently trying to influence a senior manager, Charles, to gain commitment to major innovations in the use of information technology systems and marketing. She has analysed both the organizational values and the personal values of the senior manager as follows:

- *Organizational values:* cost containment, conservative approach, fear of change.
- *Personal values:* Security, safety, caution, concern regarding risk taking.

Susan Clearly the important issue, Charles, is to continue to build on some of the developments which have been occurring over the last few years.

Tactically this is a good approach; having identified that Charles is a cautious man, she positions her ideas as part of the changes which have been taking place anyway. Selection of words is important; she talks about 'building on' rather than changing. Her use of Charles's name can be a strong influencing technique; however, a word of caution: if this is overdone it can be transparent, even irritating.

Charles Yes but I really think we need to make sure we don't move too fast; I have seen too many other organizations make sweeping changes only to have to revert back to the tried and tested methods eventually.

This response does not come as a total surprise to Susan who was prepared for the cautious approach. Fortunately she has thought of some possible responses.

Susan I agree, I too have seen some examples of organizations that have attempted some quite revolutionary approaches to branding; many have fallen into some of the classic traps such as not analysing likely market response. Maybe we should look at some of the lessons that can be learnt and at the same time look at some of the success stories . . .

Although this response may seen innocuous, Susan is using a number of effective influencing techniques. She has recognized that with Charles a directly forceful or 'hard sell' approach will not work. She needs to recognize his style and values. She starts by agreeing with his objection, which in itself is a legitimate approach; by agreeing in part she openly shows support and may draw Charles closer to her when he may be expecting more of a confrontation. What she then does is to use the same argument in support of her own ideas by suggesting they look at lessons learnt. This is likely to appeal to Charles, who is cautious and conservative. She uses a tentative word in 'maybe' which gives Charles the opportunity to build on her suggestions rather than feel that he is being railroaded.

The key principle in the above example is that to be effective in an influencing context it is essential to try to anticipate matters concerning the personal style and underlying values of the other person.

Admittedly we are not always in a position to identify these issues in advance of the meeting, i.e. when meeting a person for the first time. As previously stated, it is even more important to be able to identify the same factors through a process of skilful questioning and observation in the early part of the interaction and we will pick up these skills in Chapter 8 which covers these competencies under the diagnosis stage of the EDICT model.

If you feel that you know the individual you are trying to influence reasonably well, you might like to consider their style against the four key categories we have identified below. If you are able to categorize the other person in terms of our definitions, then some suggested influencing methods are provided.

We also consider the situation where you are the manager attempting to influence a subordinate who has a predominant style, and where you are the subordinate attempting to influence your manager. This is not about mimicking the other person, but you are likely to be more persuasive if you can recognize their preferred style and adapt your style to theirs, rather than imposing your style on them and trying to force them to operate in the way you do.

STYLE 1—SUPPORTIVE

People who fit the supportive style of behaviour are likely believe in the importance of personal relationships. They will tend to approach problem solving from a collaborative point of view and will be supportive to other people who are less experienced. They are likely to enjoy working with others and will share responsibility and resources readily. Trust is an important issue for the supportive person and they are likely to build long-term relationships.

How to influence a person who has a supportive style

When influencing a person with this sort of style it is important to stress the worthwhile nature of causes in the long term. It may be appropriate to emphasize the relationship between your objective and their personal development. An effective technique to use with a person who has a supportive style is to ask for their help in tackling a problem. Be careful of criticism of such people; they are particularly likely to fear ridicule and failure.

How to manage someone who has a supportive style

It is important when managing a subordinate who has a predominantly supportive style to give them recognition for their ideas, achievement, and contribution. It will help to provide opportunities for them to work with or alongside others. Sharing information and being open will help in the relationship. When setting goals and targets, both parties should be involved, and the manager should make opportunities available for the subordinate to achieve these targets.

How to influence a boss who has a supportive style

If your boss demonstrates a predominantly supportive style, it is important to demonstrate your value and contribution to the organization. Sincerity and honesty will be particularly respected and it will be better to admit mistakes and seek help rather than cover them up. Willingness to participate in team activities and tasks is important.

STYLE 2—COMPETITIVE

The competitive style is one where the person tends to rely on power based on authority and position, and approaches tasks in a strongly competitive manner. The main aim of the competitive person is to achieve results, challenge others, and to get on with doing things.

How to influence a person who has a competitive style

Methods of influencing a competitive person should emphasize the opportunities being offered to the person and the ways in which they can personally raise their profile. If it is possible to give authority to this sort of person, then they are likely to respond favourably. Equally, the competitive person is likely to respond well to direct approaches and will be intolerant of 'woolly' approaches which might be seen as weakness.

How to manage someone who has a competitive style

When managing a subordinate who has a predominantly competitive style, it will be necessary to influence by giving challenges and providing autonomy and individual responsibility. It is important to give recognition for achievements. It may be necessary to define clearly the demarcation of the role so that this person does not undermine or encroach on the responsibilities of others. However, it will be appropriate to give this person the opportunity to take initiative within the given boundaries. It may on occasions be a requirement to spar on an equal basis.

How to influence a boss who has a competitive style

It will help to take a direct approach when dealing with a boss with this style. This means demonstrating your capability and showing independence, but not being afraid to recognize the boss as a resource to draw on for assistance when it is required. When you are confident that you are right, it may help if you stick to your views and meet objections head on. This sort of boss will not appreciate servile behaviour, though subordinates will often take a submissive stance in dealing with such a competitive manager. This kind of manager will enjoy a challenge and the cut and thrust of a strong argument; when influencing a competitive person you will sometimes need to mirror the direct and straight-talking approach.

STYLE 3—RESTLESS

The restless style is often seen in people who enjoy change and thrive on opportunities to be in the spotlight. Typically a restless style would be recognized by a tendency to be optimistic, active and sociable. This sort of person will tend to relate well to dealing with new and different people and situations.

How to influence a person who has a restless style

Generally it is preferable to emphasize the benefits of change when influencing someone with a predominantly restless style. They are likely to respond positively to new ideas, which is in contrast to the consolidative style described below. It will be effective to stress the excitement and emotion associated with any proposals.

How to manage someone who has a restless style

If you are managing a subordinate who has a mainly restless style it will help to take a flexible approach and to accept that this sort of person will respond best to variety rather than routine tasks. To influence a restless person offer supportive feedback and do not underestimate the impact of humour. Routines, firm schedules, and close supervision are unlikely to be effective management strategies.

How to influence a boss who has a restless style

If your boss has a restless style, then the most effective responses as a subordinate will tend to emphasize eagerness and positive open attitudes to new ventures and products. Be wary of going into too much detail when explaining things. This sort of boss will tend to have a short attention span. Key competencies will be the ability to make an impact quickly and to express oneself succinctly and clearly. You may offer to take on some of the more routine responsibilities in order to relieve your boss of these matters.

STYLE 4—CONSOLIDATIVE

The consolidative style tends to be biased towards order, routine, and detail. A consolidative person will be comfortable with policy and doing things that are in the best interests of the organization or authority. This will often mean a suspicion of change and a preference for consistency.

How to influence a person who has a consolidative style

The key to influencing someone who has a consolidative style is to demonstrate a careful and cautious approach. Clearly Charles in the storyboard above has a predominantly consolidative style; we saw how Susan recognized this and adapted her approach accordingly, rather than relying on a more competitive approach which might have worked in her previous organization.

How to manage someone who has a consolidative style

A perceptive manager will allocate certain types of responsibility to a consolidative subordinate; these will be tasks involving high levels of detail and planning. This sort of person will tend to be frustrated by changes which are made part way through projects. They will need time to make considered decisions rather than being rushed or pressurized. They will place much emphasis on being treated fairly and will prefer a pragmatic managerial style.

How to influence a boss who has a consolidative style

If your boss has a consolidative style, then you will need to be careful in making recommendations for change. A useful tactic is to stress how your recommendations are similar to or build on historical methods and systems. Arguments will be more persuasive if they stress conformity and logic. When attempting to influence, it is better to be respectful of organizational norms or standards and it is important to be well prepared and have relevant facts and information to hand; this sort of boss will want to be confident that you have explored all possible options before agreeing to your proposals.

Often the underlying values of the individual and organization are influenced by matters of national or cultural differences. We will consider the fascinating subject of cultural differences in the next section.

EXPLORING CULTURAL DIFFERENCES

The danger of talking about cultural differences in general terms is that we fall into the trap of stereotyping people and nationalities. If we try to identify generally applicable rules regarding what you should or should not do or say when you are meeting with someone from, for instance, Germany, the United States, Japan, or the Middle East, then there is real risk of getting it wrong. Cultural issues are not this clear cut and there will always be individuals who disprove the rule—so tread carefully. There has, however, been some interesting research into the subject of cultural differences, not least that conducted by Fons Trompenaars as published in his book *Riding the Waves of Culture* (1993). Trompenaars has studied cultural differences with an emphasis on international cultures. It is interesting when considering this subject to consider also whether your organization or that of the person you are attempting to influence has a culture which fits a particular type. After all, culture is really about norms for how things are done and organizations have norms just as nations do.

Trompenaars defined a number contrasts in terms of cultural differences. Here we will look at the contrast between universalism and particularism, and how this relates to the preparation stage of the influencing process.

The universalist approach tends to take a clear-cut approach to business and the focus is on sticking to codes of conduct, rules and regulations, and previously established practices. In a particularist culture, however, the relationship is actually relatively more important than the contract itself; it is considered important to allow relationships to develop over time and informality is acceptable, even encouraged.

While it may be wrong to make sweeping generalizations, you may recognize these differences if you have worked in the hard-nosed environment of a universalist American or northern European organization. Equally, you may recognize the particularist culture in southern European or Middle Eastern relationships.

In an influencing situation it is worthwhile considering the nature of the culture of the person you are trying to influence. In a universalist culture you will need to have key facts and figures to hand and it will be essential to know the background to the situation so far. You will need to know who else has been involved and what are the accepted ways of doing business. It may be necessary to use forceful approaches, so make sure you are aware of where you stand legally. Prior to meeting it could be advisable to write formally to clarify the agenda and objectives, and again afterwards to confirm what was agreed.

In a particularist culture, while this level of preparation may turn out to be equally appropriate, it will be just as important to display flexibility and not to appear shocked if the goal posts are moved and the rules seem to change as discussions evolve. This is not to underplay the importance of preparation, but it is a matter of style; the trick is to be prepared but to show willingness to adapt and to work on building a good relationship. And do not be deceived if you come from a universalist culture and the other person who comes from a particularist culture appears to be wandering off the subject; it does not necessarily mean they are ill prepared, it could simply be that they are allowing time to get to know you.

MENTAL PREPARATION

Alongside the more physical or practical aspects of preparation, our research into the approach taken by influential leaders in industry suggests that in order to stand a greater chance of achieving success, it is also critical to prepare mentally.

Frequently chief executives we interviewed described the fact that in order to prepare themselves for big events such as board meetings or important presentations, they would rehearse mentally.

This mental rehearsal would take the form of addressing the particularly difficult aspects and visualizing a successful outcome: they would actually see themselves concluding the meeting successfully, whether this meant gaining agreement from the shareholders or receiving applause from the audience of the presentation.

Other managers said that they would use other mental imagery techniques, which we describe in Chapter 5 as self-assertion statements. These individuals would visualize the situation, the location, and the people, hear the applause, and feel the sense of achievement and pleasure associated with a successful outcome.

There are some interesting parallels here with the approach to mental preparation taken by top sportsmen and sportswomen. When Linford Christie, winner of the gold medal for the 100 metre sprint in the 1993 world championships, was interviewed after the race, he was shown a replay of himself seconds before the start. He was standing absolutely still with his eyes shut. When asked what he was doing at that time he explained that he was running (and winning) the race in his head. He further explained that he had done this hundreds of times before, and every time he had always crossed the finish line first.

MENTAL PRACTICE

We have known for some time that mental practice does actually improve physical performance, yet up until now the use of such techniques appears to have been confined to the domain of sport. Our research not only confirms the original findings but explodes the myth by pointing out that these techniques are widely used by other successful individuals across a variety of different situations and circumstances.

Mental imagery and visualization is an advanced approach to mental preparation, used on the boundaries of high performance, where competitive edge is seen as critical. It is a technique that needs to be practised and perfected over time. We are convinced that such mental processes can be learned as a skill and as such can be developed to assist in improving our own performance, not only in influencing but in many other skills.

Contrast the use of these types of advanced techniques with the following example which represents the approach more often seen.

STORYBOARD 'IT'S GOING TO BE ONE OF THOSE DAYS'

Robert, a successful medical consultant, was due to give a major presentation to an international forum of 200 specialists regarding the unique findings from his latest research. He knew on a logical basis that he had some important findings to report and that this should have major implications for many of the other specialists in the audience.

On an emotional level, however, it was a different story. Robert had become gradually more wary and anxious as the date for the conference loomed. He had always seen himself as a medical specialist, which meant his strengths lay in research rather than presenting to groups and answering awkward questions.

His preparatory thoughts were revealing. It went along the following lines.

> I hope they will find it interesting; I know what that lot are like, they are bound to be really critical—they always are.
> That's the trouble with this sort of conference—people are only really there for the social gathering; nobody actually wants to listen to detailed analysis.
> The problem with my research is that it is so complex it is impossible to put it across in an interesting way. Anyway I never have been that strong on the presentation side of things.

Note the number of words and phrases here with negative connotations. Robert is evidently 'talking himself down'. Once started on this negative cycle it becomes a downward spiral and is very difficult to break. Let us look at Robert's inner dialogues on the day of the presentation as he is getting ready:

> This is it then. The big day. I must get it right. I cannot afford to screw up here. There is too much at stake—if I get this wrong, then my seniors are bound to find out. Now that would be career limiting; it could set me back years. And I know how important it is to look right. The last thing I want to do now is to cut myself shaving . . .' [Robert then proceeds to cut himself shaving]. I just knew it, that is typical of me on the big day, it is going to be one of those days.

The force of the conversation in his head was so strong that Robert actually gave himself a picture of failure, an image of the nightmare scenario, i.e. cutting himself shaving, and it was as though the actions simply followed the thoughts. This is in the worst sense an example of where thoughts influence actions but in a negative way. The problem is that having had the bad experience of cutting himself shaving, he proceeds to write off the whole day as a bad experience before it has really begun. It would be no surprise now if things did continue to deteriorate because the negative thoughts are so dominant in his thinking.

People are the things that they believe to be true. Once we develop beliefs like 'its going to be one of those days', then our own desire to act in accordance with our own beliefs tends to move us towards more and more negative behaviour

You too may recognize situations or events where your approach to preparation has been similar to Robert and you have said to yourself 'This is going to be one of those days.' In order to maximize the likelihood of success it is critical to break this negative cycle and actually take control of your thoughts, rather than allow your thoughts to take control of you.

USING APT THINKING

In order to help you take control of your thinking you might use what we call the APT technique as follows:

- **A**wareness   Become conscious of your negative thinking.
- **P**ause   Tell yourself that you are in control of your thinking process. If necessary, keep repeating in your head phrases like 'Be still', 'Quiet', and 'Be positive'.
- **T**hought selection   Now replace the negative thought with something that is more positive.

We call the process of taking conscious control of our mental processes 'meta-cognition'. This word, which literally means 'greater or more than thought', describes a collection of different mental skills that allows us to gain control of our thoughts and other mental processes, rather than seeing ourselves as some sort of victim of uncontrollable processes. This is such an important subject that we shall discuss this concept more in the next chapter.

Understanding primary appraisal

One technique for dealing with trepidation or fear as you approach a major event and feel you may be falling into the negative inner dialogue trap is to take a realistic and logical look at what psychologists call our primary appraisal of the situation.

Primary appraisal is concerned with the way our perception interprets events. Negative interpretation usually results in negative thinking and behaviour that is self-fulfilling, or meets our expectations. By contrast, if we challenge our primary appraisal, refusing to view things negatively, we often achieve more favourable outputs.

So in the example above Robert might have asked himself the question: 'What is the best thing that could happen if the presentation is successful?' In predicting the consequences as objectively as possible he might have actually answered the question regarding the best case scenario in the following way:

> The best thing that could happen is that the speech is well received by the audience. This would have an impact on the extent to which they are likely to use the findings of the research in their own work. As a result, it is also probable, that participants will find the conference both valuable and enjoyable overall. The best case as far as the audience is concerned is that they remember or accept the key messages of the presentation. The consequence would be that I would not need to find other ways of

presenting my findings. I would certainly be able to have my research published in some of the key medical journals because the findings are so significant.

This approach helps to counter some of the often irrational thought processes which lead to negative thoughts. Realistically considering the best-case scenario also enables the person to retain a realistic perspective of success. Having such a mental picture is an absolute prerequisite to achieving actual success.

It is important to note that this approach is not advocating positive thinking as a panacea for success. More importantly it suggests we focus on success rather than failure, and challenge our primary appraisal, thus making sure our thinking is not self-defeating.

Pause for thought

Firstly consider a situation where you have to influence another person or people in the future. You might also consider the context of influencing in an organization, either your own or an external one. Consider also the underlying values of the organization. Draw up a perspective specification following the guidelines provided above.

Attempt to anticipate the questions which are likely to arise and how you might deal with them.

Next, consider a major event which you had to handle recently. It might, for example, have been a speech, a presentation, a meeting you had to chair, an examination you had to take, or even a family-related event. Reflect on your approach to mentally preparing for the event. Are you aware of having actually prepared mentally? If so, how effective was your approach?

Were you aware of the nature of your inner dialogues?

Were they, on balance, more positive or negative?

Finally, consider an equally important event which is due to take place in the near future. State clearly what your objective is and what success means. Is it winning an order, receiving praise, making a sale, delivering a project? Whatever the objective is you need to be able to state it clearly and succinctly.

Now visualize yourself achieving success, taking care to focus on as much detail as possible. Attempt actually to see things clearly in you head, and to hear any sounds or noises or to feel any feeling that might go with your image. How strong is your image on a scale of 1 (weak)–(10 strong)?

In tandem with this approach to visualizing success, practise the APT technique of controlling negative thinking.

If you are working with another person or in a team it is equally possible to use the same techniques of mental preparation. For example, you might describe to each other what success looks and feels like. Positive inner dialogues can be particularly powerful in building the confidence of a team; the difference is that the 'dialogue' is actually the conversation between the team or group of people.

If you persevere with such techniques in a team situation you will find that they simply become naturally integrated into the team's behaviour; it will become a group 'norm' to talk positively in preparation for a major event. This is, of course, the method used by successful sports teams, which often refer to the importance of the 'team talk' and being 'psyched-up'.

In this chapter we have considered a number of quite different techniques for preparing for the influencing situation, ranging from the more externally focused methods, such as the perspective or information specification, to the internally focused approach of managing inner dialogues and visualization techniques.

The overall message is that the importance of *preparation* cannot be overplayed. It is the key that unlocks the door to the entry stage of the influencing process in the EDICT model.

Having done all you can in terms of initial preparation, it is now worth thinking a little more about the importance of mental readiness prior to exploring the primary competencies of impact and rapport.

REFERENCES

Calvert, R. et al. (1990) *First Find your Hilltop*, Hutchinson, London.

Trompenaars, F. (1993) *Riding the Waves of Culture*, Nicholas Brealey, London.

Weyer, M. V. (1994) Mission improvable, *Management Today*, September, pp. 66–68.

4 Mental readiness

The next two chapters are inextricably linked as both deal with issues of developing mental or cognitive skills as a prerequisite to successful influencing.

Chapter objectives

- To explain why it is critical to combine such cognitive or thinking techniques with practical skills, in order to achieve lasting changes in behaviour.
- To explore the concept of 'metacognition' as a method of supporting practical skills by taking active control of our mental processes.
- To discuss a model of behaviour which shows how negative aspects of thinking tend to result in the development of a negative self-image.
- To become aware of the power of others to influence our thinking either positively or negatively.
- To explain some of the common psychological defence mechanisms that we use to protect our self-image.

It may sound strange to think about how we think about ourselves; however, our research has shown that by controlling different aspects of our mental processes—we call this 'metacognition'—it is possible to bring about significant movement towards the achievement of personal goals and objectives.

In this and the subsequent chapter we will be considering a number of key issues and ideas including the following important concepts:

- The enormous power of our mind and the apparent boundless potential we have to improve our performance.
- Meaningful change starts inside us and works its way out, rather than starting outside and working its way in. Therefore we need to consider changing our thinking before or at the same time as we start changing our behaviour. We should not leave this process to chance.
- Perception is reality. There is only one truth, the way I see things. This may be different from your truth.
- Our self-image is the sum total of all our inner dialogues, as well as the influence of 'experts' on our thinking. Once developed, our self-image con-

trols the way we behave by acting as a type of comfort zone; that is we do things to keep ourselves comfortable.
- Mental practice actually improves physical performance.
- Experience is not bound by time; more importantly it is equal to the intensity of something plus the number of times that we think about it, or in effect experience it in our minds
- As individuals we move towards and become like what we think about. The more we think about success, the more we are likely to achieve it.

For thousands of years philosophers have pondered the nature and scope of our minds, yet the major developments in our real knowledge have probably come within the past fifty years. Indeed it is probably true to say that our understanding is still in its infancy; this point appears to be supported by the numerous different ideas and theories that appear to exist. For example, many researchers and writers have described the structure of the brain and will often give vastly varying accounts as to its size and function. This we feel in itself is not that important; what is important is that it is generally recognized that the brain is made up of an enormous number of neurons, or nerve cells, and that one of the functions of these cells is to record and then store or imprint experiences or data. These experiences may ultimately be capable of recall from our memory.

Another area of general agreement appears to be that most individuals rarely begin to exploit their true potential. In part this seems to be due to the actual size of the brain, with its possible endless number of different permutations. Also, this seems to be related to aspects of our beliefs and attitudes that may either exclude or limit our real potential.

In somewhat simplistic terms the brain can be likened to the hard disk on a computer. Like the computer, the brain records information without being concerned about whether something is fact or fiction. It just records things that it is told. Here the similarities end because our brain records information which we have interpreted through the process of perception. The consequences of this is that people act in accordance with their beliefs—and if those beliefs that we have recorded are incorrect or false, then we still act in accordance with them.

It is worth pausing here to reflect on how these experiences may have been recorded falsely or in a distorted way. This is a common phenomenon which is primarily concerned with the way our brain makes sense of the world by perception.

Perception is concerned with the way we individually, and uniquely, interpret data which is coming into our brains. The quantity of this data is enormous—a constant and consistent flood of information. We are interpreting from what we see, hear, smell, or touch. We will be conscious of some of this data, while there are other things of which we will be unaware.

Given the amount of data and speed at which we are receiving this data, it is hardly surprising that sometimes we do not accurately record things as they really are, but as we think they might be. Naturally this can cause us some problems.

We will return to this subject of perception later on when we explore ways in which we can tap into the common distortions in human interaction, and how these can be utilized when we influence others. However, let us now consider the rationale behind our suggestion that we need to take control of these internal mental processes if we are to achieve permanent change.

INSIDE-OUT

Learning may be defined as a lasting change of behaviour as a result of practice or experience. Yet for some time we were concerned that in traditional skills development programmes we did not appear to be getting the levels of transference or application of skills, from the classroom to the working environment, that we would have liked. On closer examination we were somewhat startled to discover that the problem was worse than we had originally suspected. When monitoring past participants over a period of one year after attending a traditional skills development programme we found that there was a dramatic loss over time in their ability to apply successfully the newly acquired skills. Indeed the initial study suggested that after twelve months as few as 6 per cent of individuals had achieved any significant lasting change of behaviour.

Further questioning of these individuals suggested that many of the barriers to successful application of new skills were psychological in nature. Included in this were the following reasons for poor application:

- Negative influence of other people
- 'Not really seeing myself as being able to behave that way'
- Having beliefs that were inappropriate to applying the new skill, such as: 'I've never been good at dealing with difficult situations'
- Lack of personal motivation
- Inappropriate self-image

This in itself should not have been surprising as most traditional skills training programmes tend to avoid the issue of developing mental processes, or if they are mentioned it is almost always as an afterthought. These findings brought us to the conclusion that in order to produce lasting and sustained behavioural change, particularly in the area of influencing skills, we needed to address simultaneously both skill development and the issues of internal mental processes.

These findings show that behaviour, i.e. 'what we do', is primarily an output. That is to say that behaviour is the consequence of our thinking processes either consciously or subconsciously, which in turn may give rise to specific feelings and will result in certain behaviour.

STORYBOARD   BEHAVIOUR IS AN OUTPUT

At a meeting the young executive Martin is waiting for an opportunity to explain his current project in which he has been trying to improve distribution by developing a relationship through a third party. He has been working on this project for some time and has just made a breakthrough which could result in significant profitability and is now anxious to show others the extent of his work.

The meeting goes on dealing with a whole range of what appears to be trivial issues and Martin finds himself thinking 'Why are we talking about issues like the new parking arrangements? Don't you realize we have some much more important matters to discuss?' (*thinking*)

A few minutes later the meeting suddenly seems to change direction and starts discussing the need for a new car policy. Martin thinks 'This is ridiculous, I've got far better things to do with my time than sit hear listening to this rubbish.' (*thinking*)

By now Martin is feeling somewhat irritated and annoyed (*feelings*), and these feeling are being demonstrated (*behaviour*) in his looking up at the ceiling, deep sighing, and tapping his pen repeatedly on his pad.

In the above example just forcing Martin to change his behaviour by stopping him looking at the ceiling or tapping his pen would not have resulted in a lasting change. Any change that did occur would tend to be temporary in nature. We call this kind of forced change 'white knuckle change'; that is to say a change where we are forcing ourselves to act in a certain way, and that this forced behavioural change is contrary to what our thinking dictates. In essence this new behaviour contradicts the pictures that we hold in our heads about ourselves and as a result is unlikely to last—moreover it results in high levels of stress.

In order to help Martin, we need to address issues like the way he sees things or his thinking processes. Only by taking this sort of approach are we likely to achieve any sort of enduring or lasting change. Such help might include showing him how to re-examine his primary appraisal, or by showing him how to use the APT technique to change his thinking. Once his thinking has changed, his actions or behaviour will naturally follow: what is more, the whole process will be relatively stress free.

The same can be said of any learning experience. If you truly want to develop your skills of influencing, then it is critical that you take the time and spend the necessary energy developing specific skills or competencies like listening or persuasion. However, if such change is to be sustained, then we suggest that you must also consider the need to make sure that your cognitive processes or the way you see and think about things are appropriate to what you are seeking to achieve.

We shall return to this subject later in this chapter; however, let us now consider in more detail which aspects of our mental processes are of most significance across different business situations.

BEING POSITIVE

You may have heard of catch-phrases such as 'the power of positive thinking' or 'think positive'. In some respects this notion is somewhat simplistic, yet it does provide us with a useful way of exploring the importance of positive mental attitude.

In our research we asked some of the most successful chief executive officers and senior management of major international organizations to explain the approaches they use to help build their own confidence and ensure that, in business situations, they are likely to be successful. The sorts of situations which they considered were, for example:

- Achieving desired results in meetings.
- Influencing other people.
- Removing worries of not being able to cope.
- Overcoming fears of using personal computers.
- Improving personal abilities in high-profile presentations.

What our research revealed was that there are apparently some commonly used techniques and methods, which appear to be used quite naturally by these successful managers, and the use of these techniques seemed to contribute significantly to their success.

You might be thinking 'Surely the top chief executive officers and senior management cannot all use the same methods and approaches.' Certainly we would agree, but what we did identify were a handful of common approaches that managers use either consciously or subconsciously.

We have categorized these approaches into a number of specific techniques which you can practise in order to increase the likelihood of success. We found that by introducing these techniques on skills development and management development programmes, managers significantly increase their chances of success and are more likely to develop skills that result in lasting changes in behaviour.

We present the principles behind the techniques of managing perception, positive inner dialogues, later in this chapter. The skills of using imagery, utilizing visualization, and developing the application of self-assertion statements are discussed in the next chapter. In addition, we also provide some worked examples of these techniques and a number of opportunities which will help you put them into practice.

You might like to consider at this stage some of your own personal goals. These might be related to influencing, for example, in the following ways:

- To improve ability in persuading senior management.
- To develop skills in giving feedback to others.
- To improve assertiveness in conflict situations.
- To stay controlled in difficult situations.
- To make a good first impression on other people.

Equally, you may have more personal or non-work-related personal goals, such as:

- To learn to play a sport to competition level.
- To improve relationships with neighbours.
- To raise funds for a favourite charity organization.

The examples quoted above are expressed in quite broad terms. What we will demonstrate in the next chapter is how to turn your general aims into more specific targets, and more importantly how to make sure that you achieve them.

The techniques of visualization, self-assertion statements, and positive inner dialogues covered in the next chapter focus on what happens in your mind rather than specifically on what you do. As previously explored, to increase the likelihood of achieving your personal goals you will need to address these internal issues as well as the external, skill-based competencies and techniques.

APPROACHES TO DEVELOPMENT

It is commonly accepted that one way of developing effective behaviour and learning in others is to use techniques of coaching and encouragement. Psychologists refer to this as conditioning and shaping of behaviour. For example, to improve the ability of a novice tennis player, a coach would gradually encourage good tennis strokes by working through the following sort of procedure:

1. Explain the principles of how to hit the ball.
2. Demonstrate to the trainee in stages how to do it.
3. Watch the trainee doing it.
4. Provide feedback on performance.

5. Give encouragement.
6. Allow time for practice.
7. Observe improved performance and give further advice and encouragement.

Effective coaches will deal particularly well with stages 5 and 7 in this procedure; they will give encouragement which is appropriate considering the level of the trainee. This means that it is likely that a true novice will be given praise for efforts which, compared to the professional's own standards and abilities, are actually relatively weak. Such encouragement is meant to instil confidence and persistence. As the novice starts to improve, so gradually the standard required in order to generate the same amount of praise, increases. The skill of the coach is to judge the current level of the trainee and therefore the correct positioning of feedback to develop optimum improvement. Gradually the trainee's performance is 'shaped' in the right direction.

Such an approach has been prevalent in many management development initiatives in recent years. Whether through the off job training course or coaching provided on the job by the boss, the emphasis has been placed on developing effective performance by breaking the desired task or skill down into component parts and then allowing time for practice and giving feedback and encouragement. Admittedly not all organizations and not all bosses are highly skilled in doing this, but this is the approach that has been commonly assumed to be the most effective.

Pause for thought

Have you ever been aware of how your thinking process gave rise to behaviour and how when you changed your thoughts the behaviour changed automatically?

What caused that change of thinking?

Try and identify some occasion that you actively used positive thinking to help you with a difficult or important situation. What were the circumstances? Did you get what you wanted?

Consider how you have been taught different skills and behaviours in the past. You might draw on work-related examples or examples from other walks of your life.

What would you describe as your most successful learning experience?

How does that contrast with the least successful?

To what extent was coaching used and how effective was it?

In considering the application of coaching, others have provided the following management examples that they have experienced using this conditioning and shaping approach:

- Developing skills in handling meetings.
- Improving presentation skills.
- Team supervision.
- Communication skills.
- Assertion training.

We considered how effective such approaches are in bringing about a lasting change in behaviour. As previously described, our research has revealed that traditional skills training on its own tends to result in very few participants claiming any substantial (lasting) change twelve months after the training took place. This may seem surprising and certainly it prompted us to research causes for what appeared to be an anomalous situation. This in turn allowed us to explore additional methods of development which would improve the likelihood of achieving lasting and sustained change. It was this further study that enabled us to develop a model of how cognitive processes are developed, albeit positively and negatively.

A MODEL FOR UNDERSTANDING BEHAVIOUR

Clearly it is more straightforward to study outward behaviour and to break a visible skill down into component parts than to answer the question 'What happens to you internally when you learn best?' Such questions are often considered too deep, mystical even, and certainly not lodged in the 'real' world. It is for these and other reasons that we assume cognitive skills are not overtly developed in traditional skills programmes

Our research showed that chief executives and other successful senior managers regularly described a cycle of mental processes that appeared to assist them in gaining success. This will be demonstrated in our discussion of the model which looks at how our internal mental processes relate to our external behaviour as summarized in Fig. 4.1.

This model shows the three key stages we go through, starting with reflecting on our own behaviour, and how through our inner dialogues this in turn builds our self-image, ultimately it is this self-image that often controls the way we behave. In other words we act and behave the way we know or believe we are. Effectively this is a virtual cycle of mental events.

Let us work through the model from an individual's point of view, taking first of all the frequently adopted pessimistic approach; interestingly we found that this was an approach taken by many individuals. We will then look at how the same model fits with a more progressive approach, that which we found in successful individuals. Consequently in the next chapter we will explore the

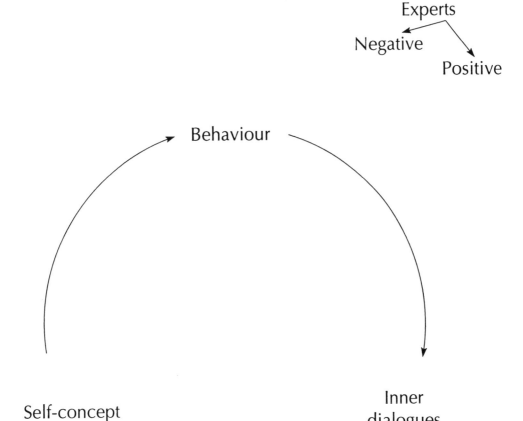

Figure 4.1 Understanding behaviour

techniques which can be practised to develop more powerful mental processes in ourselves.

Behaviour

Conceptually one could start anywhere in this circle as it reflects a continuous
process; however, we will start with the observation that 'I engage in behaviour', that is I do things.

As one of the authors, I am currently sitting at my desk typing this manu-
script. I regularly get up to look things up in my reference books or files,
and I find myself occasionally looking out the window into my garden.
I am behaving

As the reader you may be sitting reading this book while relaxing or
alternatively travelling or waiting for something or somebody.
You are behaving

The important thing to remember is that we are all behaving all the time. All
the time we are doing something or another—even sitting still is behaviour,
albeit passive behaviour.

Inner dialogues

As a result of my behaviour I frequently find myself engaging in inner dialogues, that is to say that I talk to myself in my head. This is normal; however,
often such dialogues assume the nature of background conversations where
we find ourselves almost discussing something with ourselves, as if we were
two different persons. This is particularly true in conflict situations or where we
feel under stress. Generally inner dialogues take place all the time but particularly before and after specific events.

These inner dialogues are based on our perception of reality. As we have seen
previously, perception is concerned with the way in which we interpret events.
It is notoriously unreliable and prone to distortion, and this means I do not
necessarily see things as they are but how I think they are. Consequently these
inner dialogues are not necessarily 'the truth', but they are undoubtedly 'our
truth'. As a result they are our reality, and in turn we live by that reality.

We will continue to look at how perception is distorted in more detail later in
the book.

Various studies have shown that many individuals often evaluate their own
behaviour negatively. We believe that this tendency is probably learnt early on
in our lives primarily by the influence 'experts'.

'Experts'

In addition to what I say to me about my behaviour, either positive or negative,
I am also subjected to another major interpretation of my behaviour which
comes from people who have been influential in my life: we call these individuals 'experts'.

An 'expert' might be defined as anyone I permit to influence my thinking. Early
in my life these people may include my parents, peers, or friends; in later life
these might include our spouse, boss, colleagues, or indeed anyone who we
believe has more experience or knowledge than ourselves.

The important thing in this notion of 'expert' is that it is only necessary for us to believe that the person has more knowledge than ourselves, rather than the actual existence of such knowledge. As a result it can be seen than many people who are trying to influence others will often try to give the other person the idea that they have more knowledge or experience than they actually have. In effect they will try to behave as 'experts'.

Unfortunately for most of us, we have probably had many experiences of 'experts' who have provided a negative, rather than a positive influence in our lives. If over time these negative beliefs are reinforced, then ultimately I develop a clear picture of who and what I am.

Clearly some of these beliefs are inappropriate; they have their basis not in the truth, but in our (and other people's) interpretation of the truth. In effect this is how my beliefs are developed.

Self-image

This is the sum collection of the attitudes, habits, values, and beliefs that ultimately make up my self-image: that is to say the picture that I hold in my head as to who I am. This self-image then acts in a way to control my behaviour as in general terms I usually act in accordance with my self-image, or the way I know or believe that I should act.

In consequence my self-image appears to act as a sort of comfort zone, meaning that when I behave in a way that I know and believe I am, then I am relatively comfortable. Behaving in way that is inconsistent with my self-image is likely to result in a high level of stress or discomfort.

Operating outside my self-image, or comfort zone is a prerequisite for successful personal change. Traditionally in psychology this has been achieved by two methods:

- Flooding
- Desensitizing

Flooding is where we move a long way outside our comfort zone and literally get 'flooded' with the experience. For example, a gentle person who believes that they are not particularly good at confronting others could be asked to represent the organization in a difficult confrontation with a trade union official, who is known for his aggressive personal style.

Most of us will have experienced this sort of approach: a case of 'sink or swim'. Flooding is used in many organisations and for many individuals this is a useful and expedient approach—they swim. Unfortunately some people are not so lucky—they drown! Consequently where this approach has been used unsuccessfully, then the impact on the individual is not only highly stressful but can also be catastrophic: the person may not try anything like it ever again.

Desensitizing is where the individual moves slowly, bit, by bit outside their self-image or comfort zone. This is the approach often used in traditional training programmes. Typically in a training course we would increase the degree of complexity of role-plays as the learner becomes more proficient, as in coaching we are effectively shaping their behaviour. Desensitizing is more likely than flooding to ensure success, but it can take a considerable period of time and still involves a level of applied risk-taking by the learner.

Both techniques are frequently used in clinical psychology to help individuals with specific fears or phobias; however, both are potentially damaging due to the need for the individual to change their behaviour before having achieved the necessary internal changes. The result is always stressful for the individual.

More recently studies by ourselves and others suggest that we can move outside our comfort zones by primarily managing our mental processes. In many ways this is akin to desensitizing, but takes considerably less time and is relatively stress free. We shall be describing the use of self-assertion statements, to achieve this, in the next chapter.

Where we find ourselves acting inconsistently with our self-image, then we are likely to engage in a range of psychological defence mechanisms. This matter is discussed later in the chapter. Let us now consider this model in action using a storyboard to illustrate the key stages of our cycle.

Some studies have shown that one of the things humans find most stressful is making a public presentation or speech. For example, one recent survey revealed that public speaking featured at the top of a list of anxiety-provoking circumstances, while death was listed at number three. In other words some people would rather die than make a presentation!

STORYBOARD   OVERCOMING A PERSONAL FEAR

Pauline was a successful administrator; however, she was uncomfortable whenever she was asked to make a presentation or speech.

She could trace her fear back to her childhood and an early experience in the classroom. On one occasion she had been asked to read in front of her class (*behaviour*) and due to perceptual distortions, i.e. seeing things incorrectly, and her accompanying negative inner dialogues, she believed that:

- Other pupils were better speakers.
- She was being picked on by the teacher.
- That this task was a more important event than it really was.

Even before speaking she had been heavily engaged in negative internal conversations (*inner dialogues*), saying things like:

'This is going to fail.'
'I had to read my poem before, and I was unprepared—it was a night-mare.'
It will be so embarrassing'
'The teacher ('*expert*') is going to give me a bad report.'
'What will my parents ('*experts*') say?'

Such negative inner dialogues indeed contributed to her physical manifesta-tions (*behaviour*) such as perspiration, shaking hands, aware that her heart was beating fast (she thought others could hear it), shuddering voice, and ulti-mately a rather less successful reading than might have been possible.

Overall the performance was not a total failure, but Pauline selectively noted the feedback of the more negative pupils in her class and again selectively recorded the negative aspects of the balanced evaluation from the teacher.

Over time when similar situations were encountered the same negative proc-ess was repeated. As a result she developed a self-image that contained a negative belief about her ability to make such presentations.

(It is important to remember that this belief is based on her interpretation of events, rather than on reality.)

Later in her life, despite having reached a responsible position in business she still holds this profound fear of public speaking. By now this negative belief has ultimately become career limiting.

The above illustration uses the example of presentation skills, yet it is impor-tant to understand that the same can equally be true for other beliefs including those related to aspects of influencing such as:

'I find it difficult to engage in small talk.'
'I have never been comfortable when confronting others.'
'I am naturally shy with others.'

An important issue to understand here is that in our storyboard, Pauline does not necessarily to actually have conduct further presentations for the same negative and cumulative results to occur. This is because simply by mentally reflecting on the experience, i.e. thinking about things, the negative impact increases. In other words the mental repetition is as powerful as the actual physical experience. If the experience is a particularly uncomfortable or pain-ful one, then we discover that we are much more likely to engage in this process of repetition; consequently this process of repetition then imprints the same image, which results in a reinforced belief.

What we are describing here is that in our mind reality is often based on an event that has been experienced in a very intense manner, and as a result of multiple mental repetition it becomes our truth. Hence the child who is frequently humiliated by his parents as being stupid or dim witted feels the experience in an acutely painfully way, and as a result of reflection comes to believe what his parents say about him. This situation is typical of many underachievers across many different spheres.

The other thing that is interesting in the above storyboard is that it shows that even where we have a belief that is self limiting or restricting, and more importantly are aware of this fact, we still act in accordance with the negative belief. Of course the reason is simple, we are acting in accordance with our self-image, hence we may not particularly like or enjoy our behaviour, but we are free from stress or anxiety because we are both predictable and consistent. These latter two characteristics are very important aspects of human behaviour.

STORYBOARD   DEVELOPING BELIEFS

Carol Ann was flying from Los Angeles to Auckland via Honolulu. She was well travelled and flew thousands of business miles each year; she enjoyed the whole process of flying.

As the 747 gathered speed to take off from Honolulu, suddenly there was an enormous 'bang', which sounded like an explosion. All the passengers became aware that the aircraft was braking harshly and eventually it ground to a halt. Clearly the passengers were somewhat anxious, there were no announcements as to what had happened, but generally an air of chaos existed as they disembarked down the escape chutes.

Subsequently it transpired that almost at the point of take-off a front tyre had exploded. Although in no imminent danger, the pilot had quite rightly aborted the take-off. The aeroplane had come to rest about 200 m from the end of the runway (and the sea).

Carol Ann returned to the terminal building with the other passengers. They were there for almost two hours and during that time they talked about their common experience. Every time they discussed the incident, Carol Ann found herself seeing it in her mind. In effect she was repeatedly imprinting the powerful experience.

She eventually arrived in New Zealand and once again she found herself recounting the story to different individuals. Each time she did this she continued to imprint the picture in her mind.

In effect although the incident happened only once, she probably thought about it several hundred (if not thousands) of times. As a result her subconscious recorded it as if it had happened repeatedly. As a result of this repetition, Carol Ann developed a series of different beliefs about flying which included the following:

> 'Flying can be dangerous.'
> 'You have no chance if something goes wrong.'
> 'I don't like flying.'
> 'I get headaches when I fly.'

As a result, although she continued to travel extensively, she found that the experience was less and less enjoyable and more and more stressful. This was hardly surprising as when one of the authors met her, some eight years after the original event, she was still able to recall the incident in vivid detail. In effect she was still imprinting the experience: it was still happening to her.

What the above story clearly illustrates is the ease with which any of us can develop beliefs based on intense real experiences that by repetition quickly become our reality. This is the way in which fears and phobias are developed.

COPING WITH INTERNAL TURMOIL

When we act in a way that is inconsistent with our self-image, there are a number of inbuilt defence mechanisms which the mind may bring into play in order to help cope with the mental unease of doing something that does not fit our internal pictures.

Arguably these defence mechanisms allow us to maintain our sanity, because they provide an explanation for our behaviour, or a way of compensating for it.

These behaviours take many forms. We will consider some examples of these below.

Rationalization

If I see myself as being an assertive person, capable of stating what I think, need, and feel, and yet find myself in a situation where somebody else is 'pushing me around' or taking advantage of me, then I am likely to find myself rationalizing my behaviour.

Rationalization is a way of excuse making whereby I would seek to explain or justify my actions as being normal or rational. Effectively it is about me telling myself things to make me feel better about something I did or something I did not do.

In the above example I would probably find myself saying to myself:

> 'I know I am being pushed around; however, on this occasion it is OK

because I do not want to upset this person; they have probably been having a hard time recently.'

Let us take another example. I have a self-image which says I am a fit, strong, athletic, and healthy person, and I train regularly in order to keep fit. I start out on a forty-minute run in hot weather on a route I have run a number of times. On the outward journey, after about five minutes I trip on an area of cobbled stones and almost twist my ankle; I manage to recover and continue with the run. On the return journey I am feeling particularly tired, in fact more tired than I would normally be at this stage of the run. Internally I have a conversation with myself as follows:

'I am feeling tired but I must go on to prove to myself that I can still do it.'

One minute later:

'This really is quite uncomfortable; I will see how I feel in one minute and review the situation—it may be necessary to walk some of the way.'

One minute later:

'This really is getting tough; I must remember that tomorrow I have an important day at work and I do not want to be too tired—maybe it would be wise to walk part of the way.'

Then:

'I am about to come up to those cobbled stones: definitely a good reason to stop and walk the rest of the way. If I tripped again I could injure myself and that would be bad news. Yes I am going to walk the rest of the way.'

Clearly this example illustrates the fact that several spurious reasons are thought up to try and explain the reality which does not fit with the self-concept held.

Rationalization is probably the most frequent form of psychological defence behaviour that we see in ourselves and other people. It is frequently seen in the context of the influencing situation, where an individual who has a tendency to avoid really improving their influencing skills will rationalize why they adopt a more passive or aggressive approach.

Often this is about seeking some evidence to support the outcome and engaging in inner dialogues after the event which say such things as:

'He had made his mind up, nobody could have influenced him, let alone

me; actually he is probably right, I was thinking of doing it his way.'
'Well it was not important to me anyway; it was more important to them than it is to me.'

Compensation

Compensation refers to the way in which we cover up a perceived weakness by overemphasizing another more positive trait. This is often a way of avoiding taking an honest look at one's own behaviour. In the context of influencing, the following example of compensation is often seen if a person feels a natural nervousness about being assertive and standing up for their opinions and views.

For example, suppose you were dealing with someone who was putting you down with throwaway one-line comments such as 'You would say that, wouldn't you?', or 'What do you know you are only a secretary?'

In these circumstances our inner dialogues might go as follows:

'I know that I am not confronting him; however, I prefer to use my more subtle persuasive skills. I also know that I am good at my job so I will deal with it by being really helpful trying to keep him happy.'

As a result the other person is likely to continue to act in this aggressive, manipulative manner.

Projection

This a psychological defence mechanism which involves transferring the blame or responsibility for what may be perceived as our own failure to something or somebody else. This is about failing to take ownership for one's own behaviour and protecting oneself by in effect saying 'It's not my fault, it is the other person who is to blame.'

For example, if we were failing to convince someone to take a particular course of action, then our inner dialogues might be as follows:

'I could have been more persuasive but she wasn't really prepared to listen to me. It's her fault, she is a bad listener. Also she is always aggressive, everyone knows that; I just don't need to get drawn into such unpleasant situations. I am better than that.'

As a result of this type of mental process we would probably fail to address the real issues behind one's own behaviour, which in this example could be lack of preparation, negative impact, or failure to question effectively.

Displacement

With this behaviour the individual transfers his or her anger or frustration on to another person who is probably not the source of the original difficulty.

Suppose you have a meeting in which your boss publicly rebukes you in front of other people. Although you feel he is wrong, you keep quiet rather than risk making things worse. Your inner dialogue might be as follows:

> 'There was no need for that; it was really embarrassing being shown up in front of my own team. Well if that's how they want to play it I can play the same game. I feel really angry inside.'

Later that day you have a meeting with the computer services department and you find yourself making a mountain out of a molehill with a junior engineer who has produced her development plans several days later than expected.

The interesting point is that the boss who causes the original problem is not confronted. The anger and frustration is displaced onto a weaker, more vulnerable target. The likely consequence is that the relationship with the boss will continue as it is, i.e. the same sort of public humiliation can be expected to recur. Furthermore the situation is exacerbated because relationships with the computer services department are likely to degenerate as a result of the displaced anger.

Atoning

Atoning is the term which describes the reaction that is often seen when a person feels guilty about their behaviour. We do things that are aimed at making amends or putting things right; more often, though, atoning is about the individual finding a way of internally feeling better about the situation.

For example, in the situation described above, after the meeting with the computer services department you feel you should not really have given the engineer such a hard time. After all she was only a junior person and the problems with the department are not solely down to her. You decide to go to her department at the end of the day and see if she wants to come out for a drink. She declines. You make then make offers of special assistance in order to accrue her goodwill.

Your inner dialogue might be:

> 'I'm not really vindictive, well at least I have tried to help him; if she doesn't want the benefit of my experience that's up to her. All I can do is offer.'

The consequences of this sort of behaviour are that one is seen as being manipulative, inconsistent, or untrustworthy; most people are likely to see through such behaviour and recognize that there is some atoning taking place. This is, therefore, unlikely to prove very effective as an influencing strategy.

Sympathism

This is the sort of behaviour which is often exhibited by those who in an influencing sense tend to be passive or submissive when dealing with stronger personalities. This is to do with attempting to gain sympathy or understanding from others aimed at increasing one's general feeling of worth, despite having an obvious failure.

For example, if during a meeting you fail to support a colleague when he comes under attack regarding a presentation, and then after the meeting the colleague confronts you.

You respond:

> 'Yes I know that I didn't help you but I wasn't prepared, I haven't been very well lately, and as a result I haven't been sleeping very well. I'm thinking of going to the doctor.'

In the short term this approach may result in some sympathy from some people; however, most people will see through this and ultimately it will result in lack of respect in the eyes of others and internally a feeling of guilt.

Withdrawal

This is where because of a feeling of inability to confront an issue, person, or situation, the way of coping is actually to withdraw or avoid that situation. Often this avoidance type of behaviour is very creatively disguised. Actions are taken that enable one to escape from an uncomfortable or unpleasant situation.

In the above situation you feel that supporting your colleague's presentation is simply not something you could do; you always find confrontation a thing of embarrassment and as a result a high level of stress is usually involved

Hence when you are next asked to confront senior managers in a meeting and to support your colleague, you find a plausible reason why you are unable to attend on the allocated date, or alternatively you agree to the meeting but subsequently cancel on the basis that an unexpected personal situation has occurred. The next time you actually manage to pre-empt the request by booking a vacation at the time you would have to attend the meeting.

The consequence of this type of avoidance behaviour is that, as with many of the defence mechanisms discussed, externally it may work in the short term but in the long term others will become aware of what is happening. This in turn may result in a high level of individual stress.

In many ways all psychological defence behaviours are designed to protect our fragile self-concept (ego) from hurtful or painful experiences. Everyone engages in such processes from time to time. They really only become dysfunctional when we engage in such behaviours to excess, or where the behaviours become outside the usual bounds of society norms.

For example, whereas displacement behaviour may be fairly common, when it leads to direct acts of violence, or by its frequent use results in lack of trust, it ceases to considered in the usual range of normal behaviours. Essentially such behaviours are concerned with maintaining our inner balance or peace and harmony.

UTILIZING THE TURMOIL

This discord resulting from behaving in a way that is inconsistent with our self-image, can actually help us change our behaviour.

As a result such an action could initiate and drive internal change. In effect this is the underlying principle by which self-assertion statements work; we will discuss self-assertion statements in the next chapter.

Pause for thought

How much of your inner dialogues are positive?

Who have been, or who are, the 'experts' in your life?

Have these 'experts' exerted either a positive or negative effect on you beliefs about yourself?

What beliefs do you currently hold that may be limiting your skills of influencing?

Consider a situation where you experienced 'flooding'. How successful was this?

In what circumstances would you see desensitizing as being of benefit?

Consider situations where you have used the psychological defence mechanisms covered above.

How did they help you cope?

What were the aspects of your self-image that you were trying to protect?

Which approaches do you rely on more than others?

To summarize, in this chapter we have been exploring a number of critical mental processes, a cycle that can either contribute positively or negatively to our achieving personal success. In particular we have seen that the way in which we perceive experiences is fraught with difficulties, and as a consequence we frequently misinterpret or distort events. This results in our own unique version of reality or the truth.

We have also examined the importance of positive thought, and the role of 'experts' on our thinking, and have acknowledged the way in which such thought contributes to the picture or self-image we have in our head as to who we are.

We went on to examine the way in which we tend to act in accordance with our self-image, both positively and negatively, primarily due to our desire to stay comfortable. We concluded by looking at some examples of what may happen when we act in a way that is inconsistent with our self-image. These behaviours are designed to protect our fragile self-image.

In the next chapter we will move on to explore how we can utilize some of these cognitive processes to achieve lasting change by making sure our beliefs, and self-image, are consistent with what we want to achieve.

5 Making change last

Chapter objectives

- To build on our understanding of the model of behaviour discussed in the previous chapter and examine how we can positively take control of these critical mental processes.
- To look at the psychological techniques which powerful influencers use to increase their chances of success.
- To provide information from our research which shows that successful people tend to use imagery to visualize success in their heads, as a way of moving towards new levels of achievement.
- To explain how to formulate your own self-assertion statements aimed at focusing on critical personal change.
- To consider a powerful way of imprinting these new beliefs into our self-image, thus ensuring that you build mental pictures that help you to achieve your personal goals.

In this chapter we are going to look at ways of increasing the likelihood of being successful through the use of practical techniques which help us to control the way we interpret events, think about ourselves and our world, and develop a self-image that will lead to higher levels of personal performance.

BREAKING THE MOULD—IMAGERY AND VISUALIZATION IN ACTION

Our model of behaviour discussed in the previous chapter may seem rather pessimistic. There is, though, a much more optimistic scenario. The negative vicious circle can in fact be broken, and by working against the tendency towards negative inner dialogues and using techniques that encourage positive images, the individual's self-image can be developed and effective behaviour change achieved

The two specific techniques covered here are those of drafting 'self-assertion statements' and the use of 'visualization' as a way of successfully imprinting these images as new beliefs.

These techniques have been borne out of our original research into the common characteristics displayed by highly successful individuals as well as successful influencers in organizations and are backed up by earlier findings regarding methods used by successful sportsmen and sportswomen.

But first let us consider the story of an aspiring entrepreneur which is based on a discussion we had with a successful businessman regarding the way he achieved his success.

STORYBOARD   THE ASPIRING ENTREPRENEUR

When starting my own business I did not really see myself as an entrepreneur, indeed I did not really know how business people became aware of business opportunities. Essentially I had a picture of myself as a corporate manager with big blue-chip company experience and expertise. We were always the buyers of services and I saw myself as a good buyer—after all I had plenty of experience of sitting back while the salespeople flocked to see me and I decided who to do business with.

Shortly after starting my own business it became glaringly obvious that entrepreneurial skills were going to be integral to the success of the venture. The clients were not going to simply come knocking on my door. I had a choice: either I committed myself to becoming gamekeeper turned poacher or I employed someone with strong sales skills. I seemed to know the problem on an intellectual level but that didn't seem to help me when it came to changing my behaviour or doing anything different.

As it turned out, the problem was not so much my actual ability to generate business, but more to do with my self-concept and the messages I had given myself over the years. As a result I committed to spend a few minutes each day trying to imagine myself seeing and developing business oportunities.

As a result of this type of thinking process, something strange seemed to happen, I started to see a number of different opportunities. In particular I remember one specific event that was to change the way I would 'see myself' for ever.

One evening in the early days of the new business, I was sat enjoying a meal with in a public restaurant with my family and I found myself overhearing a conversation between two businessmen. As their discussion developed, I recognized the situation they were describing and it struck me that their problem was my business opportunity. I found myself visualizing their particular organization and equally important could see myself actually approaching them in order to explore opportunities of doing business with them. My business card was in their hands before they had finished their coffee, and by then they had agreed to meet with me the following week.

Fortunately that contact not only generated some valuable early business but as a result of repeatedly going over that event in my mind (imprinting), and talking to others, it also had a profound effect on how I viewed myself.

From that time on I could not fail to see business opportunities, but equally important my new belief about myself allowed me to follow up such opportunities. Hardly a day would pass without me identifying at least one chance to demonstrate my entrepreneurial flair.

The anecdote above is drawn from our personal experiences and demonstrates in a less theoretical way the real power of the self-image in respect of how we act in accordance with the pictures that we have of ourselves (in this case self-limiting), and the way positive imprinting and repetition can lead to changes in this self-image, ultimately leading to significant improvements in performance.

The entrepreneur describes three important issues. Firstly the ability to use visualization as a way of seeing specific opportunities in order to succeed in a new job role or skill. This illustrates how insight into our own behaviour in itself is insufficient; it was the use of imagery that galvanized the entrepreneur into action.

Secondly our ability to visualize or picture success is something more than simply 'positive thinking'. If we can manage the pictures we carry in our heads of ourselves or of situations, and if we can control the internal conversations we have, then our perception will become heightened and as a result we are more likely to see the things that we want. Seeing these things is the prerequisite to taking action

Thirdly we are moved into action by the repeated use of this imagery, but more repetition produces lasting and sustained change.

To demonstrate the power of these principles, try the following simple experiment. The next time you are driving into your local town and are worried that you will not be able to find a parking space, instead of waiting until you arrive in the town centre and then getting into a cycle of negative self-talk, about the lack of parking spaces, spend about a minute before you leave home thinking along the following lines:

- Try to visualize the town centre, particularly in the area that you would like to park. Try to see as much detail as possible.
- Picture where the cars are usually parked.
- Image yourself reversing into a space somewhere in the general area.
- Imagine the feeling of relief at finding a place so soon.

As a result of undertaking the above you may be surprised at how quickly you find a parking space. This is primarily caused by your perception being heightened, resulting in you seeing things that were always there, but that you normally missed because you waited until had arrived before you started 'looking'—and so missed numerous parking opportunities.

As a result of using the above sort of technique, you will find that when you get to within 800 m of where you had been visualizing, you will suddenly start seeing all the opportunities for parking like:

- People reaching in their pockets for their car keys.
- Smoke starting to come from exhaust pipes.
- Doors opening.
- People walking determinedly towards vehicles.

In effect with this technique you are first visualizing success, and as a result utilizing the way in which perception works and locking onto opportunities that abound.

Of course the more traditional approach would be to wait until you have arrived at where you want to be, and then to be surprised at not seeing the opportunities. In this scenario, by the time you have arrived, you have already passed all the major opportunities. In this negative example, life has literally passed us by!

More specifically, successful influencers appear to possess strong imaginative skill, including the ability to picture or visualize situations. What they also do effectively is channel these skills into visualizing success in influencing situations. We believe that the use of visualization and imagery are skills which can be developed and refined.

THE POWER OF IMAGINATION

Consider the following exercise which explores your basic skills of imagery

Close your eyes and relax.

Imagine you are lying asleep in bed at home. You wake up and it is very quiet and still dark outside. Your throat is very dry and after realizing that you are not going to fall back to sleep you decide to go to get a drink.

You get out of bed and because of your familiarity with your home you make your way to the kitchen without putting any of the lights on. Standing in front of the refrigerator you pull the door open and the light makes you blink.

Looking within the refrigerator you see a lemon on the top shelf. You reach for the lemon, it feels cold and waxy in your hand. You take it out of the refrigerator and shut the door. Once again it is dark.

You open a drawer where you know you will find a knife and using the breadboard you cut the lemon in half. You reach towards one half of the lemon and move it towards your mouth. You bite hard . . .

Consider the following:

- Did you salivate?
- Could you actually taste the lemon?
- To what extent could you feel the effect it on your taste buds?
- Did you feel the waxy cold skin of the lemon?
- On a scale of 0 (low)–10 (high), what level of detail in the house were you able to see?

Successful people we interviewed scored highly in this exercise in terms of their ability to visualize the above scene as though it was real; they described experiencing the sensations of temperature, taste, and sound, and being able to see the scenario in a vivid way. In particular they tended to rate the final question as seven or above.

The interesting thing in this specific exercise is that it recognizes that when we use imagery and visualization, it is not only pictures that we see, but it may be actual things we imagine we can hear, smell, taste, or touch. Along with these sensations you may experience emotions or moods. Indeed in developing our imagery skills we should always try to incorporate as many of the senses as possible.

Pause for thought

Now let us consider the development of our imagery skills while at the same time improving our critical skills of influencing.

Firstly, below you will read descriptions of seven general influencing situations which include the key competencies as described in our EDICT model of influence. This exercise will ask you to consider these situations and by using as much imagery that you can, make the images as real as possible. We will then ask you to consider how effective your imagery skills are against four key criteria:

1. How vivid was the picture image?
2. Were you able to hear sounds associated with the image?
3. Could you actually feel yourself doing something or taking action?
4. Were you able to experience any specific emotions associated with the image, i.e. being satisfied?

Before you start these exercises it is important that you first try to relax fully. Ensure that you are sitting or laying down, make all your muscles go loose, try tightening each muscle in turn before relaxing. Take slow deep breaths and try to regulate your breathing. If necessary start using positive inner dialogues to help you relax by repeatedly using words like 'be calm', 'be still' or 'peace'.

It is only when you are relaxed that you are best able to practise your imagery skills. In doing this try to see as much detail as possible; focus entirely on the image and prevent your thoughts from wandering.

Image and visualize the following seven different influencing situations. Spend at least a minute thinking about each of the situations. Think about things like what you are doing and how you are doing it. When imagining each situation, try to see, hear, smell, or feel as much detail as possible.

- *You are preparing to influence someone who you are meeting later that day.*
- *You are in a situation where you are required to make a good first impression on another person.*
- *You are quickly building a trusting relationship with another person.*
- *You are showing powerful listening and questioning skills.*
- *You are giving feedback to another person and it is being well received.*
- *You are using strong persuasive techniques, including the use of appropriate body language.*
- *You are in a situation where you are easily able to confront another person in a manner that is assertive, and you are able to control the way you respond when the other person becomes either manipulative or hostile.*

When you have finished imagining each situation, please rate your level of imagery skill using the following questionnaire, by circling the response that most describes your level of achievement. Remember that for the purpose of this exercise, image is taken to relate to any sensory experience albeit seeing, hearing or feeling

Self-assessment rating

1 = Not able to see an image

2 = An image but not very clear

3 = Moderately clear image

4 = Extremely powerful image

Using the above rating scale, answer the following questions in respect of your imagined performance in respect of each situation.

How clearly did you see yourself doing this activity?	1	2	3	4	5
Could you hear any sounds?	1	2	3	4	5
Could you feel yourself taking any specific actions?	1	2	3	4	5
How strong were your feelings?	1	2	3	4	5

Next think about the specific situation and the effectiveness of your performance in the context of using the influencing skills. On the scale of 0 (low)–10 (high):

- *How effectively did you feel you performed with the skill?*
- *Consider how could you improve your performance?*
- *What could you do differently to make things more powerful?*

Finally repeat the process of using imagery in these seven situations. Keep repeating this process and continue to rate both yourself against the self-assessed imagery rating, as well as the perception on your performance. This way you should be able to monitor your progress as you improve both your imagery and visualization skills as well as the actual competencies of influencing.

SIGNIFICANT FEATURES OF OUR RESEARCH

Overall, our research into the thinking processes of successful people led to investigations beyond the group of chief executives. We also conducted extensive interviews with high achievers from a broad range of backgrounds including the following:

- An international professor of creativity and creative leadership.
- A young retired senior army officer who had overcome considerable educational handicaps and difficulties of social class to achieve significant status in the establishment hierarchy.
- A 2 hour 35 minute marathon runner with a long history of social and psychological difficulties.
- A socially disadvantaged, uneducated, unmarried mother who in the space of ten years turned her life 180 degrees and is now happily married, running a successful business and classified in the top 1 per cent of earners.
- The owner of a small business who had received national acclaim for her achievements since being left destitute after the unexpected death of her young professional husband.

There were some interesting patterns in terms of thought processes and ability to visualize. These high achievers tended to show the following significant similarities:

- Heightened awareness of the impact of other people on their inner dialogues, particularly the negative impact of these.
- Regularly engaging in the use of imagery, and an ability to experience actual feelings and see detail when fantasizing or using imagery.
- Frequently using 'internal coaching' to improve performance.
- A tendency to encourage themselves either before, during, or after doing something—particularly in threatening or potentially difficult situations.
- Recognition of the potential impact of negative thoughts and how vulnerable they could be if such thoughts were not managed.
- The regular use of repetitive imagery of success to create or visualize how things might be in the future.
- The ability to visualize big pictures but with the capability of homing in on fine details.

APPLICATION IN HUMAN ENDEAVOUR

Our findings are supported by some of the research into the achievement of human potential in the sporting word, where it has been known for some time that mental practice and visualization can improve physical performance.

As long ago as 1965 experiments in examining methods of gymnastic coaching discovered that it was possible for people to learn gymnastic skills simply by reading a mechanical analysis of the skills combined with mentally practising (Jones, 1965). What was particularly interesting in these results was the fact that this approach applied even when the learner had no previous experience of the skill.

Other more anecdotal examples include, for example, the recollections of the golfer Jack Nicklaus, who in his book *Golf My Way* (1976) describes his use of imagery as follows:

'I never hit a shot, even in practice, without having a very sharp in-focus picture of it in my head. It's been like a colour movie. First I "see" the ball where I want it to finish, nice and white and sitting up high on the bright green grass. Then the scene quickly changes and I "see" the ball going there: its path, trajectory and shape, even its behaviour on landing. Then there's a sort of fade-out, and the next scene shows me making the kind of swing that will run the previous images into reality. Only at the end of the short, private, Hollywood spectacular do I select a club and set up the ball.' (p. 107)

Similarly in the clinical field, work with stutterers highlighted the fact that stutterers held a stronger self-image of themselves as stutterers than as non-stutterers, and that because of this they felt more comfortable relating to the world as stutterers (Fransella, 1971).

It was shown that with mental practice and visualization techniques the problem could be significantly alleviated.

In the medical context there is a growing body of evidence to indicate the effectiveness of imagery in treating a whole spectrum of conditions ranging from depression to chronic pain (Schultz, 1978; Jaffe and Bresler, 1980).

OTHER INTERESTING CHARACTERISTICS

Given that some people appear to have strong visualization capabilities, one review of the existing literature (Barber and Wilson, 1979) showed that these people tend to engage or experience the following type of experiences:

- Extensive vivid fantasies
- Hallucinatory fantasies
- Pretending to be someone else
- Sensory motor experiences
- Vivid personal memories
- Telepathy and other psychic experiences
- Out-of-body experiences
- Automatic writing
- Religious visions
- Healing
- Apparitions

Of those high-achieving individuals that took part in our research, at least 53 per cent stated that they had experienced one or more of the above phenomena at some point in their life.

USING IMAGERY IN PRACTICE

We also asked those with strong powers of visualization whether their use of imagery is linked to any context or particular time of day. The majority said their strongest visualization experiences were when they were relaxed or semi-conscious, and were particularly vivid when in a state of limbo between wakefulness and sleeping in the morning or last thing at night. This is what is sometimes referred to as the 'alpha state', when the body is relaxed but the mind is still working though with slower brainwaves.

It is clearly possible consciously to harness these powers that appear to be so frequently used by both high achievers (including sportsmen and sportswomen) as well as those individuals who are strong powerful influencers.

The primary technique that we can utilize to help us with this mental readiness is that of self-assertion statements.

USING SELF-ASSERTION

Self-assertion statements are concerned with defining success as a goal, yet they are written in a certain specific way, which through the use of visualization can result in the goal being imprinted so it becomes our new belief, and ultimately with repetition, our new reality.

Self-assertion statements can be either temporary or permanent, and repetition can help us achieve lasting and sustained change in our behaviour.

Self-assertion statements are simply statements of desired outcomes or behaviours which are written down and then imprinted on the mind. They accelerate the process of moving towards the achievement of personal goals and objectives by taking the time to imprint only images that we want into our subconscious, rather than other, less helpful messages.

Self-assertion statements are about establishing new beliefs and counteracting old beliefs about ourselves by effectively programming our subconscious. This programming is a normal and natural process; however, by using self-assertion statements we are taking control of the process, rather than leaving things to chance.

Key steps of using self-assertion statements

The technique for using self-assertion statements follows three critical steps:

1. Identify and define the desired change, i.e. recognize what needs changing.
2. Draft the self-assertion statements (making sure that they subscribe to the principles as described below) and ensuring that they specify successful outcomes.
3. Imprint by reading the self-assertion statement at least twice a day, thus using imagery to produce powerful changes in beliefs and subsequently behaviour.

How they work

Self-assertion statements work by initially creating discomfort with our self-image, or how we see ourselves. This discomfort increases the more we imprint the new images. Eventually, by repetition we start to create a new dominant picture of reality as well as an increasing level of discomfort. Slowly we start to change our behaviour to match the new image or dominant picture of ourselves, and consequently we actually begin to act in accordance with the new picture or belief.

STORYBOARD   USING SELF-ASSERTION STATEMENTS

Phil was concerned because he had a self-belief that he was not particularly willing to develop others in his team, compounded by the fact that he felt he was not very good at developing others. This belief would often show itself by his subordinates frequently giving signs that they needed his help, but in general terms he ignored such signals.

After some time, this characteristic was picked up by his boss and Phil committed himself to do something about this problem, but he knew it would not really be easy not least because he did not really think he could do much actually to help his people.

Phil knew about the power of self-assertion statements; he had already used them to improve aspects of his performance, so he decided to draft a new statement as follows:

> 'I am proud that every day I take time to help my people grow and develop.'

Each morning and each evening he read the statement and each time he tried to visualize a different image related to his helping develop his people. What he did not do was try to force himself to change his behaviour, he believed that if you changed the picture first, the behaviour would follow.

After a period of about ten days he became aware that he seemed to find himself doing something that provided him with an opportunity to provide development for one of his staff. However, he did nothing and as a result of this he found himself feeling uncomfortable and engaging in various psychological defence mechanisms. His own favourite was rationalization: 'I would have helped him, but I have to get ready for that meeting tomorrow.'

The more he read his self-assertion statement, the more his discomfort or stress seemed to increase. Consequently, after a period of about three weeks Phil found himself unconsciously changing his behaviour to match his new picture of himself.

In the above example Phil changes his behaviour to escape from the stress that he is experiencing by repeatedly reprogramming his self-image. The change is first made within him, and the behaviour then follows. Phil will need to keep using the assertion statement for some time to really ensure that what he has is a permanent change.

Developing powerful statements

There are a number of important principles for producing effective self-assertion statements which, if adhered to, are likely to produce results.

Make them your own

You can only affirm for yourself. Do not try to affirm qualities or changes in other people or to correct or alter situations you cannot control. In writing your self-assertion statements, you are changing your self image, or how you see yourself. Only you can deliberately control the input of information and the visualization that brings about the change of your subconscious self-image. Therefore, in most cases, your self-assertion statement will start with the word 'I'.

As with most guidelines, there are exceptions. When you and another person have agreed on a joint goal, it is possible to write a 'We' affirmation. For example, you and your team could set an agreed joint goal; in this case you will need to affirm both the 'We' joint goal as well as your individual part of reaching the goal.

Particularly positive

Only write out your self-assertion statements in a positive way. Do not describe what you are trying to move away from or eliminate. You must vividly paint the picture of your subconscious image of success in a positive statement. For example, do not make an affirmation like 'I am no longer poor at making social small talk', but make a positive statement like 'I make an immediate impact on people I meet', to enable you to picture the change you desire.

Only in the present tense

Write out your self-assertion statements in the present tense. The reason we only use the present tense in describing our affirmation is that this in the only timeframe the subconscious operates on. Statements like 'some day', 'maybe I'll', 'tomorrow ' will create pictures that make you feel detached from the behavioural change you want to experience now. You want to feel like the change is already happening and that you are experiencing the change inside your own mind and body.

Avoid comparisons with others

The technique of self-asserting is a personal process. You are a unique person and if you attempt to compare your behaviour to people, it will give you no personal way of measuring your growth progress. You may become discouraged by not measuring up to others, or you may get false clues as to the change in your self-image by being better than someone who is less capable. Do not affirm that you are 'as good as' or 'better than' anyone else—just strive to bring about the changes in your self-image that you desire by asserting the qualities that are best for you.

Paint the picture

Describe the activity you are asserting in terms that create pictures of you performing in an easy and anxiety-free manner. Your subconscious actions should be described by statements that start with 'I easily', 'I quickly', 'I enjoy', 'I love to', 'I thrive on', and 'I show'. Statements like these carry a picture of action and accomplishment that does not cause you to feel either threatened or pushed. The result is that you keep moving towards success with confidence.

Do not indicate just the ability 'I can' in your self-assertion statements because this will not produce change. You already have that ability. What you must indicate strongly is actual achievement. Statements like 'I am' and 'I have' clearly express to the subconscious the picture of the behavioural change that you desire. By using self-assertion statements you are assuming on the subconscious level that you are already acting like the person you indicate you want to become. The more you subconsciously act as if you are already in possession of that quality, the faster will your self-image make it evident in your daily actions. By seeing success you also help eliminate some of the stress usually associated with trying to achieve a goal.

Particularly powerful words

Try to put as much power and excitement in the wording of your self-assertion statements as you can by vividly stating your behaviour in colourful terms. Words that spark an emotional picture in your subconscious help to make the experience in your assertion more believable and attractive. Write out your self-assertion statements in a manner that creates emotions such as fun, pride, happiness, and accomplishment. Incidentally, the more emotion, the faster the change. Some examples of starting phrases include: 'I warmly', 'I happily', 'I lovingly', and 'I enthusiastically'.

Realize the achievable

It is important for you to assert only as much as you can honestly imagine yourself becoming or performing. The basic rule is do not overshoot or undershoot. Try to have such a clear and vivid picture of the end result you want to accomplish so that you accurately stay on course to your goal.

In writing out your self-assertion statements, do not try to assert perfection. It is generally self-defeating to make assumptions about yourself or your accomplishments that you know have very little chance of ever happening or lasting. By using terms like 'I always', 'every time I', or 'I'll never' you can place unrealistic demands on your performance reality.

Clearly if you were to set a self-assertion statement which said 'I enjoy the feeling of winning the London marathon', then simply reading the statement and waiting for the victory will lead to disappointment. It is important to combine physical training with the psychological technique. It is worth noting, though, that top athletes, who are often very close in terms of physical ability, will use psychological techniques such as self-affirmation statements and visualization to give them the physical edge over the competition.

You should remember that your personal self-assertion statements should be for yourself only because people may constantly try to remind you of your 'old self-image picture'. Without really meaning to hold you back, the people around you may get upset when you start changing. If we reveal our personal goals and self-assertion statements to others, it allows them to work against us and very often causes us to fail to accomplish our goals. Use good judgement: only reveal your self-assertion statements to those people who need to know them and who can help you to realize them more quickly.

Finally, a word of caution: we believe that self-assertion statements are a powerful psychological tool that support behavioural change by throwing your mental equilibrium into disorder. In view of this we suggest that when writing your statements you seek to write a number of different statements relating to various aspects of your life. These might include the following areas:

- Health
- Job
- Family
- Leisure
- Finance

Using this approach you are less likely to find yourself becoming so goal oriented that everything else gets forgotten!

SOME EXAMPLES OF SELF-ASSERTION STATEMENTS

The following are four different sample self-assertion statements that may be helpful. There are some that may fit your work situation, others which focus on improving aspects of your influencing skills. If some of these self-assertion statements fit your personal needs, please use them, but be sure to rewrite them if necessary so that they sound like you talking to you.

Management self-assertion statements

1. I am an expert at delegating responsibilities and seeing our people experience the achievement of results.
2. I always find the satisfaction which comes from developing my people extremely rewarding.
3. I enjoy the results that come from positive thinking.
4. I consistently receive tremendous gratification from 100 per cent customer satisfaction.

Team self-assertion statements

1. We treat all our customers like they were our only customer: the effect is that people come back to us, which really gives us a buzz.
2. We are true professionals in our approach to all our job activities and we like the feeling of respect which this generates.
3. We pride ourselves on our company image in the community.
4. We easily keep our records up to date so that information can be quickly found.

Personal self-assertion statements

1. I like and respect myself. I know I am a worthy, capable, and valuable person.
2. I enjoy my life, my profession, and my relationships with other people and have a good balanced lifestyle.
3. I show others that I am a person who does not give things up easily
4. I have many successful experiences of using self-assertion statements and I take temporary setbacks easily.

Influencing self-assertion statements

1. I am proud that I always make a positive impact on others and that people warm quickly to me.
2. I am pleased that I am able to build relationships quickly.
3. I am grateful that I only confront other people using an assertiveness approach.
4. People always listen to me; my personal style is friendly and persuasive.

When you are satisfied with the wording of your self-assertion statements, transfer them to your diary, personal planner, or personal computer so they will be easy to access. You may wish to make several copies—one to carry, one for your desk at work, and another set for the bedside. Organize them in any way you wish. Recognize that you will be changing them frequently as you achieve existing goals and define new levels of success.

IMPRINTING YOUR SELF-ASSERTION STATEMENTS

Reading and using visualization are the actions required to imprint your goal on the subconscious and can be seen as a three-step process of reading, imaging, and feeling.

Reading

Read the words of your self-assertion statements as many times as you can each day; this provides a consistent trigger resulting in reinforcement. The best times to read and imprint your self-assertion statements are generally early in the morning, soon after you wake, and just before you go to sleep. Alternatively you can read them at any time during your day, ideally when you are relaxed and have the available time. Repetition of the self-assertion statement is essential.

Imaging

As you read your self-assertion statements you should be trying to imagine vividly or picturing yourself clearly having accomplished the change you want or the success you intend to create. You are displacing old self-images with new pictures of how you want to feel and act. Remember you are practising and experiencing the change consciously to begin with, but through your imaging you are recording your images into your mind. Very quickly you will find yourself moving easily and naturally to the newly imagined levels of performance.

Remember to try to use visualization that helps you imagine sound, smells, the touch of something, or how you might feel

Feelings

Feeling the emotion you want is very important for imprinting. Gather up the feelings that you know will accompany the accomplished goal and enjoy them each time you imprint your self-assertion. The assertion will affect your system in a positive way in direct proportion to the frequency with which you use vividness of imagery and emotional involvement.

Generally speaking, the impact of imprinting of your affirmation can be broken down in the following way:

Just reading affirmation	10 per cent impact
Reading and picturing	55 per cent impact
Reading, picturing, and feeling	100 per cent impact

> **Pause for thought**
>
> *Consider your own goals—try to identify at least two work-related and two personal goals and three in relationship to improving your influencing skills.*
>
> *Now follow the guidelines above for writing good quality self-assertion statements.*
>
> *Practise the three steps of imprinting:reading, imaging, and feelings.*

Think about how you might be able to use self-assertion statements when working with others.

Practise drafting a team self-assertion statement.

In Appendix 4 you will find an exercise that will help you to reflect on your own thought processes and which focuses in particular on your personal beliefs regarding your own influencing ability.

So far we have considered the use of self-assertion techniques that are basically of a permanent nature, that is to say they are very useful in helping us challenge inappropriate beliefs that may be deeply held within us. They tend to require fairly extensive imprinting, and may need to be repeated over a considerable period of time. Nevertheless, usually if we are imprinting regularly, then we might expect to see some measure of improvement within about 21 days.

An important concept in the process of using self-assertion statements is that during their use, it is important to realise that you should not try to force a change in your behaviour. Keep reading the self-assertion statements, keep imprinting but do not initially do anything different. If such change is forced, then it will be similar to that which we discussed early in the chapter as being 'white-knuckle change'. The result of this is that we become stressed and are unlikely to continue with the change.

Eventually when the time is right, that is to say when you have reprogrammed your beliefs and established a new dominant picture of reality, then the necessary change will just happen naturally. What we are describing here is change that starts within us, and works its way outside into our behaviour. This will be achieved without unnecessary stress.

Our research showed that while successful individuals used these sorts of mental processes to achieve significant and lasting change related to their self-image beliefs, they also used what we have described as temporary self-assertion statements prior to particularly difficult situations.

A chief executive of an international petrochemical company described sitting down before a shareholders' meeting and using visualization to picture a successful result. Such an outcome might include seeing and hearing the meeting applauding him, or alternatively seeing smiling faces.

Another executive from an international brewing organization stated that he would usually make himself relax before using imagery prior to doing something demanding like informing people of major restructuring or redeployment. In such circumstances he recognized the importance of seeing a successful outcome as the critical output

An international business professor explained that he had recognized the link between his thinking prior to starting an assignment and the eventual out-come. In particular he found that where he was able to visualize people wanting his help, or where he saw himself as being made welcome and quickly encouraged to contribute, then he found that the outcome was infi-nitely more favourable. By contrast, the opposite was also true. Consequently he developed a habit of using instant positive imagery on his way to the cli-ent's premises.

The use of these sorts of techniques are similar to more permanent self-asser-tion statements—the primary difference is that they are not written down nor are they necessarily repeated. However, the principles of how they are devel-oped are still valid, i.e. first person, present tense and positive, etc.

As such, these temporary self-assertion statements appear to be of particular value when there is little time to prepare. They are also useful in supporting other more formal permanent statements—indeed, it is these circumstances in which many successful sports persons use this technique.

Finally we can use these temporary self-assertion techniques when dealing with others. For example, when our staff come to us with specific problems we might try this response: 'What does it look like if you didn't have this prob-lem."

This sort of response forces the recipient to describe (and see) success. As we have discussed, this is the fundamental prerequisite which is the critical start-ing point necessary for achievement.

Pause for thought

What is the best method of recording your self-assertion statements?

Are your self-assertion statements balanced across all aspects of your life?

When or how would be the best time for you to imprint them into your subconscious?

How long are you prepared to use these statements to help you achieve lasting change?

In what circumstances would you feel that you could use a temporary self-assertion statement?

Practise using this technique on something that you are going to do later on today.

To summarize, we can draft and, by imprinting, use self-assertion statements to change aspects of our own beliefs about ourselves that we have identified as being self-limiting.

These techniques are ideal when dealing with significant or deep-seated beliefs about our self-image. In a similar way we can use temporary assertions when we are suddenly faced with a difficult situation or where we have little time to prepare or need to support a more formal self-assertion during a specific situation.

Having now spent some time looking at this subject of mental preparation, we will now go on to explore the importance of the first impression we make on other people.

REFERENCES

Barber, T. X. and Wilson, S. C. (1979) Guided imaging and hypnosis: theoretical and empirical overlap and convergence in a new creativity imagination scale, in Sheika, A. and Shaffer, T. (eds), *The Potential of Fantasy and Imagination*, Brandon House.

Fransella, F. (1971) *Personal Construct Psychotherapy and Stuttering*, Academic Press, New York.

Jaffe, D. T. and Bresler, D. E. (1980) Guided imagery:healing through the mind's eye, in Shorr-Sobel, J. E. and Connells, J. A. (eds), *Imagery: Its Many Dimensions and Applications*, Plenum Press, New York.

Jones, J. G. (1965) Motor learning without demonstration of physical practice under two conditions of mental practice, *Research Quarterly* vol. 36, pp. 270–276.

Nicklaus, J. (1976) *Golf My Way*, Penguin, Harmondsworth, Middx.

Schultz, D. (1978) Imagery and the control of depression, in Singer, J. L. and Pope, K. S. (eds), *The Power of Human Imagination*, Plenum Press, New York.

6 The first four minutes

Chapter objectives

- To discuss the techniques associated with making an impact on others.
- To look at 'impact killers' which are to be avoided if one is to make a good impression.
- To explore the subject of how relationships develop in order to help identify how to accelerate the process of building rapport.
- To explain the techniques for building rapport.

To recognize the importance of understanding cultural differences in the early stages of influencing.

In the previous chapters we have explored various aspects of *preparation*, which are normally the prerequisite to the first step of gaining entry to the influencing process.

The next consideration, and to complete the entry stage of the EDICT model, we will explore the primary competencies of 'impact' and 'rapport'.

IMPRESSIONS MANAGEMENT

The ability to make an immediate impact on the person or group you are intending to influence is absolutely critical to success. Consider the implications of some of the research into first impressions which suggests that people form 90 per cent of their opinion of another person in the first 90 seconds (Pease, 1984). We see this in the recruitment interview where interviewers often describe having a 'gut feel' about the candidate right from the start of the interview. The interview itself might well be viewed as an influencing opportunity; however, in a general sense the importance of making an impact right from the start of any meeting cannot be underestimated.

The significance of first impressions

We often hear expressions such as 'first impressions count', 'make a good impression' and 'you do not get a second chance to make a first impression'. In a similar vein there are some interesting connotations associated with expressions such as 'all that glitters is not gold', 'a wolf in sheep's clothing', and 'do not judge a book by its cover'.

Implicit in these sayings is the fact that it is quite possible to be deceived by first impressions.

We will refer to this concept of managing the impressions that others form of ourselves as 'impressions management'. This is a key concept fundamental to the subject of influencing, and impressions management has applications in a number of areas other than just first impressions. Throughout the book we will look at several ways in which perception of reality can be distorted, and how knowledge of this and judicious application of suitable techniques can actually help increase the power of personal influence.

First impressions are an aspect of impressions management that suggest that it is possible to capitalize on the fact that as a result of distorted perception, we can positively encourage others as to how they interpret events or see us.

It has been suggested that by using techniques to capitalize on the 'distortion' of first impressions, we are supporting a deceptive strategy. This is not our intention. It is, however, a fact, that whether we like it or not, when we meet others for the first time, they will form a first impression of us. At the extreme ends of the spectrum this may be a good first impression or a poor one. Impressions management is about ensuring that we give ourselves the best possible chance of giving the right impression.

The positive aspect of managing the first impression is that we can actually take some control over the nature of the first impression formed by others.

The competence we call rapport follows naturally from that of impact and is essentially about building trust quickly so that the other person feels that a strong relationship exists and that there is some bond between the two parties.

Some people are naturally strong in their ability to do this, whereas others find this the most difficult aspect of influencing. Rapport needs to be established in the early part of the relationship and then reinforced continually throughout. We will be looking at some of the techniques which effective influencers use in order to build rapport.

Cultural differences are an important consideration when attempting to make an impact and create rapport. As with the competence of preparation, we will look at some of the researched cultural differences which have implications for how we might adjust our approach to making impact and building rapport when doing business with people from different cultural backgrounds.

MASTERING IMPACT

Why is it that some people simply make an impact when they enter the room? It is said of these rare people that 'He just has charisma' or 'I cannot explain why, but other people just sit up and listen to her.' Often people talk about these qualities as though they are genetic; you either have it or you do not. It has previously been considered that these charismatic traits, often associated with successful leaders, are natural rather than learned. Without debating, here, the classic argument of whether our personality is determined before we are born or shaped by subsequent learning, suffice to say we strongly believe that the ability to make an impact is something that can be learned and improved with practice.

In order to make an impact there are a number things you can do and equally a number of things you should definitely not do. In a sense these are the more straightforward techniques to learn and practise. Then there are the things you possibly or probably should or should not do, depending on circumstances; these are really dependent on the style and cultural background of the person you are trying to influence, and this is where a degree of judgement and a good deal of common sense are called for.

Promote yourself

Frequently in our culture one hears British children being told 'not to show off'; there is a cultural norm which says that talking about your own successes is immodest and could be seen as arrogant. Even if someone else compliments you on an achievement or strength you are expected to respond in a suitably humble manner. In some cultures and societies the roots of such behaviours and norms can be traced back through history. This is borne out by the following statement from the Victorian Mrs Humphry in *Manners for Men*, who wrote in 1897:

'The truth is that society demands a never-ending series of self-denying actions from those who belong to it, and the more cheerfully these are performed, the more perfect the manners.' (quoted in Jessop, 1994)

In a similar way Mark Twain said:

'Good breeding consists of concealing how much we think of ourselves and how little we think of the other person.' (quoted in Pease, 1994)

For children who are heavily socialized in this way some similar behaviours are transferred into adulthood. This is often the reason that we hear people respond to praise in the following way:

'Oh its nothing really.'
'Thanks, but I was just lucky.'
'Actually I'm not that good.'
'It wasn't all to do with me—I had a lot of help.'

Contrast this with the approach taken by one American multinational consumer goods giant which has actually built official bragging into its performance management system. If you feel you have achieved something out of the ordinary you are encouraged to complete a 'brag sheet' where you literally brag about your success. This is submitted to your manager, who if he or she feels the achievement is sufficiently notable, will send it to the head office in the United States. But the system does not stop there; if the senior managers are suitably impressed they will send the brag sheet back with a written note of praise.

Those who are successful in terms of making impact do not feel guilty about letting others know about their successes. They will be their own best public relations agent.

Clearly if it is possible to have someone else 'sing your praises' to a third party, then this will prove to be an even more powerful way of making impact. This is the reason that often a senior manager will be accompanied by a more junior colleague on a business meeting. The junior can behave suitably in awe of the omniscient senior manager. Similarly if you are making a high-profile presentation, try to arrange for someone to introduce you officially, and brief them regarding your achievements and successes so they give you a strong introduction.

In informal discussion do not be afraid to promote yourself. This could mean talking about a recent project you were pleased with, or a project you are proud of. If this is done in a suitable tone without being overbearing, then it need not seem too egocentric and opinionated; if you sound confidently surprised and pleased with your achievements, then your enthusiasm if likely to spread. And to ensure you are seen to be entirely reasonable and balanced, talk about the success which the other person has had; this will also help with building rapport.

A final point on making impact and building rapport is to remember to build your personal credibility slowly. This means rather than letting everything about you be known when you first meet, slowly let additional things be known; this is done best in an almost oblique manner through half references or innuendo.

Choose your words with care

The actual words you choose to use when attempting to make impact are very important and it is worth considering the effect that certain words are likely to have on others, rather than simply relying on your own interpretation. Some words are likely to make others sit up and listen from the start and this has to be a key consideration for the entry stage of the influencing process. Other words which may even have a similar meaning are less likely to gain attention. The words that make impact are sometimes referred to as power words. A list of power words and phrases and equivalent 'weaker words' is shown in Table 6.1.

In a similar way there are some words which have emotive connotations for the person hearing them despite the fact that they are used without the intention of stirring such emotion. A good example of this is the use of the word 'but'. This is a commonly used word which can be interpreted as a blocking and negative word, whereas the words 'however' and the word 'and' actually hold a similar meaning without such potential for negative interpretation. When you hear yourself about to say 'but', try to use 'however' or 'and' which convey a more supportive approach.

Similarly the use, early in a discussion, of the word 'problem', particularly if couched in terms such as 'your problem' or 'the problem you have is . . .' can seem quite accusational and threatening. The use of the word 'issue' may achieve the same purpose in a less threatening way: 'The issue we need to address is . . .'. Notice here the use of 'we' rather than 'you'; again this is less confrontational and may help in setting the appropriate tone early on in the discussion.

Power words/expressions	Weaker words/expressions
Definitely	Possibly
Clearly	New
The only option	The latest thing is . . .
Leading edge	Big
Pioneering	I believe
The new technology is . . .	What I mean is . . .
Giant	Well known
Achievement	I believe/I think
Specifically	Impression
Renowned	As soon as possible
Success	Maybe
Power	Perhaps we
Impact	False
Immediately	Mostly I've found

Table 6.1

Get noticed

We are not proposing here that it is necessary to dress up or to act in order to appear different but in order to make impact at the start it does help to look distinctive. This could be demonstrated through subtle detail such as interesting cufflinks, buckles, or brooches, or even a distinctive fountain pen. Some people have made certain characteristics their trademark such as unusual ties or loudly coloured handkerchiefs; the danger here is that the feature, if it appears as a gimmick, actually becomes more of a focus of interest than the person or their message.

Undoubtedly an important consideration with regard to dress and appearance is to have some understanding of the cultural norms for the organization, profession, or nationality of the people you are attempting to influence. While it may not be sensible to mimic the dress conventions of the other party it may prove helpful to modify or adjust your appearance in order to show some identification with them. If consulting with a client organization in a British government department in London, anything other than dark or formal clothing may seem revolutionary. The expectation may be that in order to continue to work with this organization conformity is essential; this means that any attempt to be noticed will need to be discreet and subtle. Conversely it is possible to visit a creative advertising agency in the same street where it will be expected that one should wear bright colours and informal clothing. In this environment the dark suit which would have been entirely appropriate for the government department would actually be viewed as staid and unimaginative. The corollary of this is that an assumption will be made that the personality and attributes of the person are also unimaginative and lacking in creativity—qualities which are actually considered important in this sort of organization.

Many successful influencers we have interviewed have described the importance of being able to demonstrate 'chameleon' like qualities—in other words the ability to adjust one's appearance and style according to the people or group one is attempting to influence. The trick is be able to strike a balance between blending in with the environment but retaining some distinctive and memorable qualities or features.

Speak up

In group discussion situations it has been found that those who speak first tend to be viewed by others as influential. It is the early intervention which makes a major impact even though the more reserved members of the group may have more to contribute. It is vital to speak up from the start, though this can sometimes prove difficult.

If you are unsure what to say or fear that you may make a fool of yourself by saying the wrong thing, then try simply stating the objective of the discussion, or building on and adding to the comments of another early speaker.

Frequently the problem with making an early contribution is that it is difficult to find an opportunity to 'get in' because other, more forceful characters tend to dominate. There are some interesting lessons to be drawn from these more dominant people, though: how is it that they manage to have their say early on and others seem to listen? Some interesting techniques are as follows:

- Speaking but avoiding eye contact with other people, thereby making it more difficult for others to signal non-verbally that they want to interrupt. This takes a degree of confidence and it is necessary to suggest through a deliberate tone of voice that you are not going to stop.
- Prefacing the input with a 'trailer' which raises awareness and interest in what is to follow, e.g. instance comments such as 'And do you know why this is important? I'll tell you why . . .' or 'Here is the real issue . . .'. This draws attention and raises expectation that there is more to come.

Agreeing with another person and adding to their comments but 'adding value' to their comments with some personal examples from your own experience. An example of this would be a comment such as: 'Of course you are right Michelle—in fact I have found the same problem in my experience. The approach I took was . . .'.

And then there is the obvious but frequently neglected technique of simply raising the volume of the voice. Some people have a voice which naturally carries, whereas for others it is more difficult to physically 'speak up'.

- An even more effective technique is to start by grabbing attention by raising the volume and then deliberately lowering the volume so that the listeners, having gained interest, have to work to hear the quieter contribution. It is as though the quieter voice, contrasting with the early contribution, suggests a conspiratorial or secret discussion which others will not want to miss out on.

This early part of the discussion is often found to be difficult when communicating with people from a different culture to our own. This is due to the existence of strong cultural norms which we may not be aware of, or even if we are, then we tend to work from our own cultural frame of reference.

In an Anglo-Saxon culture, for example, it is normal for one person to speak, complete their input, and then for the other person to start speaking. In a Latin culture, by contrast, it is more common for the inputs to overlap. In an Oriental culture, however, silences between inputs are more common. It should not come as a surprise, given these cultural norms, that a German, plunged into a meeting with a group of Italians, may feel uncomfortable in the discussion because of the difficulty of gaining entry; the German will be waiting for an appropriate opportunity to make a contribution, whereas the Italians are likely to operate in a much more dynamic way sometimes with four or five people talking at once. The opportunity for a formal input may never come; it may be a question of simply recognizing the cultural difference and rather than fighting it, working with it.

Of course these cultural differences work both ways. If one of the Italians was invited back to the German's organization the same difficulties could be experienced but on this occasion with the Italian feeling uncomfortable with the formality of structured inputs at predetermined times.

Use body language

Body language, the non-verbal cues and signals we give out, sometimes consciously, often unconsciously, are incredibly powerful in terms of impact. This is why at the early stage of an interaction it is critical to portray positive body language. It is body language that other people are likely to work on for interpretation and meaning, even more so than the actual words which are spoken. Examples of positive and negative body language are shown in Table 6.2.

Clearly it is simplistic to suggest that these positive examples of body language taken in isolation will always be interpreted in a positive way; it is more likely

Positive body language	Negative body language
Smiling when appropriate	Grinning (may be seen as patronizing) Scowling (may be seen as aggressive)
Shaking hands or bowing confidently	Hesitant handshake (may be interpreted as weakness)
Sitting or standing upright	Slouching back (may be seen as disinterest)
Varied intonation—use of range of tones	Monotone voice (may be interpreted as disinterest on the part of the speaker or as though the subject is boring) Quiet, low volume (may be seen as uncertainty or lack of confidence)
Making eye contact	Staring (may seem intrusive) Looking away (may be interpreted as disinterest or viewed with suspicion)
Open gestures such as facing the other person and raising eyebrows	Crossing legs and arms (may be viewed as defensive)
Upright or slightly tilted head to show listening	Bowed head (may be seen as shyness or nervousness)

Table 6.2

that the person you are attempting to make an impact on will look to a number of sources or 'clusters' of non-verbal behaviour for the real message. So they will piece together evidence from sources such as facial expressions, sitting position, gestures, and tone of voice. When trying to make an impact, consider whether the non-verbal signals you are giving are consistent with the verbal message and whether they are likely to enhance or diminish your profile.

See the signals

The danger with focusing on making a major impact at the start of the influencing process is that we overemphasize the importance of portraying messages to the other person at the expense of reading the signals which others, either overtly or inadvertently, are giving out. It can be very informative to look for the non-verbal messages and consider how to adapt accordingly. For instance:

- Are they looking anxious?
  It may be necessary to spend more time putting them at ease or making 'small talk', or it may help to try to identify the source of the anxiety.
- Do they seem preoccupied?
  It may help to try and find out the real issues they would like to discuss rather than just the stated objective.
- Are they giving out hostile signals?
  If you know the source of the hostility it may help to bring this discussion out into the open, or if you are uncertain of the source it may take some gentle probing to identify their perception of the problem.
- Do they look disinterested?
  It could be that you need to raise their interest by relating the subject to them personally or you may need to make a high-impact statement such as 'Do you realize some of your colleagues have doubled their salary in the last year by focusing on this issue?'

It is always worth paying close attention to the actual words and terminology used by the other person. Often this means looking for subtleties or 'neon signs'. These are signals that other people give us that basically are designed to prompt us to ask additional questions. Consider also, for instance, the following issues: in their organization do they talk about departments, units, sections, or divisions? Do they distinguish their territory by regions, districts, or areas? Are there certain words or expressions which you can identify as taboo? For example, managers in an organization may prefer to talk about development reviews rather than performance appraisals. The two expressions could be used to refer to the exact same process, but the organization may have a history of a failed 'performance appraisal' scheme. If you can pick up the language used by the other person, then try to echo back the same words when presenting your own points of view. This may mean working from the other person's frame of reference rather than purely from your own, but it will certainly help in encouraging the other person to identify with you.

LESSENING IMPACT

Just as there are a number of techniques you can deploy in attempting to make a positive impact, there are also a number of 'impact killers' to be aware of. These are mistakes which are often made without even knowing it. The following sections give examples of impact killers.

Self-deprecating comments

These are the comments, often used to preface a statement, which lower the status of the speaker. Often self-deprecating comments are meant to demonstrate modesty but in fact they do little more than weaken the impact of the statement which follows.

Examples of self-deprecating statements would be 'I don't really know much about this but what I think we should do is . . .' or 'I am certainly no expert in this field, but why don't we consider . . .'. In contrast to this approach our studies of successful influencers have shown that they will be very cautious about putting themselves down publicly. This does not mean covering up weaknesses and attempting to portray omniscience, but it does mean showing respect for one's own views and opinions and not sharing negative inner dialogues with others.

Compromising on quality

If you are seen to compromise on quality, the chances are that it is likely to show. This is to do with taking short cuts or ignoring mistakes. Examples of compromising on quality would be making a presentation with well-prepared slides but allowing one or two slides with spelling mistakes to be used rather than correcting them. Or it could be demonstrated by the acceptance of low standards in others which might be shown through comments such as 'Oh that will do' or 'This will be good enough'.

Mispronouncing or misspelling names

This can be a tricky matter, particularly when working in an international environment, but mispronouncing the name of the person you are attempting to influence is one certain way of making a negative impact. You may be lucky and find the other person is forgiving or understanding because they recognize they have a name that can easily be mispronounced. You will gain more credibility, however, by checking you have pronounced their name correctly or asking how it should be pronounced and making a point of getting it right. It is a dangerous strategy to guess.

Not being well informed

Being ill-informed is another certain impact killer. This could mean having out-of-date information or not knowing about important changes in the other person's circumstances or organization. Conversely actually demonstrating you are well informed and up to date will help in establishing impact. It is not always possible to have the latest information or the insider knowledge and if you are aware there may some news you are unaware of, then exercise some caution when attempting to demonstrate your knowledge. If you are uncertain of facts and figures that you are expected to have to hand, it can be a mistake to try to bluff; a much better tactic would be to promise to seek out the information and provide it a later date. You will gain more credibility by actually honouring your commitment than trying to suggest you have knowledge which you do not.

Allowing repeated interruptions

Finally the other main impact killer is allowing constant interruptions. Some people have a tendency to allow others to interrupt them repeatedly. While allowing the occasional interruption may actually demonstrate an ability to listen to the other person, allowing repeated interruptions will eventually be interpreted as lack of self-esteem and self-respect which will clearly reduce impact in an influencing sense.

Pause for thought

Think of someone who made an immediate positive impact upon you.

What was it specifically they did or said which contributed to this impact?

What were the non-verbal messages they conveyed?

Now consider someone you have taken an instant dislike to.

What was it specifically they said or did which contributed to this dislike?

What was it, if anything, about their appearance you disliked?

What assumptions were you making about these people based on first impressions?

If you got to know this person better, how well founded were your assumptions?

We have considered a number of ways of making impact which, to be effective should be demonstrated, if possible, in the first four minutes of an interaction. That is not to say the techniques of making an impact do not apply throughout the influencing process, but it is the first four minutes which really count in terms of making a powerful first impression.

We will now look at the competence of building rapport, which effectively follows on from making impact.

LAYING THE FOUNDATIONS—BUILDING RAPPORT

Rapport is about building trust or laying the foundations of a relationship, and consequently enabling the other person to feel that they have something in common with you. There are some specific techniques for building rapport which are used by powerful influencers and can be defined and practised. But before we look at the techniques, it will be helpful to discuss a model which looks at how relationships are formed and strengthened.

How relationships develop

If the ability to build rapport is really about being able to accelerate the development of a human relationship, then it is helpful to look at the process by which relationships are built.

The model shown in Fig. 6.1 is, in its title, an interesting example of how the psychologists who developed the model have used one particular influencing technique to great effect. Although the name of the model, 'Johari window', suggests some complex and even mystical meaning and source, it is actually a combination of the first names of the two psychologists, Jo and Harry, who created it. While this is quite an amusing fact there is a real message here regarding the subject of influencing. This method of establishing expertise by using 'technical' or pseudo-technical language can be a very effective persuasive technique for establishing credibility and perceived expertise; we will look at this influencing technique in more depth later in the book.

The Johari window model uses the concept of windows to show how we tend to relate to other people around us. Using the metaphor of windows, the model says that there are essentially four windows which exist in our relationship with others. The horizontal axis shown on the top of the windows refers to what is known by others about ourselves. The vertical axis shown to the left of the windows refers to information known by ourselves about ourselves. Each window represents a certain amount of information about ourselves.

So the arena represents all that information about 'me' which is known by me and by others; it is the arena in which we operate. When we first meet another person the arena tends to consist of psychologically safe information which is invariably of a factual nature. This would include information such as names, job roles, locations, nationalities, and other personal, but not too personal information.

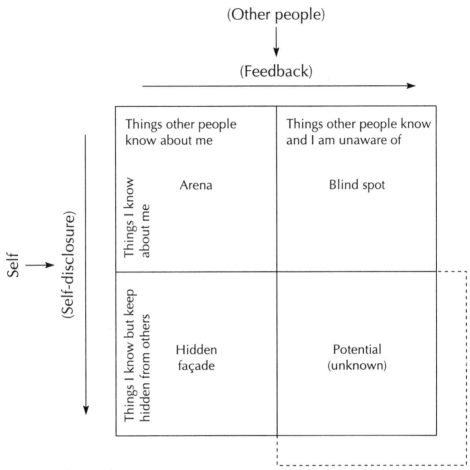

(Other people)

(Feedback)

Things other people know about me	Things other people know and I am unaware of
Arena	Blind spot
Hidden façade	Potential (unknown)

Self

(Self-disclosure)

Things I know about me

Things I know but keep hidden from others

Figure 6.1 Johari window

Then there are the things in the top right window which are known by others about me but which I am unaware of. You may be thinking: how can others have such personal knowledge yet I do not possess this same knowledge about myself? Surely I am the authority on myself? Well possibly, but this window is referred to as the blind spot because it contains a whole lot of information regarding, for instance, mannerisms, habits, and behaviours which others are actually more conscious of. The only way to increase our consciousness of these factors is through a process of feedback, be it requested or imposed.

Then in the lower left window is what is often referred to as the hidden or façade. This is the window concealing a lot of personal information which we, in most superficial relationships, tend to keep hidden. This could include information regarding our personal tastes, beliefs, religious views, upbringing, childhood, personal relationships, weaknesses, and more. This sort of information may remain concealed from all but a handful of people, and even then those who are aware of what lies behind the façade are likely to be those who are nearest and dearest to us. Alternatively we may expose different parts of this window to different individuals.

Finally there is the lower right window, which represents our potential; this contains information that we neither necessarily know about ourselves nor are others aware of. This signifies the potential we could achieve, if, conceptually, we are able to reduce the blind spot and façade. Here is the crux of the model; in order to reduce the blind spot we need to seek feedback, and in order to reduce the façade we need to reveal more information to others so that they have a better understanding of why we are the way we are.

Of course this can seem quite threatening because if we receive feedback we may not like what we hear, and if we disclose personal information, then others may not like what they hear.

In some cultures, such as in the Middle East, self-disclosure is frowned upon because it may mean exposing weaknesses, and there is an underlying fear that others could use this information in the future to their own advantage and to the disadvantage of the person self-disclosing.

We said that this is a model of how relationships develop because as we become closer to certain individuals, whether family friends or partners, there is a tendency to disclose more information and to give and receive more honest feedback.

Now let us consider ways of building rapport with those we are attempting to influence; we will refer back to the model of the Johari window.

Those who are particularly effective in their ability to develop rapport in a short space of time tend to use certain techniques in order to establish trust and the impression that there is a bond or relationship between the two parties.

Critical in this rapport-building process is the very early part of the relationship or discussion. This is not to say that rapport building takes place and is then forgotten; strong influencers will continue to build rapport throughout the discussion and will refer back to some of the subject matter discussed early on as a way of continuing to move closer to the other person.

The primary place for starting to build rapport is, as with impact, within the first four minutes. This is the stage when both parties, irrespective of status and experience, are likely to feel apprehensive about how the relationship is going to evolve. If there is little or no knowledge of the other person, then normally the very early part of the interaction will be marked with formality and caution as each person attempts to weigh up the other.

Using small talk

The most effective rapport builders will at this stage invest time trying to break the ice, often through conversation which may seem trivial in relation to the real agenda. Conversation at this stage is based around the safe arena discussed in the Johari window model above. This level of conversation might be referred to as 'small talk'.

In the United Kingdom small talk tends to revolve around the weather, at an interview the small talk is often focused around the interviewee's journey, and before a business meeting it could be to do with share prices. The subject of the small talk is in fact not so important; what is important is that it does take place. In many ways the blander the topic, the more neutral it is likely to be, and therefore the more likely it is to be a safe subject where both parties are able to operate on a level basis. It is unlikely that one person will have a competitive advantage or significant expertise over the other person when talking about such neutral subjects. It may be possible to find other neutral topics which are of interest to both parties; this could be the latest sports results or discussion of a recent news item.

A good next stage, having spent some time on small talk, is to try to find a subject which is of particular interest to the other person and again invest some time discussing this topic. A favourite, and one that is guaranteed to work in a Western culture, is the family and in particular the other person's children. Tread carefully with this subject in a certain Eastern cultures though: the family tends to be a very private matter and taboo in business relationships. Sales executives are often taught to systematically gather non-work-related data on the other person and to make sure they demonstrate their personal knowledge of the client or customer as soon as possible; while this may seem rather mechanistic and phoney, there is some useful learning here regarding the power of being able to relate to the other person from their point of view. It is possible to be caught out, however, if you fake knowledge or understanding which you do not have; what do you do if the other person decides to discuss these subjects in depth? It could prove worthwhile, though, knowing what is the other person's favourite sport, pastime, or team; just a few exchanges on the right subject can accelerate the rapport-building process immensely.

Showing the similarities

Strong rapport builders are also very quick to pick up on areas of common interest or experience. They will identify such commonality very early on simply by picking up on information discussed in the normal 'arena' in Johari terms. They will then make a point of overtly declaring this common interest in order to identify with the other person. It is surprising the extent to which it is possible to find that you have something in common with the other person even if they are quite different in terms of personality and style.

As with first impressions, where perception tends to be distorted, so our perception is distorted by a concept we will refer to as 'attracted to like'. The concept of 'attracted to like' explains why if we were to mingle freely among a mixed group of people in as large room, then after five or ten minutes we would become attached to someone with a strong common bond: maybe we come from the same country or town, possibly we are the same gender or have the same background, profession or educational background. In an influencing sense it is possible to use this perceptual distortion to ensure that the other person sees some common bond or identification with you as an influencer.

Consider even using the occasional expression like 'You are like me', 'I am like you in that sense', or 'That is where we are similar': this may sound transparent and obvious, but if these comments are integrated with good identification skills they can be extremely effective.

Using self-disclosure

The next technique for building rapport really plays on the fact that self-disclosure, as discussed in the Johari window model, can be a good way of building trust. If we are prepared to take the risk of disclosing some information which might normally be kept hidden behind the façade, then there can be some positive benefits. The chances are that the other person will feel that they can reciprocate and this is how trust is gradually built. Trust building is a process of reciprocal self-disclosure based on the premise that the other person will not abuse the privileged information they are privy to. In the early stage of influencing a small amount of self-disclosure can help begin trust building. This could be as simple as sharing a concern or giving away some personal information. The emphasis is on a *small amount* of self-disclosure here, because clearly if someone starts to self-disclose too much too soon, then there is a danger that questions will be raised. The person on the receiving end of the self-disclosure may consider this suggests insecurity on the part of the discloser or that incorrect assumptions are being made about the nature of the relationship.

STORYBOARD MAKING IMPACT AND BUILDING RAPPORT

As James dressed he carefully selected a suit that was in keeping with the client he was meeting later that day. In his mind he knew that the organization was highly traditional with conservative values; consequently he chose a grey, pin-striped suit with a white shirt and a plain, simple dark-blue tie.

Two hours later he checked his appearance before he entered the office of his client. He smiled widely, and extended his hand in greeting. 'Good morning Al, how are you? (*impact*) Goodness what a journey; it doesn't seem to get any easier—still it's nice to see you again. How's business?' (*rapport*)

James listened attentively while Al described the recent reorganization in his company. He tried not to interrupt other than to seek clarification or to provide some empathetic response.

'You certainly have your hands full, I can't say I envy you. Never mind, think positively: you will soon be on the Algarve playing golf. Anyway, joking aside, what can I do to help you?' (*rapport*)

After describing his difficulty in introducing the new performance appraisal system, James said 'I can see that the issue of communication would be a problem; however, when I worked for Ultracorp we had the same difficulty and we found that rather than viewing it as a communications problem, we treated it as a training issue'. (*self-disclosure/rapport*)

In many ways the above example demonstrates that issues like impact actually start in the competence of *preparation* because clearly if James was inappropriately dressed he would not have created a positive first impression. In a similar way it can clearly be seen that the competence of impact involves basic human attentiveness skills like looking at the other person, greeting, and smiling; whereas rapport is concerned with making the other person feel important. Techniques for doing this can vary from using the other person's name, to asking what you can do to help.

Of course the other person may not want to engage in the process of rapport; instead they may wish to get straight to the point. In these circumstances do not force the issue, but be prepared to respond to their specific needs. Ultimately you may be able to build rapport at a later time.

Put simply, rapport should never be rehearsed or it will appear stilted or false, but it should focus on picking up cues either from the other person or the current situation or from circumstance.

Another consideration in building rapport is to establish some sort of banter with the other person; this could be fun discussion, or playful one-line comments. When you have sufficient confidence that your sense of humour will translate and that the other person will understand the fact that you are taking a jovial approach, this can be a good technique. If in doubt, though, do not risk this approach: unless the other person is on the same wavelength it will surely cause more problems than benefits. Humour does not generally travel well; while the use of understatement and irony may work well in a British culture, it may not translate to, for instance, a Germanic or Dutch culture where supposedly humorous comments are likely to be interpreted more literally.

A HIERARCHY OF ATTRACTION

An alternative way of looking at the issue of building relationships is to consider the process as a kind of hierarchy. Our research suggests that as our relationships progress, we pass through several clearly defined stages which each have their own characteristics:

- Awareness
- Interest
- Knowledge
- Liking
- Preference

Awareness is about the other person becoming aware of our actual existence. Clearly this level is primarily concerned with making positive impact and creating the appropriate first impression. Interest is the stage at which the other person identifies a value in the relationship, and knowledge is the level at which the other person is starting to gain a real understanding of our uniqueness as a human being. Liking occurs when the other person feels an affinity or closeness with us. This is probably as a result of the other person recognizing the similarities between ourselves and them. At the highest level of preference, the other person identifies our unique ability to meet their needs, and influence is achieved as the other person trusts our integrity and readily accepts the suggestions that we make.

We are frequently asked how long one should spend on the rapport stage of influencing. As a generalization those managers who we have worked with in order to develop the competencies of influencing tend to spend far too little time creating rapport. Even if they do spend some time at the start using the above techniques, they will often move promptly into the 'real' business and presume that because some time has been spent developing rapport it will not be necessary to backtrack and the rest of the discussion can focus purely on the business in hand.

A useful guideline in respect of how long to spend building rapport is to consider two key issues (see Fig. 6.2):

- How personal is the issue we are going to discuss?
- What is the requirement to continue to work or have contact with this person after this discussion?

Where the answers to the above are 'highly personal' and 'a potentially long relationship', then the need to create rapport becomes paramount. For example, if I am about to discuss a personal habit of a colleague such as their need to use a body deodorant, then I will need to take much longer building rapport than I would if I was asking a service engineer to help me understand some new software.

All issues of communications have cultural implications. In what Trompenaars

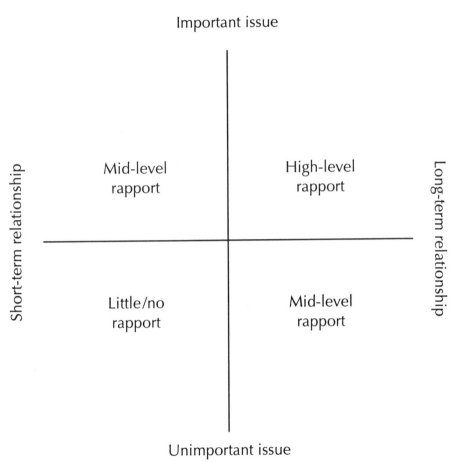

Figure 6.2   Building rapport

refers to as a 'specific' culture, such as that of the North American and North-ern European countries, the main emphasis in a business relationship is placed on the business issues which have to be dealt with. The norm would be to spend a minimal amount of time on small talk because this could easily be seen as irrelevant. By contrast in a 'diffuse' culture such that of the Latin, Ara-bic and Southern American countries, the emphasis is quite different. Here the relationship is considered to be with the whole person and it is not viewed as simply a contractual relationship. In this sort of diffuse culture rapport building could take months rather than minutes, and for someone used to the 'specific' environment the danger would be showing impatience with the seemingly circuitous nature of early discussions. So one consideration when deciding how to build rapport is that of culture.

Of course the other issue about building rapport is that as relationships never stay static, so the need for rapport continues. Over time it is the style and nature of the rapport that changes

So far we have explored the three competencies which constitute the entry stage of the EDICT model of influencing, namely preparation, impact and rapport. Effective management of the entry stage will lay the foundations for subsequent success and will ensure that the person you are attempting to influence will be co-operative in the next stage: diagnosis.

REFERENCES

Jessop, J. (1994) *The Victorians*, Coombe Books, Surrey.

Pease, A. (1984) *Body Language*, Sheldon Press, London.

Question time

WHAT DO YOU REALLY MEAN BY PUSH AND PULL STYLES OF
INTERVIEWING?

> The push style of influencing is where you attempt to impose your views on
> the other person, rather than trying first to understand their views. With the
> pull approach you identify the other person's beliefs, attitudes, or even values,
> and then influence by using arguments which appeal to their values not yours.

IS THE PULL APPROACH ALWAYS THE BEST?

> Generally speaking, yes. Persuasion using the pull approach is likely to be
> longer lasting. Using the push approach might work if you have position
> power to rely on, but the other person may not remain persuaded in the long
> term. Influencing by using the pull approach is likely to lead to the other per-
> son remaining influenced on a more permanent basis.

WHAT IS MEANT BY A PERSON'S UNDERLYING VALUES AND WHY ARE THEY
IMPORTANT?

> It is suggested that we only have a hard core of approximately six underlying
> values which tend to determine our beliefs and attitudes, which in turn deter-
> mine our behaviour. If we can identify the other person's basic values, then we
> have more chance of knowing how to influence them by appealing to their
> values. Examples of values might include the following: family values, the work
> ethic, independence, integrity, safety and security, and a belief in the ability to
> shape one's own destiny.

WHAT IS A PERSPECTIVE SPECIFICATION?

> This is an approach to preparing in advance of an influencing situation. It in-
> volves attempting to see the situation from the perspective of the other people
> involved by listing against a number of headings your estimate of their per-
> spective. This helps deal with the natural tendency we have to influence only
> from our own perspective and is particularly useful when it is known that there
> are different views held by the different parties.

HOW IS CULTURE RELEVANT TO PREPARATION?

Cultural awareness is important at all stages of the influencing process; however, at the preparation stage it is helpful to consider whether there is any strong cultural difference which you may need to recognize and be tolerant of. Examples would include whether the other person sees the relationship as essentially a contractual and formal one or a 'friendship'. Equally it is important to understand something of the cultural norms for the person you are attempting to influence. Beware, however, of stereotyping the other person and saying 'Because they are from X country or culture they are bound to . . .'.

WHAT ARE SELF-DEPRECATING COMMENTS?

These are comments which demean the status of the speaker. For instance 'I do not know much about this . . .' or 'I am no expert but . . .'. Often these sort of comments are made unwittingly and have a negative impact in terms of influencing.

HOW LONG SHOULD I SPEND CREATING RAPPORT?

This depends on the importance of the issue being discussed and the length of the relationship. While it is important to focus on building rapport in the early part of the interaction, it is also essential to continue the rapport-building process throughout the discussion.

Part 2

Diagnosis

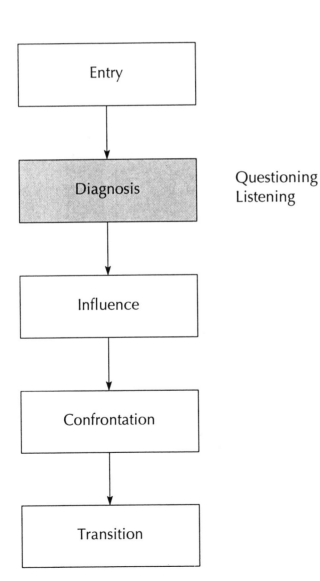

Entry

Diagnosis

Questioning
Listening

Influence

Confrontation

Transition

7 Managing the barriers

Chapter objectives

- To identify and explore the common barriers to the influencing process.
- To examine ways in which these barriers can be successfully managed.
- To continue to consider the cultural differences affecting the influencing process.

In this chapter we will consider some of the common barriers to influencing. It is these barriers, which are not always obvious or overtly declared, that can make the difference between successful influencing and failure; the frustrating feeling associated with failure is often compounded by not knowing why a particular approach to influencing has not worked. It may be possible to anticipate some of the potential barriers in the early stages of influencing and this will help determine how they might be overcome in the later stages.

The identification of potential barriers is a key part of the diagnosis step of the EDICT model. Having identified potential barriers, these might then be confirmed or otherwise through the skilful deployment of the competencies of listening and questioning skills, which we will look at in the next chapter.

Here we will consider several of the barriers and how they might be overcome, again recognizing some the major cultural differences that can obstruct the influencing process.

SELECTIVE LISTENING

By this we mean that people hear what they want to hear, rather than what is actually said. It is a common perceptual distortion, which can easily be managed by checking understanding or asking the other person to repeat something back to us.

We are naturally selective in our listening; you may have heard of the expression 'She only hears what she wants to hear' which sums up selective listening quite succinctly. In truth, selective listening is often used as a survival tactic; we are exposed to so much information, much of it through sound, to the extent that the only way to make sense of the world is through selective perception.

Listening is likely to become more acute when something is of personal interest or for that matter a threat. Have you ever been in a crowded, noisy room
where it is difficult to pick out specifically what anyone is saying, and then
suddenly you hear someone on the opposite side of the room mention your
name? That is selective listening operating at a subconscious level. People will
also filter out information more consciously particularly when they are hearing
things that they do not like the sound of.

Throughout the influencing process it is worth trying to identify whether the
other person seems to be filtering certain information out. You may need to
confront them on this.

Similarly there is a danger that you will selectively listen to the what the other
person has to say. We will look at personal listening skills in the next chapter.

Another part of this difficulty may be caused by our not valuing the source of
the information.

OPINIONS

Preconceived ideas and opinions will be a barrier to effective influencing.
There is no easy way to overcome this problem other than asking overtly for
people to be open-minded or to suspend judgement. Where this problem
seems to occur regularly, then a useful technique is to allow the person to
criticize openly only after they have provided at least three positive statements
in support of what is being said

LANGUAGE

Often language presents a significant barrier to influencing—and we are not
here simply referring to the national language spoken but also to the terminology and jargon that tends to pervade working life in most professions and
disciplines. It may be possible to anticipate or guess the likely language issues
before the meeting but it is just as important to look out for the sorts of words
which are used by the person you are attempting to influence.

In most organizations there are certain expressions and terms that are used
more than others. One organization uses so many three-letter abbreviations to
describe anything from procedures to job titles that it has published an internal
book of what it refers to as TLAs! While you may question the value of developing such a secondary language when there are often enough difficulties
coping with different national languages, understanding the buzz-words of
those you are trying to influence can have significant advantages. It may be
appropriate occasionally to echo back the same terminology in order to encourage identification, though obviously caution needs to be exercised in
using this approach.

More often the problem is understanding the terminology used by people who are members of other groups than our own, such as a different organiza-tion or profession. In this case it is imperative to question the other person as soon as possible to clarify meaning; the trick is to commit such language and meaning to memory for the future.

Conversely it is advantageous to recognize the jargon you tend to use and to question whether the person you are attempting to influence will understand your 'language'.

One should recognize, however, that often jargon is deliberately used and created in order to create an impression of expertise as a way of influencing the other person. Some professions make an art form of this, converting the simplest issues into the most complex sounding concepts. Such terminology may be presented in such a tone as to suggest that the person should under-stand what is meant and that they should not dare to ask for interpretation. If you sense this technique being used by others on you, try asking what is meant; you may be pleasantly surprised by the response!

Pause for thought

What jargon do you use?

Consider jargon which might be specific to the following groups you are related to:

  Educational
  Professional
  Vocational
  Organizational
  Peer group

Consider the people you attempt to influence. To what extent do you use terminology which may actually hinder the communication process?

What alternative terminology could you use which might be more effec-tive?

Next consider the deliberate use of jargon and supposedly 'technical' terms. When might others have used this as an influencing technique on you?

How effective was it?

When have you used this approach on others?

How effective was it?

COMMUNICATION OVERLOAD

A frequent barrier to effective communication and influencing is overload. It has been shown that most people are able to hold onto and retain between five and seven pieces of different information at the same time. Because of this it is worth presenting information in small quantities rather than in bulk. Where it is received in bulk, the other person is likely to switch off.

This is in some ways related to selective listening. It may be that the reason a person is selective in their listening is due to the sheer amount of information coming at them. The quantity is too much and has to be reduced.

This issue has implications for how information should be presented to those we are trying to influence. It should be possible to summarize arguments, views, and ideas succinctly Over-embellishment is only likely to lead to confusion. Review carefully the length, complexity, and relevance of your message. This issue is particularly important when presenting written information.

Another critical issue in any influencing discussion is to build in some process of review and reinforcement. This can be done by the use of summaries or seeking clarification of understanding.

TIME BARRIERS

Frequently the opportunity to influence is set within tight time constraints. The more pressure there is in terms of time, the less likely it is that a true pull type of influencing strategy will be possible; it is probable that more forceful approaches will have to be used. Alternatively it may be possible to make more time available and actually to question the validity of the time constraints being imposed.

CULTURAL BARRIERS

We have already looked at some of the cultural issues that exist in relationships; here we will consider those cultural barriers which can cause serious problems in influencing situations. Again the Trompenaars research provides some useful models.

It was explained earlier that in a specific culture as contrasted with a generalist culture there can be significant differences in terms of how rapport is addressed. Additionally there are contrasts between 'achievement' and 'ascription' oriented cultures. In an achievement-oriented culture, respect tends to given primarily to those who have achieved through their own efforts, almost regardless of issues such as age and experience. By contrast, in an ascriptive- or position-oriented culture, the main focus of respect is on the position that people hold in the hierarchy which is largely determined by age and experience. Status is ascribed due to the position, level, age, and even family background of the person. Scandinavian, British, and North American cultures tend to be more achievement oriented, whereas Middle Eastern and Asian cultures tend to be more ascriptive. In Japanese culture the ritual of the first meting is an overt display of respect for the ascribed status of the two parties. The ritual demands that the two people hold their business card out in front of themselves and in a synchronized way bow deferentially and exchange business cards. The cards are then studied for some time while each party respectfully notes the job title and level of the other person and even discusses this before actually moving on to the start of the meeting.

These differences clearly affect the influencing situation in a crucial way, and here again the issues tend to surface when someone from one culture is attempting to influence a person from another culture. So if a young, dynamic, self-made American were to travel to the Middle East to do business with a senior and significantly older team of Arabs, there could be some immediate problems in terms of credibility. The American would do well to emphasize his years of experience rather than the fact that he is the youngest senior executive in the organization. He might actually gain more kudos by emphasizing that he is related to the chairman in his organization than actually talking about his personal achievements.

Similarly a key variable between cultures is that of 'individualism' as opposed to 'collectivism'. In an individualist culture the main focus of attention and indeed power is usually the individual. The individual manager makes decisions, as opposed to the collectivist culture where the group is considered to be more important than the individual and where decisions tend to made on a group basis.

So the instinct of our young American manager may tell him to target the decision-maker in order to strike a deal, whereas a more appropriate approach would be to openly recognize the various levels of manager based on their title and to show some patience in awaiting decisions.

Another major principle to recognize as being of major importance in some cultures is that of allowing other people to save face. In, for instance, an ascriptive culture the more junior members of a team are likely to offer close support to their seniors and privately provide answers and assistance if they fear there is a danger of the senior members being embarrassed. They will then be quite content for the seniors to take the praise because this respects the hierarchy. As someone attempting to influence in this environment it may be necessary to 'play the same game' and ensure that, although a senior person is incorrect or wrong in their understanding of a situation, it would be more appropriate to confront them privately afterwards than in front of their peers or subordinates.

It is clearly difficult to give specific advice regarding what to say and do when influencing across cultures; what is important is to try to assess what the cultural ground rules or norms are, before or during the early stages of a discussion. While it will be inappropriate to change one's own culturally influenced behaviour radically, it may be appropriate to make modifications and accept that there are differences. It is these chameleon-like qualities which are becoming increasingly important in order successfully to influence others.

STATUS DIFFERENCES

Differences in the relative status of two people can cause major blockages to the effectiveness of an influencing exercise. This is highlighted by the example below, which is drawn from a real case.

STORYBOARD—STATUS BARRIERS

Hans was a new graduate recruit who had joined an international electronics company as a graduate trainee direct from his university degree course.

He was delighted to have been accepted onto the training scheme and the first week had been an interesting one; he had met a number of other trainees on the same programme and had enjoyed the graduate induction course.

It was the final day of the induction course and the company had arranged a social evening at the organization's own social club. The idea was for the new recruits to mingle socially and to meet some of the older and more experienced employees.

Hans was enjoying a drink at the bar with another employee whom he estimated was probably in his mid to late fifties. The conversation proceeded along the following lines:

Hans Yes the induction course has been really quite good fun—I've met a lot of people and they all seem good to work with. I even discovered that one of my old friends from school is on the same scheme.
Anyway enough about me—what about you? How do you find it working here?
Employee Oh I have always enjoyed it here—we obviously have our ups and downs though. The past year has been quite encouraging.
Hans So I hear—can I get you another beer?
Employee Thanks a lot—I'll have a small one.
Hans So what is your background then? Are you an engineer by training?
Employee Yes, electronic engineering; I studied in Germany and then got a lot of my early experience in the Far East.
Hans How long have you been working here then?
Employee Oh, just over twenty years.
Hans Well it can't be that bad then—what do you do now?
Employee I'm the Chief Executive actually.
Hans Oh . . . no . . . I mean I am sorry . . . no I don't mean I'm sorry

about your job . . . Oh dear, I am not expressing myself too well . . . how can I say . . . I am sorry that I didn't know who you were . . .

At this point Hans, who until now had been communicating very effectively with someone whom he assumed to be of similar status, started to fall apart in terms of his communication and influencing skills. His voice started trembling, he became stuck for words and started muttering and stumbling around.

The only reason for this was his knowledge that he was one of the most junior people and he was talking to the most senior manager in the organization. He had already proven his social skills and was making a good impression on the chief executive while his perception was that they were on a similar level. As soon as he became aware of the status differential, he temporarily lost all of his social control and poise.

The above example highlights the principle of 'frames' which suggests that everything we do is influenced by the frame or context we put around it. Every interaction or discussion depends on a context for its meaning; the fact is that the context is subject to an interpretation. In the example of the discussion above, at the start the context as far as Hans was concerned, was two employees of a broadly similar level having a drink and an informal conversation in a bar. When, however, he found out that he was talking to the chief executive, his frame changed dramatically. Suddenly the frame was of a formal interview situation where he considered he was of considerably less value than the other person.

Using reframing

One way of dealing with this sort of situation, and this is a technique which particularly lends itself to dealing with intimidation and fear of others, is deliberately to 'reframe' the situation. So instead of Hans thinking of his colleague as a chief executive, he might reframe the situation and think of him as a family man who enjoys a social drink with his family and friends, or even as a friendly old uncle!

This may sound rather like we are suggesting we should move into the realms of fantasy, but this is a very practical approach which entertainers and major performers use to help them cope with situations that would otherwise be frightening.

In a business context it may be that you reframe the situation whereby you picture the people you are trying to influence in less formal clothing, in a family role, or even try picture what they were like as children. You will find that when you discover a reframe which works for you personally, this can be a very powerful technique. In many ways your ability to reframe will be partly determined by your powers of visualization and your ability to use imagery; as previously discussed, our research shows that these skills can be developed with practice.

SELF-FULFILLING PROPHECY

The concept of the self-fulfilling prophecy is especially relevant to situations where we are attempting to influence those over whom we hold higher status or position or those to whom we may serve as role models.

The phenomenon of the self-fulfilling prophecy was identified by psychological experiments carried out on a class of schoolchildren. They were identified at the start of the year by psychologists, who then categorized them into those considered to be intelligent and likely to perform well, and those who were less bright and more likely to fail. In fact these were a random group of children. The teacher was not informed that this was an experiment but told of the supposed result of the 'tests'. The psychologists left, only to return at the end of the year to study end-of-year test results. It was discovered that, as predicted, those categorized as intelligent succeeded, whereas as those put in the less intelligent category were less successful.

It was then revealed that the two categories defined by the psychologists were in fact spurious and the split was entirely a random one. The research found that it was actually the expectations of the teacher which translated into actions and attitudes in the way the pupils were treated, which in turn affected the behaviour of the pupils.

The term 'self-fulfilling prophecy' is used to describe the way that we can influence the performance and behaviour of others simply through the way we deal with them and through our expectations: the prophecy becomes self-fulfilling. Further research then revealed this phenomenon in a number of other areas, including in the organizational world.

The self-fulfilling prophecy concept frequently has negative connotations. Consider the impact parents have on their children using terminology such as 'She's not too academic' or 'He is the world's most untidy child', and how after hearing this several hundred times the child then incorporates this as a self-belief and acts in accordance with it. Obviously this contributes to how self-image is formed.

The upside of the self-fulfilling prophecy, of course, is that it can work in a positive way. In fact many of the successful people we interviewed in our research suggested that their success was driven by a strong positive belief held about them by others, be they a sports coach, a parent or a senior manager. Interestingly some also described the fact that they were able to channel some of the negative beliefs held by others into achieving positive outcomes in order to disprove the negative views. One memorable example of this came from the one of the highest-paid chief executives in Europe during the economic boom of the 1980s, who said he was primarily driven by overhearing a

Figure 7.1   Force field analysis

conversation his parents were having with friends where he heard his mother say 'Oh Rolf will never achieve much. He is a lovely lad but it is his sister who has all the brains and concentration.'

In the context of attempting to influence others we should consider what sort of expectations we have of them and the extent to which we demonstrate these expectations. It should not come as a surprise that if we try to influence a subordinate to develop certain skills or attitudes, but we believe they are unlikely to make the change, then to find that they fail.

A useful approach if we are dealing with problematic behaviours and attempting to bring about a positive change is to use positive terminology and to create strong pictures of what success looks like, rather than dwelling on the existing negatives.

BREAKING DOWN THE BARRIERS

There is potentially an endless number of barriers which may be encountered when attempting to influence. We have covered some of the major barriers in this chapter, but equally there are numerous others which may need consideration.

What is most important in order to tackle the potential barriers in an influencing situation is that they are identified in the first place. Having identified the barriers as part of the diagnosis stage of influencing, a worthy technique to apply is *force field analysis*.

The force field analysis model works on the basis that people resist change because of a state of equilibrium which exists between the forces pushing for change and those resisting it. If we can identify these forces and estimate their respective strength, it should be possible to move towards the goal by reducing the resisting forces of increasing the driving forces. Figure 7.1 shows a worked example of a force field analysis which has been completed by an employee who is attempting to persuade her boss that she should receive a pay rise.

A number of forces favouring a pay rise have been identified and a number of forces against; clearly the subject of some of these are related, such as future business looking good yet current performance being poor. Having identified these forces, the force field analysis technique now requires you to consider how forces for can be increased and those against can be weakened; in this example, which is very much an influencing situation, the requirement is to look at ways of building on the arguments for and playing down or countering the arguments against.

To summarize, a key part of the *diagnosis* step of the EDICT model of influencing is to attempt to detect the potential barriers which exist in terms of one's ability to influence others. Some of these barriers can be identified through skilled analysis before the influencing discussion takes place, based on information which is available and sound judgement. The possible pitfall, however, is that of making false assumptions about the other party before actually hearing and understanding their point of view. This is a trap that is best avoided; it is a question of striking a balance between thorough early diagnosis and pre-judging the situation. Next we are going to look at the key competencies of diagnosis: 'listening' and 'questioning'. Questioning and listening are very much related skills which need to be marshalled well in order truly to understand where the other person is coming from. Advanced skills of listening, which we will refer to as empathy, and of questioning, which we call three-level questioning will be addressed in the next chapter.

8 Gaining insight into others

Chapter objectives

- To identify the different types of question relevant to the *diagnosis* stage of the influencing process.
- To explain the concept of three-level questioning and how it can be used to identify core values of other people.
- To look at the practical skills of the competence of 'listening', and explain the techniques which can ultimately help the effectiveness of the influencing process.
- To explore the different levels of listening and the skills associated with developing empathy.
- To examine the notion that by identifying the thinking patterns of others we can improve the way we influence.
- To provide guidance on how to build a joint vision of the outcomes we wish to achieve.

PUSH V. PULL STYLES

Hold up the palm of your hand and ask your friend to do the same; do not tell them anything, but slowly start pressing towards the other person What happens? Nine times out of ten the other person will resist or push back at you, and as you intensify the strength of your push they are likely to match you. What you are seeing is really the equivalent of what frequently happens when we are attempting to influence someone. We push our view, they push theirs, and the stronger they push theirs, the stronger we push ours.

If the other person has a point of view which we are diametrically opposed to, then a natural reaction as soon as we detect this is to present vehemently our counter-argument. The problem with this push approach, though, is that it is quite possible to misunderstand the other person's view or to miss out on a different perspective which could be enlightening.

The key competencies which we need to develop are those of listening and questioning. As such these two competencies are inextricably linked

Listening in an influencing context is to do with more than just hearing; it is about understanding the words and interpreting the messages being conveyed. Furthermore it is not sufficient to remain content in the knowledge that we have listened effectively; in influencing we must demonstrate to the other person that we have understood the message, as they intended it to be received. This should not, of course, be confused with agreement.

You might argue that a negotiating tactic would be to summarize incorrectly what the other person has said, adding your own interpretation—but remember we are addressing here the *diagnosis* stage of the EDICT model. The aim with diagnosis is to improve our own understanding.

As previously mentioned, very much linked to the competence of 'listening' is the other key diagnostic competence of 'questioning'. Here we will look at not just the type of questions to ask and when, but also how to formulate a line of questioning in order gain a complete picture of the other person's perspective.

Listening and questioning can both be approached at various levels and we will look at how, through deeper-level listening and questioning skills, it is possible to understand not just the message but the feelings, emotions, motives, and underlying values of the person you are attempting to influence.

In order to influence effectively it is vital to understand the other person and have a clear picture of their perspective. It is only when we are armed with this understanding that it becomes possible to use what is important to them as a way of influencing rather than an influencing strategy that is based on what is important to us.

Finally in this chapter we will look at how to summarize our understanding of the diagnosis step by building a joint vision which establishes the outcome sought by both parties and which can be expressed in terms of a joint output statement.

QUESTIONS WHICH PRODUCE RESULTS

One of the major misconceptions about questioning skills is that there are hard and fast rules regarding which sorts of questions should and should not be used. In the context of influencing, this is simply not the case. The successful influencer needs to be aware of a whole range of types of question and should be able to use different types of question according firstly to their objective, and secondly to the nature and style of the other person. So while it may be necessary to ask open-ended questions in order fully to understand someone else's point of view, asking such questions to a person who needs help in structuring their conversation because they have a tendency to digress will simply fuel the problem.

Here we will look at the use of questions at the diagnosis step of the influencing process, where the overall aim is to ensure an accurate picture of the other person's point of view.

Later in the book we will consider the issue of questions that address the subject from a rather different point of view, i.e. the use of certain types of question in order to persuade or lead the other party to accept your ideas or proposals.

There are a number of categories of question which can be used at the diagnosis step, and each type of question is treated in turn below.

Informational questions

The informational question aims to draw the person out by phrasing the question in such a way that they are unable to respond with brief answers and are obliged to provide information regarding their own perspective. Such questions tend to be prefaced with words such as 'How . . .', 'Why . . .' and 'Tell me . . .'.

The intention of the questioner is not to make any judgements or to present one's own view at this stage, but simply to understand where the other person is coming from. Listening skills are also critical. In handling the response, it is essential to assist the speaker with supportive, but neutral words and gestures such as selective head nods, non-verbal 'noises' such as 'uh-hu . . .', 'mm-mm . . .' and comments which demonstrate listening like 'I see' and 'I understand'.

Some examples of how informational questions might be phrased are:

'Tell me about it . . .'
'How do you feel about this . . .?'
'What are your views on . . .?'
'What do you mean by . . .?'
'Is there anything else . . .?'

These sorts of questions make it rather difficult to evade the issue and to withhold information unless the person is being deliberately awkward. Such questions are particularly relevant when it is proving difficult to gain information either because the person is naturally introverted and quiet or because tactically they are 'playing their cards close to their chest'.

Some caution needs to be taken with those who have a natural tendency to talk, maybe they are normally extroverted or are trying to baffle you with lots of information; in this case asking informational questions which are not sufficiently focused can serve to exacerbate the situation.

Probing questions

Probing questions seek to explore a particular subject in some depth. Probes might start with phrases such as:

'Can you give me some examples . . .?'
'In what way . . .?'
'Specifically what was your role . . .?'
'What did you enjoy/not enjoy about . . .?'
'What evidence do you have for that?'
'Tell me more . . .'
'How would you support this comment . . .?'

The aim with a probing type of question is to seek more information on a subject which has been discussed superficially. In effect it is about trying to ascertain the depth of understanding. Certain comments or non-verbal behaviours may trigger a need to probe. It could be that the person seems a little evasive or cautious, or you may be picking up signals that suggest they are withholding important information or even 'being economical with the truth'. In these circumstances it is necessary to probe and to demonstrate that you are not going to accept anything other than the whole story.

In addition you may find that the individual presents you with a 'neon sign' statement. As mentioned earlier, these are statements that people make, which tend to invite the other person to ask another question. Frequently they are used because the person does not want to raise an issue explicitly, but would prefer that the other person asks the question.

Examples of this might include the following:

'It would have been on time, but things have been difficult recently . . .'

In this example the person has been unwell and is using this as an excuse for explaining away work that is late; however, they do not want to be seen as making excuses.

'Unfortunately we didn't really get all the help we needed . . .'

Here the person feels that the system personnel failed to get the system working in time, but does not want to be seen publicly criticizing them.

'Our market data was not as good as we had hoped.'

What this person is really saying is that the marketing department gave them data that was incorrect, and as with the previous example they do not want to be seen as disloyal or critical.

All these sorts of statements beg for a probing response. But a word of caution: sometimes people will present you with neon signs in order to be able to
respond in a manipulative manner. However, whenever we become aware
that we are seeing a neon sign, we do not necessarily have to respond to it.
We might just note it and come back to the issue later.

A useful technique to use if you are getting short answers when attempting to
probe is to phrase questions in 'relative' terms in order to seek comparisons.
For example, a question such as 'Which of the reports are you more comfortable with and which are you less comfortable with? Why?' is likely to draw out
more information than 'Which is your favourite report?', to which a respondent could more easily say 'I don't have a preference'.

Behavioural questions

A behavioural question seeks information regarding how an individual be-
haves in a specific situation. Behavioural questions need to be focused on real
or actual situations providing evidence of actual behaviour drawn from experience rather than on hypothetical situations.

The difficulty with a hypothetical or 'What would you do if . . .?' type question
is that it often elicits a response based on how the respondents would like to
see themselves behaving rather than on how they would really behave: the
two are not always the same.

Seeking information regarding previous behaviours is the best predictor of
how a person is likely to behave in the future, and as such this approach can
provide valuable information regarding the nature of the person you are dealing with. If you are able to predict how they might respond to a certain
situation, then this may well shape your influencing strategy.

In order to maximize the value of a behavioural question it is usually necessary
to follow up with prompting question to draw out more information.

Examples of behavioural questions are:

> 'Tell me about a situation where you have had to cope without resources
> and under time pressure? What happened? How did you cope? What did
> you do?'

> 'Tell me about how you responded when your staff were upset about the
> reorganization? What did you do? What did you say? How did you han-
> dle it? What was the most difficult aspect of this incident?'

> 'How did you persuade your boss to increase your budget? What did
> you do? What was your approach? What objections were there? How
> did you handle them?'

Pinpoint questions

Pinpoint questions seek specific information and fall into two categories. First of all there are the occasions where you will want to clarify specific information and only a direct question will do. In this case the response is likely to be short and factual. An example of pinpoint clarification questions are 'So are you saying the price is $3000 including service or excluding service?' This really leaves little room for manoeuvre on the part of the respondent and enables the questioner to fill in pieces of the jigsaw.

Then there are questions which seek to deal with the deliberately vague statements which are often made by others in an effort to exert some influence and add weight to their arguments. Pinpoint questions in this situation cause the speaker to clarify and indeed justify his or her comments. In this way they aim to pinpoint the missing or vague areas and may even cause the speaker to come forward with information which might otherwise have been withheld. The only problem with pinpoint questions is that they can often sound very direct and abrupt and the danger is that without some 'dressing' to soften them, any rapport which has previously been established can quickly be destroyed. Some examples of the phrases to look out for and to tackle with pinpoint questions are shown below. Examples of the pinpoint questions are given and then an example of how the questions might be 'dressed up' in order to maintain rapport is given. Another important issue in terms of maintaining rapport will also relate to the way in which the question is asked and this will be determined by the intonation, facial expressions and body language of the questioner. A supportive and interested style is clearly more appropriate than an abrupt style which may be interpreted as hostile.

Vague verbs and nouns

For example	'They keep pushing me around.'
Pinpoint questions	Who are they? What do you mean pushing around? Could you give some examples? How often does it happen?
Dressed up	I understand it must feel pretty uncomfortable . . . Who are the main people causing the problem? What do they do? How often does this sort of thing happen?

Sweeping generalizations

For example	'Everybody knows she is always complaining—she will find anything to complain about.'
Pinpoint questions	Everybody . . . have you personally interviewed everybody on this?!

	What do you mean always?
	When did she last complain?
	What was the reason?

Dressed up   That sounds tiresome. I know it would irritate me if someone kept complaining. What does she complain about? Have you got any examples?

Exaggeration

For example   'He is the world's worst dresser.'

Pinpoint questions World's worst?
Surely not?

Dressed up   His dress sense may need some attention. What specifically do you feel the problem is? Is it to do with style or colour co-ordination for example.

Definitive statements

For example   'We could never get approval.'

Pinpoint questions Who said?
Have you tried?
Never ever?

Dressed up   Yes, it must be tricky in this climate? I wonder if it might at some stage get easier?

DEALING WITH FALLACIES

Pinpoint questions are of particular value in dealing with fallacies or false arguments. These arguments are frequently used in confrontational or conflict situations and include the following types of irrational thinking approaches when trying to influence other people.

Appeal to pity

Here the individual assumes that you will feel sorry for them or their circumstance. This may or may not be the case.

Building false assumptions

With this fallacy the individual builds an argument on a series of false or unproven assumptions. These can be easily explored and recognized through the use of pinpoint questioning.

Self-interest

Where an argument is plainly positioned to satisfy an individual's self-interest, pinpoint questioning can expose this situation

Catch-22

Here the individual apparently presents an alternative that is clearly no alternative. Careful questioning will highlight the anomalous situation.

False linkages

With this fallacy the individual makes a false connection between different issues which are not actually related.

Either/or

Here the individual presents an argument that indicates extreme opposed solutions. Pinpoint questioning will quickly show that things are rarely so clear cut.

When considering the use of pinpoint questions, there are certain words which tend to be used by others and are particularly relevant. For instance, words such as: never, always, they, everyone, nobody, impossible, worst, best. Seeking clarification can only serve to enhance the communication process if it is handled skilfully and ultimately this will lead to a clearer diagnosis of the other person's perspective.

THREE-LEVEL QUESTIONING

Figure 8.1 shows how a line of questioning might be developed in order to attempt to identify the other person's values. This is a process of digging ever deeper and continuing to ask why they do what they do. As discussed previously, being able to identify the core values which are driving the person you are attempting to influence has major advantages in that it is then possible to use this knowledge in formulating an appropriate influencing strategy.

Techniques which approach influencing by appealing to the other person's value system are likely to be much more successful than attempting to impose one's own values.

The three-level questioning model suggests that there are, broadly, three levels at which it is possible to question.

At the basic level, level one, the objective of questioning is to obtain basic information of a more factual nature. This is the level of questioning which is considered normal on an initial meeting, where there is likely to be an ex-

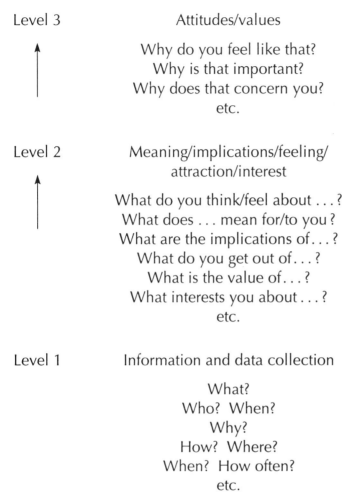

Level 3   Attitudes/values

Why do you feel like that?
Why is that important?
Why does that concern you?
etc.

Level 2   Meaning/implications/feeling/
                    attraction/interest

What do you think/feel about . . . ?
What does . . . mean for/to you ?
What are the implications of . . . ?
What do you get out of . . . ?
What is the value of . . . ?
What interests you about . . . ?
etc.

Level 1   Information and data collection

What?
Who? When?
Why?
How? Where?
When? How often?
etc.

Figure 8.1   Three-level questions

change of non-threatening information often to do with, for instance, roles, names, locations, jobs, and organizations.

The second level of questioning seeks to probe a little deeper and identify some of the underlying views, opinions, feelings, and interests. This will reveal more about what motivates the person.

Then there comes the third level where the objective is really to identify the ultimate values of the person; where does the inner drive come from which determines that the person has a particular interest and is attracted to certain roles and activities.

So to take an example, if one is to attempt to identify the core values in order to influence another person by using their own value system, the conversation might take the course shown in the following storyboard:

STORYBOARD   LEVELS OF QUESTIONING

Pierre So tell me a little more about what you do? (level 1)
Marianne Oh I work as a sales executive. We sell pharmaceutical products mainly to hospitals and clinics.
Pierre Interesting. What sort of products are you involved with? (level 1)
Marianne Well its mainly vaccines and some of the new drugs for inoculation of children.
Pierre So what does this mean for you? (level 2)
Marianne Actually it means a lot of time away from home. Lots of travel—visiting all sorts of different organizations—hospitals, clinics, day centres.
To be honest, despite all the hassle, I really enjoy it?
Pierre What is it you particularly enjoy? (level 2)
Marianne The thing that gives me the most satisfaction is the fact that I personally decide where I go and who to meet. I have a great deal of scope to decide on the sales strategy. If I want to do something, I just do it. It really is so different to my last company where everything I did had to be approved by a director. I couldn't even get approval for a carphone and I was a sales executive on the road 80 per cent of the time.
Pierre So why is it so important for you to be able to decide on where you go and who you meet? (level 3)
Marianne That's a tricky question—I guess its to do with independence. I've always had this need to do my own thing. I've always wanted to be my own boss. I just can't stand feeling constrained. I truly believe that everyone has potential if they were allowed to get on with it, instead of people interfering.

What Pierre has identified through this process of three-level questioning is that Marianne has a core value of independence. In attempting to influence her, it is important to emphasize the fact that she would have scope and personal discretion; the danger to guard against would be imposing too much control. This might be quite different, for instance, if Marianne revealed a strong need for security and safety; in this case the fact that there is close supervision to fall back would be an important point to make.

LISTENING AND UNDERSTANDING

As the first learned and the most used of communication skills it is surprising that listening is the least taught. Listening is also one of the most misused terms. Have you ever had the experience of someone saying 'Carry on . . . I am listening' and you hesitate to continue because you are not convinced that they are actually listening? Conversely have you ever been in conversation with someone else and found your mind wandering on to another subject or tuning into someone else's conversation? Or have you had a discussion with someone close to you where they have said '. . . But you just don't understand'. If so, then you have personally experienced some of the difficulties associated with listening.

Listening breaks down for several reasons. It may be that the person trying to listen to you is simply receiving more information than you can digest at any one time. In this situation it is not really helpful to blame the speaker for not being able to express himself or herself well enough; you have a joint responsibility to ensure that the process of communication is effective. One approach would be to help the speaker by giving structure to the discussion with interventions that address the process of the discussion. For instance:

> 'I am having some difficulty following you here—could we first of all cover subject "x" and then move on to "y'?"

Or it may be appropriate to ask the speaker if they mind if you take a few notes, which incidentally will buy you more time to think as you are writing.

Emotions can easily get in the way of effective listening, and in this case it may be better to admit to the other person that you are feeling angry, upset, or even too overjoyed to be able to listen properly. It may help to take some time out and come back to the subject when the sense of emotion has subsided. Sometimes just one word used by the other person can have major emotional impact, often for personal reasons. This may be related to powerful previous experiences, good or bad, which come flooding back and obstruct the listening process.

Another reason for failure to listen could be related to who is speaking; if we do not like them or have a certain opinion of their worth or value, then we are likely give the same value to what they say. Or it could be that we categorize the other person in terms of a stereotype.

We are all susceptible to the dangers of stereotyping, i.e. our tendency to label other people or make generalized assumptions

"We fit people into the stereotypical image for that category of person. Stereotypes are based around a number of issues such as gender, race, religion, age, and profession or occupation. It is, however, possible to make serious misjudgements about people because of the tendency to stereotype." (Hale, 1993)

So we may have a stereotype view of an academic which says that all academics lack common sense and tend to be preoccupied with theory, and when we are given a practical piece of advice, which in actual fact is very relevant, we would dismiss this advice before listening to it for what it is. The key here is to recognize which stereotypes you hold and how they might get in the way of understanding the individual.

It is also important to note that other people hold stereotype views of ourselves, and it is therefore useful to consider how these may get in the way of our influencing

Pause for thought

What type of questions do you usually use?

How effective are they at giving you a real understanding of the other person

What are the stereotype views that others might have of you based on gender, nationality, and occupation?

What parts of these stereotypes are positive and what parts are negative?

What, if anything, can you do to optimize the positive aspects of the stereotype while minimizing the negative aspects?

Another common cause of failure to listen is what psychologists refer to as 'cognitive dissonance'. Cognitive dissonance is described as 'the feeling of discomfort that a person has when he or she holds conflicting attitudes towards the same stimulus' (Wittig and Belkin, 1990) This explains why, for instance, if a person believes two different but opposing viewpoints on an issue, e.g. 'Drinking and driving wrecks lives' and 'I am a more confident and competent driver after a few drinks', then ultimately the feeling of discomfort will become so intense that one of the beliefs will be eliminated. In the context of listening we often receive conflicting messages from another person and therefore fail to receive the real message. So if you are used to someone constantly giving you good news and they then try to give you some bad news, you may fail to hear accurately the real message.

Another major factor affecting one's ability to listen is driven by the characteristics of memory and recall. Figure 8.2 shows the normal level of attention and recall of information provided over a period of time. This shows that during the period of an input the listener tends to be more attentive at the start and end with some high peaks of attention and recall throughout, which is known as the von Restorff effect. This pattern is often seen in formal presentations where the audience attention levels are high at the start and then drop off, attention then peaks if a subject particularly strikes a cord with the listener, and then there is an increase as soon as signals are picked up which suggest the presentation is nearing an end. As a listener the significance of this phenomenon is that one should be conscious of the dangers of missing key information from the main part of the input. As a speaker it is clear that in order really to influence the audience, one needs to make a major impact at the beginning and at the end, which is why presenters are often taught to

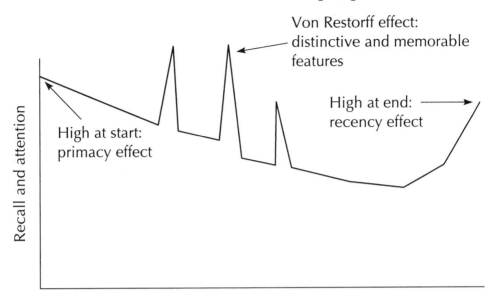

Figure 8.2 Recall and attention

develop powerful introductions and conclusions. Also it may be possible as a speaker to increase the peaks and reduce the troughs by incorporating a number of beginnings and endings by introducing breaks and intervals.

Figure 8.3 shows the common response of a listener attempting to listen to a speaker in a one-to-one discussion. This shows that when a speaker is talking, the listener typically spends the first part of the input listening, the second part formulating a response, and the final part trying to gain entry to the discussion. This clearly has implications regarding how effective the listening actually is. If the speaker is presenting an argument or point of view that the listener disagrees with, then it may be that the listening time is reduced still further. Again for the speaker the implication of this is that key messages need to be delivered succinctly and early on.

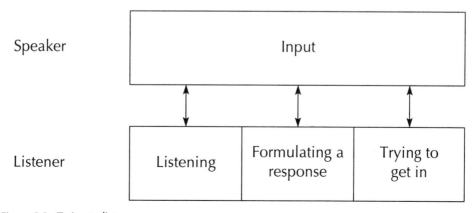

Figure 8.3 Trying to listen

Levels of listening

Basic

Listening skills can take place at various levels. At a basic level listening is about 'shutting up' or stopping talking. This an obvious but often neglected first step and should be accompanied by concentration on what the speaker is saying. In terms of body language the behaviours which should support concentration are selective head nods and supportive noises such as 'uh . . . hu' and 'mm'; most people tend to do this without even thinking about it but have you ever had the experience of talking where the listener provides no supportive 'noises'? It can be quite disconcerting and if this happens when you are communicating by telephone you might wonder whether the person is actually still there on the other end of the line because you do not have the benefit of being able to look at the other person for feedback though facial expressions.

Also at a basic level it can be helpful simply to restate what the speaker says, though clearly some caution needs to be exercised because simply repeating the last few words like an echo can be irritating if overworked. Repeating key words and then pausing, though, can prove to be a very good way of assisting speakers and encouraging them to give more information; this is a technique often used to good effect by interviewers. It is incidentally also useful in giving the receiver time to formulate a response.

Intermediate

At an intermediate level the techniques of listening involve rephrasing of paraphrasing what the other person is saying. By doing this it is possible to check that you have correctly received the message, which can be reassuring for both the speaker and the listener. Paraphrasing means reflecting back what the other person has said using your own words, without changing the meaning. Equally, seeking clarification on a specific point or fact is another aspect of listening and a way of demonstrating that you are listening.

Advanced

At an advanced level, listening is about developing empathy with the speaker. Empathy can be defined as 'the quality of feeling as another feels, to experience another's reality from that other person's point of view' (Wittig and Belkin, 1990). In a regular discussion the two parties tend to focus on the content of the discussion and there may be an undercurrent of emotions and feelings experienced by both parties. Often these feelings and emotions are never actually discussed, because an assumption is made that one should keep focused on the discussion in hand. Showing empathy means seeking to identify how the other person feels about what they are describing and then demonstrating to them that you understand the feeling. If it is possible to demonstrate genuinely that you have an understanding of the feeling and emotion they are experiencing by mentioning your own similar experience, then this will enhance the relationship. This shows empathy through the technique of identification and self-disclosure which can be a way of building trust.

A three-step approach to showing empathy is:

1. Recognize the emotion (e.g. are they angry, excited, upset, frustrated, sad?)
2. Check that you have interpreted the emotion correctly (e.g. 'You seem pleased about this', 'This has clearly upset you')
3. Show understanding and empathy (e.g. 'I can understand how you might feel. I had a similar experience and I was also angry/upset/angry')

As previously discussed, sometimes the other person will signal in a subtle way that they are seeking to disclose some information, particularly if the subject is tricky or personal in nature. Often the signal is hidden in some seemingly innocuous statement which they are hoping you will pick up on so that they can then disclose more information; we previously referred to these statements as 'neon signs'.

Neon signs in themselves actually mean nothing but they may prompt you to ask exactly what is meant so that more information can be disclosed; they tend to be used when someone has something important to say but does not quite know how to get into discussion of the subject.

Pause for thought—empathy

Using empathy, develop an empathetic response to the statements below. Formulate a response which demonstrates empathy; remember you will need to identify the feeling, show that you recognize it, and find some way of identifying with it.

Remember at this stage we are just focusing on a response which shows empathy, not attempting to solve the problem or even make recommendations. This is something which might follow after having demonstrated understanding and empathy.

Example   'I keep getting interrupted; I am simply not getting enough done and I am slipping behind schedule.'

Empathy response   'I can imagine you must feel quite frustrated; I know when I have had to work on important projects and I have been disturbed that it can be really stressful.'

1. *'I just cannot handle any more of this—I am working in lunch hours and after hours. I have a life outside of work too you know.'*

2. 'We have got this really important meeting tomorrow, and I know the senior management are going to be there. I really haven't got all my information together. I know I am not as well prepared as I should be, but I have just been so busy lately.'

3. 'Everybody is talking about changes around here. I even heard the Chief Executive was leaving. Nobody knows what to believe any more. You just don't know what is likely to happen—the next target could be our department.'

4. 'They broke into my car and not only did they take the radio but they even stole my work case. I mean what use is that to them. I just cannot believe what society is coming to.'

5. 'I've been working for six months now without a break. And the amount of work has been building up gradually over that time. What is more, family life has not been too easy—what with the new baby and the house move.'

6. 'Instead of just leaving me to do it my way, everyone seems to have some smart suggestion about how things could be done better. Why don't other people keep their noses out of my business and let me try my best. OK, if I get it wrong, then that is my problem and I am prepared to accept the consequences.'

7. 'It's really strange before I retired I was so busy and now life just seems kind of empty. The other thing is people used to recognize me and give me a good level of respect. Now I am just the same as the man on the street.'

8. 'Only one week to go and then I have a month touring around the world. I just can't wait—I'm counting the hours. I don't know how I am going to contain myself over the next few days. And the other thing is, it means it is extremely difficult to concentrate on work.'

Understanding at a higher level

An advanced form of listening to and understanding others has been developed as part of the concept of *neuro-linguistic programming* (NLP). This was developed in the early 1970s by Richard Bandler, a mathematician, psychotherapist, and computer specialist, and John Grinder, a linguist. They studied the work of leading psychotherapists who were consistent in their ability to facilitate powerful and lasting change and personal improvements in others. NLP focuses on close study of the behaviours which develop relationships between people. While some aspects of NLP can seem rather tangential to the business environment, there are some interesting and relevant concepts regarding how to understand the thought processes of others.

It has been shown that, by understanding something of how the person we are attempting to influence thinks, we can use this knowledge to improve rapport and build the relationship. This approach might be seen as an advanced form of listening as it proposes that we can detect and then use some of the very subtly disclosed cues which the speaker will reveal regarding their thought processes.

The 'neuro' part of the term neuro-linguistic programming refers to the neuro-logical processes of the five senses, i.e. seeing, hearing, feeling, tasting, and smelling. It is believed that humans use these same senses to help with their internal thought processes just as much as to experience external factors. The term 'linguistic' refers to the way that people use language to organise internal thought processes, and 'programming' relates to the fact that thoughts and behaviour can be actively managed.

In NLP terms the use of certain senses tends to dominate our thinking and this is often revealed in terms of the language we use. Our thinking preferences may be biased towards one of the following sense, though normally the domi-nant tendency will be towards one of the first three:

Sight	referred to as *visual*
Sound	referred to as *auditory*
Touch	referred to as *kinesthetic*
Smell	referred to as *olfactory*
Taste	referred to as *gustatory*

People tend to use words in speech which are influenced by and suggest their preference in terms of thinking. So comments and expressions such as:

'I see what you mean.'
'I can picture the person.'
'We should look at this . . .'
'It's a black/dark picture.'
'You must keep things in perspective.'
'She's a colourful/bright/character.'

would reveal a preference towards visual thought processes.

Comments and phrases such as:

'The message is received loud and clear.'
'This behaviour is unheard of.'
'It just sounds right.'
'It is music to my ear.'
'His clothes are so loud.'

would suggest an auditory bias.

Comments and phrases such as:

'Let's touch base on this.'

'It does not feel right.'
'He is a smooth/warm/cool character.'
'Don't push me.'
'We need to pull him into line.'

would suggest a predominantly kinesthetic thinking preference.

Clearly we all use all of our senses to some degree in our thinking, but it is likely that if our language was monitored over a period of time, then a predominant thinking preference would emerge. Furthermore there are other ways of identifying thinking preferences by interpreting non-verbal signals. So a visual thinker will tend to look up when speaking, an auditory person will tend to 'sing' more when talking, and a kinesthetic thinker will tend to speak in a slower, deeper tone, keeping their head down. Again these non-verbal signals are general guidelines rather than absolutes.

The real benefit of this knowledge is that if we can identify the other person's thinking preferences, then it is possible to strengthen the sense of rapport by using similar sensory styles in our own speech; this is often referred to as mirroring.

The following examples are ways of saying the same thing but making adjustments to suit the thinking preference of the other person.

Visual	'Can you picture the situation if you take this option—it will really bring some colour to the department.'
Auditory	'I can hear the reaction now—they would be singing out with joy.'
Kinesthetic	'It is bound to trigger some action—it is the sort of kick that they all need.'

It may take some time to be able to pick up (*note this is actually a kinesthetic phrase*) the signals and to formulate relevant responses, but with practice this will become more natural, and in the meantime you can have some fun identifying the thought patterns of others.

This is really an advanced approach to listening; what might be described as a 'meta-listening' strategy which seeks to listen to information over and above the obvious subject matter and to tune into (*an auditory phrase*) the other person's thought processes.

A note on notes

Taking notes can be one way of visibly demonstrating to the other person that you are listening. Note-taking can also help considerably in the listening process. There is also, however, a danger that note-taking can hinder the effectiveness of communication by causing a distraction for the speaker and confusion for the note-taker.

As the listener you will need to make a judgement about how necessary it is to make notes; this will depend partly on the amount and complexity of the message and on how important it is to record and retain detailed information. In a formal situation such as an interview, it is preferable to inform the speaker that you would like to take notes and to explain why you are doing so; for instance, is it to help with your own memory or to record key facts?

A common problem with note-taking is writing too much, to the extent that the task of taking notes overtakes and hinders the actual discussion. When this does happen it would be a useful exercise for the listener to look objectively at the notes taken after the discussion and to ask whether it was really necessary to write so much. More often than not one finds that a lot of excess words have been recorded, as opposed to key words which would be sufficient to trigger the memory.

The other problem with taking copious notes is that, if the note-taker is working across the page and down the page as information is disclosed, then the notes will make little sense when read. This is because we tend to talk in line with our thought processes, which are more creative, disordered, and illogical than our writing.

An approach which works with the thought processes and is less distracting to the speaker because it involves less writing is the mind map approach as advocated by Tony Buzan (1989) . In summary a mind map is completed spontaneously and works in a similar way to the way we think, which tends to be in key words and images and in a creative rather than just logical way. Taking notes from a discussion using a mind map would entail putting the person's name or the subject matter in the middle of the page and then working outwards as the discussion unfolds, noting key words only and developing a kind of spider's web of lines linking key words where there is a connection. The trick is not too spend too much time taking notes when mind mapping; the mind map could be massaged into shape in a more logical form after the discussion.

This is an approach which can seem quite awkward at first, especially if you are 'left brain' biased which relates more to logic, order, sequence, and symmetry than the creative 'right brain' approach. With practice, though, you will find this approach much more manageable because you can write in a relevant part of the page as the conversation flows rather than worrying about recording information out of sequence.

BUILDING A JOINT VISION

Finally in this chapter we will look at how to summarize the analysis from the *diagnosis* step by building a jointly agreed outcome statement which can be expressed in such a way that the likelihood of achieving it is increased.

Having used diagnostic skills such as listening and questioning, you should have explored the other person's perspective of the problem or situation and it may be appropriate to consider how their understanding of the problem matches your own and then to summarize the outcomes that are sought by both parties. The significance of overtly agreeing the desired outcome is that it is often the case that the different parties will approach an influencing situation with different outcomes in mind and this may not even become apparent to the other person until it is too late.

Outcome statements should seek to describe what a successful outcome looks like; the intention is to build jointly a picture of success which both parties can buy into. In an informal situation which is limited by time it may only be possible verbally to agree this through a brief discussion. Examples of outcome statements are:

> 'We are going to agree the rates for this contract in a way which pleases both parties so that we can continue to build our successful business relationship.'

> 'We will find a way to overcome the grievance which you have raised so that you remain suitably motivated and keen to continue to enrich the work of the department.'

The outcome statement should be phrased in a positive way that highlights the desired result rather than dwelling unduly on the negative aspects if a problem exists. The difference is subtle but important; it should state what is wanted rather than what is to be avoided or overcome In the same way that self-assertion statements, as discussed previously, help the individual to move towards a successful outcome, so do outcome statements build a picture of success.

As with self-assertion statements, outcome statements are even more powerful if there is an appeal to the senses or emotions. Try to relate to the feeling associated with success: this could be pleasure, fun, excitement, satisfaction or even relief. Also ensure that specific words are used, rather than vague comments such as 'We want to achieve a successful outcome' or 'We aim to bring about improvements'; it is important to be able to define what success looks like so as to be sure when it has been achieved.

The process of jointly building the outcome statement can have an integrating effect in itself. By involving the other person in agreeing the wording of an outcome statement they are more likely to feel committed to working towards it.

We have now considered the key skills associated with the diagnosis step of the EDICT model. Diagnosis is about ensuring that the problem or issue is discussed from the other person's perspective before making any potentially dangerous assumptions. This can mean a measure of self-control, particularly if the other person seems to have a different perspective to your own. Objective questioning and strong listening skills will be called for and we have looked at a number of techniques here. Of course, listening and questioning skills are essential throughout the influencing process, as indeed are all the competencies we discuss; however, listening and questioning are critical at the diagnostic stage.

Having drawn out a sound understanding of the other person's point of view and their aims, you then seek to clarify and integrate these with your own perspective in a mutually acceptable and inspiring outcome statement.

This brings us to the *influence* step of the EDICT model and we will now look at the skills which will enhance one's ability to influence the other person, starting with the fascinating subject of body language.

REFERENCES

Buzan, T. (1989) *Use Your Head*, BBC Books, London.

Hale, R. (1993) *How to Introduce Target Setting*, Kogan Page, London.

Wittig, A. F. and Belkin, G. S. (1990) *Introduction to Psychology*, McGraw-Hill, New York.

Question time

WHAT IF I AM FINDING IT DIFFICULT TO ENCOURAGE SOMEONE ELSE TO ACCEPT CHANGE?

> People go through a number of stages in accepting change, and a normal first stage is to deny the need for change and then to adopt an antagonistic stance. Be patient: attempts to force personal change on others are unlikely to have a lasting effect. Try to help them visualize what the new situation might look like.

HOW SHOULD I DEAL WITH CULTURAL DIFFERENCES?

> It is unrealistic to expect that you will be able to radically change your own behaviour, which is culturally influenced, or for that matter change the behaviour of others. A realistic approach is to try to identify whether someone's behaviour might be linked to cultural differences and to accept these differences. Be wary of making sweeping generalizations about cultural differences though, because you can easily fall into the trap of stereotyping people and making erroneous assumptions.

WHAT IS MEANT BY 'SELF-FULFILLING PROPHECY'?

> This is the term used to describe the phenomenon whereby people tend to act in accordance with the expectations that others have of them. So if you frequently demonstrate through your words and deeds that you believe a subordinate has high potential, it is likely that they will demonstrate high potential. This works in a negative sense too where we demonstrate negative beliefs about others which ultimately become reality.

WHAT IS EMPATHY?

> This is an advanced form of listening which can be effectively used when another person is showing signs of having strong feelings or emotions about something. The skill is to recognize the emotion, check that you have interpreted it correctly and then to demonstrate that you understand how it might feel for the other person. This is different from sympathy, which tends to be associated with actually feeling the same emotion.

146

WHAT IS NEURO-LINGUISTIC PROGRAMMING?

NLP is a school of thought in the field of communications which studies in considerable detail the interaction between people. A number of practical techniques have been developed which help to enhance the process of communication including how to develop rapport and how to use body language in order to improve understanding.

WHAT IS THREE-LEVEL QUESTIONING?

This is a process for developing an understanding of someone's underlying values or beliefs whereby we start by asking for basic facts, then ask about underlying meaning and ultimately gather information about what drives and motivates them. Three-level questioning means progressively asking 'why?'.

Part 3

Influence

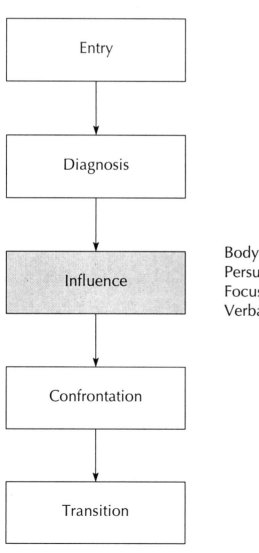

Body language
Persuasion
Focused feedback
Verbal skills

9 The significance of signals

Chapter objectives

- To explain the importance of the signs and signals of body language as the critical component of communication.
- To consider the impact of our own non-verbal behaviour on other people.
- To explore the need to ensure our body language is consistent with our verbal message.
- To look at a technique called 'mirroring' which can help develop our influencing relationship.
- To explore the subject of cultural differences and body language.

Arguably non-verbal behaviour or body language is our original language, that is to say in the history of mankind our use of language is a relatively recent feature of our communication. Indeed it is assumed that prehistoric man primarily communicated mostly by signs and signals, interspersed with different kinds of grunting noises.

In this chapter we are going to discuss the importance of non-body language with a particular focus on how it relates to the influencing situation. Specifically we will consider how one can interpret the body language of others in order to obtain an accurate picture of their feelings, and conversely how it is possible to use one's own body language in order to add weight to the analytical and verbal skills of persuasion and influence.

As a subject body language is one where we are frequently asked for the definitive interpretation of a particular gesture or behaviour. This is, we feel, an inappropriate approach to the whole subject because, for instance, if we take the example of trying to interpret what it means when someone crosses their arms, this gesture in isolation could give clues to a number of possible feelings. It could be that the person is being defensive, feeling comfortable, nursing a sore elbow, or has cold hands. This example is given in order to highlight the danger of looking at one aspect of body language and trying to put a label on it.

In the interpretation of body language, a more reliable—though not infallible—approach is to seek to identify what we will call 'clusters' of behaviour. We will consider some of the important clusters of behaviour to look out for when interpreting the body language of the person you are trying to influence. We will also discuss the importance of ensuring you demonstrate effective body language which is compatible with the verbal message you are conveying.

Body language is one topic which is extremely culture sensitive and we will look at some of the significant cultural differences which can lead to major misunderstandings if ignored and which can make the difference between failure and success if interpreted correctly.

THE RELEVANCE OF BODY LANGUAGE

The significance of non-verbal communication in conveying an influential message cannot be underestimated.

A number of studies have been conducted on the relative importance of words and behaviour in making impact or enhancing the comprehensibility of the communication. Among these findings are those of Albert Mehrabian (1971) who reported that only 7 per cent of the impact came from the actual words which were spoken, 39 per cent from the intonation and 55 per cent from the non-verbal communication (see Fig. 9.1).

This may seem a surprising set of statistics; however, have you ever had the experience of listening to someone saying what is probably the right thing to say but feeling that they do not mean it? It could be the waitress who says 'Enjoy your meal' while looking over to the next table and sounding as though she has said the same thing a thousand times already that day. Or the subordinate who, when you ask if your instruction has been understood, says with a quivering voice 'Yes I understand what you are saying', while looking down and frowning in a confused way.

If these examples sound familiar, it is likely that the reason you doubted the spoken word, even though the right verbal messages were provided, was because you intuitively interpreted, on a subconscious level, the non-verbal communication.

The power of the non-verbal channel of communication can be seen if you study the communication process when the opportunity to observe visually the other person is removed. Take, for example, the telephone as a means of communication. Here one has no choice but to rely on words and intonation. Have you had the uncomfortable experience of talking to someone on the telephone who fails to provide any non-verbal grunts or other things to give you encouragement when you are talking? It is the 'Uh . . . hu's and the 'Mm mm's which say nothing but actually encourage the speaker.

It is interesting that telephone sales people and telephone receptionists are

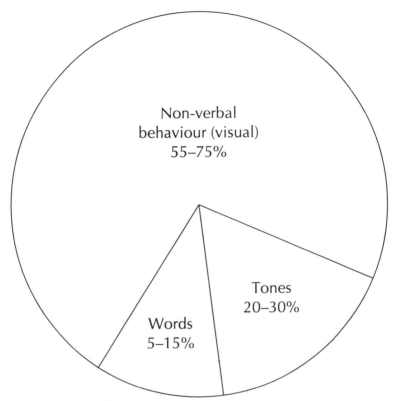

Figure 9.1 Impact in communication

often trained physically to smile when they speak to the customer or client by telephone; the implication is that the smile will be reflected in the tone of voice, and make a positive impact on the other person.

If you have you ever tried to give someone directions by telephone you may have found yourself with the handset balanced between your shoulder and ear while you wave your hands about to help you to visualize the roads and turnings. This example shows the importance of non-verbal communication in actually helping the speaker to express himself or herself.

OUR TERRITORIAL NEEDS

How close do you let other people get to you physically?

If you reflect on this question you will probably recognize that this depends on a number of different factors To begin with it is likely to depend on how well you know the person you are with. If you know them in an intimate way it is likely that you will allow them into your 'intimate zone', which could range from physical touch to an area half a metre away from you.

Outside of our intimate zone we also have a 'personal' zone; this might be between half a metre and one metre around us. This is the distance at which we tend to operate when in friendly conversation with people we feel comfortable with, like our friends or close acquaintances.

Beyond this distance we have what might be considered the social zone. This would usually be between one and three and a half metres around us and in which we would tend to operate with people we do not know people too well.

Finally there is the broader public zone which we work in when in bigger or more formal groups; clearly this would be any distance beyond our social zone.

To explore this idea of zones, try observing the way in which people select their seats on a partially empty train, or select their place on a crowded beach. Usually each person will sit in a seat or space that is almost always an equal distance from the other persons. Such behaviour is almost always unconscious.

Another interesting example of how critical space is for individuals is to study what happens when another person invades our personal space, such as in a lift. This is where people we do not actually know are forced into our intimate or personal zones.

The usual response is for people who are unable actually to distance themselves physically, to try at least to distance themselves psychologically. Consequently they will look away, trying desperately to avoid eye contact, and instead study advertisements intensely or stare at the floor or lights as though they have some deep meaning.

In a similar way, when you are in conversation with someone you know well, try moving back away from them into the social rather than the personal zone; it is likely that they will notice this and attempt to close the gap.

As with many aspects of non-verbal behaviour, however, this matter of physical space is culturally affected. So, for example in a Latin or Middle Eastern culture it may be normal and quite acceptable to stand physically close to the other person even if they are not well known, and it may even be acceptable to touch them.

In a British culture and some Northern European cultures this approach may be considered far too familiar, and more distance is recommended until the relationship is well established. Again, as with many of the cultural differences we have discussed, it is advisable to recognize that the differences exist and accept that others may not behave in the way that you would. It may feel uncomfortable to change one's own approach and to adopt the other person's approach, but it may be possible to modify one's own behaviour.

Apart from these norms, which we see in terms of the physical space between people, there are tactical considerations.

Humans tend to be very territorial in their nature and often we see some interesting 'prowling' and 'staking out' of territory in the early part of a meeting. Leaning against objects, or sitting or touching things may signal 'I belong here.'

In a similar way, a person trying to establish a dominant position may demonstrate the following types of behaviours:

- Talking down—holding the chin up and looking down to the other person, maybe using spectacles to achieve the same result.
- Turning the shoulders in the direction of the person, to suggest they are being ignored because they are not important enough to command attention.
- Crowding out—imposing oneself physically, leaning over or looking down at the other person
- Putting something into the other person's desk or territory.
- Sitting with feet on a desk, maybe while leaning back with hands behind head.

Clearly these are quite aggressive techniques, but some people do use them to establish early dominance. It can be quite amusing if you see two people both playing the same game.

If someone else uses these techniques on you, then you have essentially three choices: you could back off, do nothing, or take the same approach. Backing off is a passive approach and will reinforce in the mind of the other person that you are prepared to be intimidated; this is more likely to lead them to intimidate you in other parts of the discussion.

Not responding but 'holding your ground' is likely to demonstrate that you are not prepared to be pushed around and may result in the other person dropping such intimidating tactics.

Using the same approach, i.e. meeting aggression with aggression, could be a high risk approach; the other person may react by backing off or the non-verbal conflict may escalate into more overt confrontation.

SEATING AND POSITION

The other territorial issue worthy of consideration relates to the physical surroundings and furniture layout. Consider that you are visiting a senior manager on their territory and the room layout is as shown in Fig. 9.2. You enter the room and notice that the manager is at the top desk and you have choice of chair 1, which is near the door and at the furthest end from your host, or chair

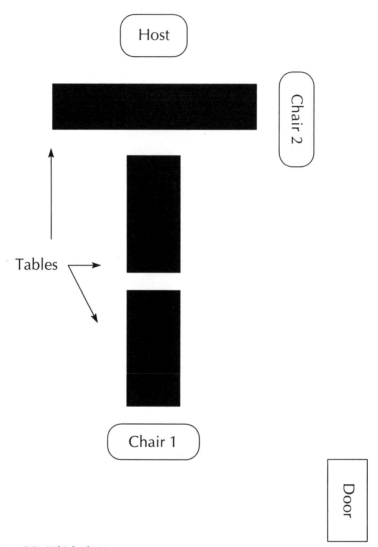

Figure 9.2 Which chair?

2, which is on the top desk on a diagonal from his or her chair. Where would you sit when invited to take a seat?

Clearly this room layout is a 'power set up'; the layout of the large desk with a row of tables running off from it to form a T shape suggests that the manager is making a point right from the start, which is 'I am the boss, and people come to consult me as an authority.' If you select chair 1 you are clearly putting yourself in a subservient position and it may be difficult to establish sub-sequently that you want to work on a equal basis. Conversely if you were to select chair 2, you are entering a more personal zone and by sitting at a diagonal angle adopting more of a consulting position; this could be a high-risk strategy if the manager actually wants to keep a physical and psychological distance, or it could break down the barriers of formality right from the start. The importance of sitting positions and room layout should not be underestimated. In order to influence effectively it is necessary both to be aware of the messages we may be giving others, and to interpret the messages they are giving us.

Below we list a number of commonly used seating arrangements and situations where they might be appropriate or otherwise.

DIRECTLY OPPOSITE

Possible interpretation	Confrontational
	Business-like
	Formal
When to use	When seeking to establish tackle someone head on
When not to use	When seeking to create rapport or break down the barriers

CORNER TO CORNER

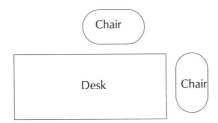

Possible interpretation	Less formal
	Joint problem solving
	Equal footing

When to use	When offering help or when trying to break the ice if the other person may be intimidated (e.g. interviews). And when there is a need to have a writing surface
When not to use	When it is important to establish that you are in charge or when you want to use an autocratic style

NO BARRIERS

(Chair)

(Chair)

Possible interpretation	Informal Counselling Closeness Co-operative Could seem threatening as there is no barrier to 'hide' behind
When to use	Counselling situations Side by side is the usual position on car journeys which tend to be good for listening and sharing information
When not to use	When the other person may be expecting a more formal approach

Another interesting aspect of sitting positions is the actual way the person sits in their chair. One classic, if rather extreme, sitting position is the 'chair straddle'; this is where the person turns the chair around and sits so that the back of the seat forms a supposed arm-rest which is in fact a barrier behind which to hide and from which to take a superior or even aggressive position in the discussion. Another dimension of sitting positions is the extent to which the person will make themselves actually seem bigger or smaller than they really are; this may sound rather absurd but the two extremes are the person who will lean forward and sit upright and push their torso outwards in order to show dominance, and the person who will shrink back into their seat, hunch their shoulders and look downwards in order to show submission or lack of confidence. The message here is that if you want to make a powerful point with impact, then you need to look the part, and sound the part even if this means dominating physically and raising your voice occasionally.

HONESTY AND DECEIT

In the neurological field there have been some fascinating studies on the subject of eye movements. It has been shown that if a person is trying to remember a real event, then they are likely to glance to the left as they use the right side of their brain to recall a picture of the event. If, however, a person is trying to create a situation in their mind, then they are more likely to look to the right. So if someone is making something up, or attempting to fabricate, then they are likely to look right as they access the left side of the brain in order to assemble a logical argument. To test this you might like to observe the behaviour of leading politicians when you suspect they are being 'economical with the truth'; do they look to their right or to their left?

In addition to this there are a number of other non-verbal signs which, when observed in clusters, could provide strong evidence that you are hearing something other than the entire truth. Being aware of this fact is clearly advantageous in influencing situations. Having identified that someone is not telling the truth is the first step; the next step is consider why they might be reacting in such a way, The reasons could be numerous, including;

- Fear of telling the truth and the effect it could have on you (consider whether you intimidate them and whether with effective listening and questioning skills you could get to the real issues).
- A passive approach and lack of ability to say 'no' (this is often linked to lack of ability to be assertive, and we address this in Chapter 11).
- A feeling that they are being pressurized (consider whether you are taking too much of a 'push' approach as opposed to a 'pull' approach to influencing).
- They are prone to fantasize and exaggerate (you are unlikely to change this trait because it is often used as a personal psychological defence mechanism, but it may be appropriate occasionally to challenge them).
- Reasons outside of their control, often to do with organizational politics, which mean that they are unable to tell the truth at this stage (it may be best to be patient or actually to confront the issue of other influences which may be in play).
- They are trying to influence you in a forceful or coercive way and are willing to use any means to achieve their aim including deceit (challenge the approach directly by stating that you recognize you are being coerced and question whether this is the sort of person or organization you should be dealing with).

Essentially the key to identifying if someone may be withholding information or not telling the truth is to look for lack of consistency between the verbal message and the non-verbal communication. The reason why this approach is so reliable is that while it is quite possible for someone to lie verbally, it is extremely difficult, almost impossible, consistently to deceive with one's body language.

Have you ever watched a play or film and said 'That actor is unconvincing'? If so, then it is likely that what you detected was a lack of consistency between the verbal and non-verbal components of the message they were trying to communicate. Often what differentiates a brilliant actor from a mediocre one is the ability to match the verbal messages with effective use of clusters on non-verbal communication.

There are, though, some recognized patterns which we can watch out for in order to tell whether someone is telling the truth.

STORYBOARD   EVERYTHING IS NOT NECESSARILY ALL THAT IT APPEARS

Patrick was unhappy: the negotiations had not gone exactly the way that he had anticipated. In part he felt his client had not really listened to what he was saying. Now it seemed that he was going to have to concede on the issue of improved delivery to ensure that he could meet their mid-December deadline.

He pushed his chair back from the table, sat back, and closed his notebook (*withdrawn*): 'Of course it's not a problem for us', his eyes looked down at the floor (*being evasive*), 'I said before we can meet any of your delivery times to meet your needs.'

His client then when on to explain how they were rescheduling their production on the new line and how this new schedule would really help them manage their inventory and costs better.

Patrick fidgeted in his chair, his arms and legs were crossed (*defensive*); he forced himself to smile and look interested but it was noticeable how he was unable to maintain eye contact. His hands alternately played with the end of his tie or the ring on his finger (*anxiety*).

He suddenly had an idea. He sat up, raised his hand as if to speak (*keen*), and said: 'If we were able to increase your stock holdings without you incurring additional costs, would you be able to maintain the existing production schedule?'

His client moved forward, adopting a similar body posture (*interest*): 'Tell me more.' Patrick went on to explain further his proposal. He noticed that as his client was listening, his head was slightly inclined (*listening*). This, he thought, showed that he was listening; in a similar way he saw that he was nodding his head in agreement. As he noticed his client's behaviour, he suddenly became aware that he was also nodding his head (*encouraging agreement*) although it was himself who was doing the talking)

He moved closer still, yet his voice got quieter as his persuasive style continued. His client pulled slightly away, this worried him; however, his smile and his response of 'Good, good, excellent' reassured him that he was turning things around.

In the above example Patrick allows his negative behaviour to reflect his disappointment that the negotiations were not going his way. After initially pulling away from the client, he exacerbated the situation by showing anxiety by playing with his tie and the rings on his fingers. However, he did pull it around and used both mirroring and mimicking. While doing so he became aware of the behaviour that the client was demonstrating.

COMPONENTS OF BODY LANGUAGE

It is possible to break body language down onto many component parts such as eye movements, sitting positions, and facial expressions. However, the importance of hand gestures is often overlooked. In terms of honesty and deceit, open palms, i.e. facing the hands upwards, is a sign normally associated with honesty. The most obvious sign of this is where the person overtly and consciously raises their hands upwards in order to say 'I am being honest' or 'I am telling you all I know'. Frequently, however, the same sort of gesture is seen but in a modified form, often as subtle as turning one's hand upwards on the desk or table during a meeting. Conversely, if someone is attempting to deceive, they may turn their hands downwards or even seek to hide their hands beneath the table or behind their backs.

If you are making a proposal and the person you are trying to influence is explaining why he or she cannot accept your recommendation, and you notice these hand gestures, it could be that they are actually giving some invalid reason or excuse rather than a genuine objection to your proposal.

When used in the context of trying to deceive, the downward facing hand gesture is often also linked to other mannerisms such as averting eye contact and hand-to-face gestures.

In children the gestures tend to be more exaggerated: a child who is lying may very obviously avoid looking the parent in the eye and may literally cover his or her mouth. In adult behaviour similar gestures are often seen but in a less obvious way. Examples of gestures that when grouped with other non-verbal behaviours might denote deception or lack of certainty about what is being said are: covering the mouth with one hand or a few fingers, touching the nose, or rubbing the eye, neck, or ear.

Of course it important to be careful in the interpretation of non-verbal behaviour. Not only should one seek supporting evidence of the interpretation by looking for clusters which back up the initial assessment, but one should be aware of the significance of cultural differences. In some cultures, for instance, looking away and averting the gaze from the other person is considered disrespectful and could been interpreted as meaning lack of honesty, whereas in other cultures the opposite is true and it is considered respectful to look away and down from the other person.

Showing assuredness

Just as there are certain clusters of behaviour which suggest uncertainty or deceit, so there are behaviours which suggest control and assertiveness.

Here there is sometimes a thin line between signals that suggest confidence and those that might be interpreted as aggression. Consider, for instance, the difference between asking someone to do something with your hand held out with palms up (open gesture) and with your hand facing downwards (suggesting a directive approach) or even with one finger pointing (often interpreted as aggressive).

There are a number of significant hand gestures which provide valuable information regarding the other person's frame of mind. If their hands are clenched, this often suggests some degree of frustration or that they are feeling negative and trying to resist direct confrontation. If you are attempting to influence by using a 'pull' approach and you detect such 'holding back' signals, it is worth considering whether you need to invest more time understanding the other person's perspective; this would suggest the need for further listening skills and demonstration of empathy.

The pushing of the fingers from both hands together in an upward direction in order to create a 'steeple' or 'roof' type structure is often associated with a person who is giving of the signals of being or feeling in control or in a superior position. It may be that in your attempt to influence you wish to adopt a superior stance and would use such a gesture; however, if you are attempting to operate on a 'level playing field', then this will give entirely the wrong message.

Again a word of caution, because this sort of action is also sometimes associated with a quite different meaning, that of evaluation or consideration. Again if you are attempting to interpret the body language of the person you are trying to influence, the trick is to look for other evidence to support your initial assumption. So if you suspect a superior attitude and you see steepled hand gestures, the head raised upwards, downward glances, and a superior tone of voice, then you have reliable data on which to make your assessment of a dominant attitude.

If, however, the steepled hand gestures were demonstrated at the same time as a pensive frown and 'thinking sounds' such as 'Mmm-mm', then you are more likely to be faced with someone who is considering your idea or proposal and is working it through in their mind before pronouncing a judgement or raising an objection.

Aggressive	Passive	Assertive
	Avoiding the handshake	Initiating the handshake
Squeezing the other person's hand in a 'vice-like' grip	Offering a hand like a 'wet lettuce leaf', i.e. limp and floppy	Matching the other person with a strong and confident handshake
Staring at the other person for protracted periods	Normally averting eye contact, only making the occasional sideways glances	Regularly making eye contact but focusing more on the forehead or bridge of the nose rather than staring directly into the eyes
Looming over the other person and invading their 'personal space'	Shrinking back in the chair or if standing making oneself seem smaller and diminutive	Sitting or standing upright
Finger pointing and wagging at the other person	Hands facing upwards and moving the body backwards	Hand facing downwards
Arms crossed and fists clenched	Touching one's own hand, arm, cuff or rings	Forearms on the desk or table, hands generally still unless using them to give support to a comment

Table 9.1

In order to demonstrate confidence in a situation it is as a general rule necessary to give strong, assertive, non-verbal messages without seeming aggressive. Achieving the right balance can be quite difficult; Table 9.1 lists some examples of aggressive, passive, and assertive non-verbal behaviours.

MIRRORING AND PACING

One very practical application of non-verbal communication awareness is the use of what are known as mirroring and pacing techniques.

Mirroring, as the name implies, is simply the process of copying the body language of the other person. This may sound rather like 'ape' behaviour and if taken to extremes this is indeed how it might be interpreted—in which sense it could seem irritating. However, there is no doubt that when two or more people are engaged in a discussion and they are getting on well together, they will start adopting similar sitting or standing positions and will use similar gestures and mannerisms and even the same terminology or verbal expressions.

Successful influencers will intuitively pick up on these points and will start to replay them back to the person they are attempting to influence. Equally it is possible actually to practise the skill of mirroring the other person in order to demonstrate that a strong rapport exists. This is really about taking your cues from the other person. Such mirroring behaviours could include the following:

- Sitting down when they sit down.
- Getting your papers or notes out at the same time.
- Engaging in small talk if they give the signal that they wish to.
- Standing, sitting or leaning in the same way.
- Using similar gestures.
- Using some of the same verbal expressions or terms as them.
- Using a similar tone, speaking at the same level.

In a similar way it is possible to identify the pace at which the other person is operating and to adopt a similar pace in the discussion.

In order to influence effectively it is necessary to be sensitive to such matters and at least in the initial stage to operate at a similar pace. There is nothing to be gained from racing ahead with your point of view if the other person is not mentally ready.

In the same way if you pick up the signs that the other person wishes to move the discussion on at some pace, then it is important to recognize this and to respond accordingly, rather than pursuing a protracted line in small talk. Having recognized and matched the other person's pace, it may be possible to the lead the pace, in other words to increase the pace of the discussion or to slow it down to suit your needs.

Proponents of neuro-linguistic programming (NLP) would suggest that it is possible to mirror and pace right down to the level of the other person's thinking and breathing pattern, though here we are concerned with some of the more obvious and clear-cut patterns of non-verbal behaviour.

Pause for thought

What signs do you show when you are being defensive?

Consider and list the types of positive body language you use when you are influencing somebody?

When you are next attempting to influence, consider the following:

How often do you change position?

Are any of your gestures similar to theirs?

Can you detect the pace at which they want to move through the discussion?

Try matching their non-verbal behaviour without mimicking their every move. Also look out for whether they actually start 'mirroring' your non-verbal behaviour.

Consider how you feel this effects the process of communication.

IMPACT OF CULTURAL DIFFERENCES ON BODY LANGUAGE

Earlier in the chapter we referred to the importance of recognizing that there may be significant cultural differences in terms of how people communicate non-verbally and regarding the interpretation of specific approaches.

A useful distinction has been made by Trompenaars between what he refers to as 'neutral' and 'affective' cultures. In neutral cultures, often associated with the United Kingdom, the East Coast of the United States, Japan, and Scandinavia, the tendency is towards more neutral non-verbal behaviour. Here the emphasis is on self-control, and overt displays of feelings tend to be frowned upon. In this sort of culture hand movements tend to be more restricted and the tone of voice more even throughout the discussion. A kind of unwritten code of conduct is likely to exist regarding who speaks when, and interruptions are likely to be quite discrete. If a person feels angry or upset, then this is less likely to be shown through frequent displays of emotion. This is not to say that emotion is never shown, but that it is more likely to be held inside the individual for as long as possible. The consequence of this is that it may then be displayed in the occasional cathartic dumping of emotion or even channelled into people or activities other than those causing the emotion.

By contrast, in affective cultures, more often associated with Latin, Arabic, and South American countries and the West Coast of the United States, there is much more animation in the process of communication and emotions are more likely to be displayed overtly, even to relative strangers. So in affective cultures people are likely to rely heavily on body language such as facial expression and hand and arm gestures in order to support the verbal messages being conveyed. Tone of voice will tend to have a wide range of modulation and it is considered quite acceptable to interrupt and over-talk the other person without them taking offence. Also it is not unusual to see a high level of physical contact in communication. Back slapping, patting, touching, and hugging, which might seem rather over-demonstrative in a neutral culture, are all a normal part of communication in an affective culture.

So if these are accepted as cultural norms, then what are the implications of this for the influencing situation?

Simply being aware of the differences is an important starting point. It is unrealistic to suggest that if you are working in a culture different to your own, then you will be able to change the way others operate in order to fit in with your own cultural norm. What is more likely is that you will need to be sensitive to

the differences and make allowances. So an Italian working in the United Kingdom may naturally feel the people to be more frosty or formal in their style of
communication; conversely a British subject working in Italy could find discussions too unruly and emotional. Similarly a Californian working in Japan could
feel frustrated at the lack of non-verbal feedback when giving a presentation.
The key is to question whether any frustration which is experienced could be
due to broader cultural differences rather than for personal reasons. While it is
difficult to change radically one's own behaviour—and indeed there is an argument that we should celebrate our cultural diversity, it can be helpful to
modify one's own behaviour in the direction of the other person.

An interesting question to consider is whether organizations, as well as nations, have neutral or affective cultures. Certainly some organizations are
much more ordered, clinical, and unemotional in their style, whereas others
encourage emotion and expression of feelings. Again it is worth considering
the norms for your own organization and for those in which you do business
because radical differences could be presenting significant barriers to the
process of influencing.

We have looked at the importance of body language and how it can impact
on the *influence* step of the EDICT model, and have explored how the way we
behave is even more important than the words we use.

In order to influence others successfully it is important to be able to be aware
of the signals that we give to others as well as being able to read and interpret
the body language of others. The secret here is to look for clusters or groups of
behaviours rather than pinning all the meaning on just one characteristic.

In the next chapter we will consider some of the powerful verbal techniques
which can be combined with body language in order to increase the chances
of successfully influencing others.

REFERENCE

Mehrabian, A. (1971) *Silent Messages*. Wadsworth, Belmont, CA.

10 Persuasion in action

Chapter objectives

- To discuss the distinction between logical and emotional approaches to persuasion.
- To explore a model to help understanding of the stages of the process of persuasion.
- To continue to explore issues of impressions management.
- To examine a number of verbal persuasive techniques which are frequently used by influential people and look at the factors which tend to increase demand or desire by others to accept our ideas.
- To recognize the secondary competencies of focused feedback and verbal skills.

We will in this chapter look at some of the detailed techniques we have seen used by some of the most influential people we have met in our research. These techniques are often subtly deployed but let there be no doubt that they are used consistently by those with the power of personal influence.

It could be argued that the use of such techniques in order to persuade others smacks of manipulation. To explore this, perhaps it would help at this stage to agree a working definition of the term 'manipulation' in order to define clearly the approach we are advocating in the influencing context.

> Manipulation is the use of covert techniques, where the aim is to confuse or deceive another person(s) with malicious intent, in order to gain an advantage for self or others.

The important point in the interpretation of this definition is that manipulation may describe an approach which aims to result in an 'I win–you lose' outcome. Often people who are manipulative will use other people and create circumstances in order to achieve their goal. The fact that their goal is seldom declared means that the person being subjected to such manipulation is often an innocent victim and there is usually some dishonest intent. Let us look at a real example.

STORYBOARD   THE MANIPULATIVE MANAGER

Steven was determined to get his boss to accept the need for a trip to the parent company in California; however, he realized that this needed to be within the next few months as he knew next year's budget was going to be tight.

He figured he deserved the trip; after all, most of his colleagues had managed to visit the plant, and on all accounts had had a great time in the process. It was generally accepted that such a trip was part of the senior management reward package. Steven knew that getting this finance was not going to be easy, primarily because of all the recent overhead reductions.

On thinking this over Steven realized that his only real chance of getting finance for the trip would be to try to use existing money, rather than attempting to get hold of a new budget. His best hope seemed to be to cancel a forthcoming planned training programme and to reallocate this budget to allow him his visit.

Sue was his subordinate manager, and it was she who had originally wanted the course. She was extremely keen to provide training for all her department, particularly in the area of improving teamwork. She had been instrumental in designing the training programme and had used an agency to identify a suitable venue. Regarding the venue, she had publicly stated that she felt this was critical, because creating the correct environment was crucial in issues of team building.

Steven knew he would find it difficult to cancel the training arbitrarily , particularly as his boss seemed to be increasingly keen on training. Subsequently he needed to get the line manager to cancel the event, while at the same time absolving himself of any responsibility.

He arranged to meet with Sue, and prior to the actual meeting he let it be implied, via one of her colleagues (*third-party influencing*) that he wanted to discuss a couple of matters of serious (*power word*) concern regarding the forthcoming training event (*attitude structuring*).

Although Steven had no strong feelings either way as to the value or otherwise of such training, he started the meeting by vociferously supporting the concept of team building (*enhanced personal credibility*). He also acknowledged her previous comments about the importance of the venue (*supportive*) as the critical factor enabling a successful outcome (*anxiety provocation*).

He then said:

'I heard from my friend Bill (*valued third-party reference*) over at INCO that they used the same hotel; however, they were very very (*repetition*) unhappy at the level of service. Apparently they found that there was a big difference between the rhetoric and the reality' (*alliteration*).

He went on to say:

'I know you would not want this to be a failure (*assumption*), not least because you are doing so well at the moment' (*coercive threat*).

Sue was clearly worried 'What are the alternatives?' Steven moves closer and his voice becomes almost conspiratorial. He says "We have several options, let's not rush anything" (*collaborative*).

Sue agrees in principle but seems hesitant; Steven keeps repeating the message:

'Let's not rush anything' (*repetition*).

While she is clearly thinking out these issues, Steven starts to throw out a list of other questions (*discrepancy*):

'Is the agenda finalized?
What arrangements have been made for the briefing?
How are we going to measure success?
Who else have you got to support the programme?
How are we justifying the costs?'

These additional issues seem to be distracting Sue from the apparent original difficulties of the hotel.

Clearly Steven's tactic is not to give her time to think while at the same time raising her anxiety level (*anxiety acceleration*) and having done this he ultimately offers her a lifeline (*psychological relief*) by suggesting the training should be postponed until these issues can be successfully resolved.

Steven further adds:

'If we postpone the programme say six months, then maybe we can pull in some of the other teams.'

After a few minutes more of these sort of manipulative persuasive techniques, Sue agrees that postponing the programme until some of these issues have been resolved is the best solution.

Even now Steven can feel that Californian sun!

What is apparent from the above example is that the manager has used a number of covert and arguably devious ploys in order to achieve his aim. Let us explore some of these in more detail, making particular reference to our definition.

Clearly Steven's motives were at best dubious, at worst dishonest, yet it was interesting to note how he structured the expectations of Sue even before the meeting, by getting her to listen to the comments of another person.

This can be a powerful influencing technique, unfortunately in this example (like most of the other techniques used here) it was applied in a negative manner. As a result of using these pre-meeting tactics, Steven had begun to prepare her to change Sue thinking.

During the meeting he deliberately gave explicit vocal support both to the programme as well as to her recognition of the importance of the venue. It was critical that he did this in order to be seen to be 'whiter than white' and acting only in the best interests of the company. This issue about the importance of the venue was then used against Sue.

In his meeting Steven tended to use a variety of different persuasive techniques including repetition, anxiety provocation, and implicit coercion. While using these techniques, he simultaneously continues to suggest a collaborative approach by using words like 'we'. This gives conflicting messages and as a series of behaviours is inherently deceptive.

Steven achieves success by the use of a particularly subtle technique. He continued to increase Sue's anxiety by throwing a number of different issues at her (while not giving her time to respond) and when this is at its highest pitch, he offers her psychological relief by showing her a solution to her problem. This is ultimately accepted because Steven offers Sue a sweetener from which she can not only maintain her own self-esteem but also gain some additional kudos.

SOME ETHICAL ISSUES

The above case was relatively clear-cut; however, it might be suggested that some forms of manipulation are legitimate because the ends justify the means. This is not an argument to which we could subscribe.

In general terms many of us use techniques that might border on manipulative; where doubt exists, then a useful framework as provided by our definition might be helpful. Alternatively we might consider our original definition of influencing as follows:

> Influencing is the process of getting other people to accept our view(s) and feel happy about it; and for them to remain persuaded and enthusiastic enough to positively influence other people.

People who regularly use such techniques of manipulation to influence others will sometimes get away with it because they often choose an easy target, but in the long term people tend to become wise to their style and treat them with extreme suspicion.

The second point is that such manipulative people are quite likely to find that other people will attempt to manipulate them, and a whole lot of time is therefore wasted playing games with each other.

We are thus not advocating manipulation as an influencing style; however, we do recognize that we present below a number of techniques, all of which could be used in a manipulative way and all of which could be used in a positive influencing manner.

The important issue is the way in which such techniques are used. If we adopt a pull approach to influencing and follow the EDICT model, then there would be an open discussion at the start regarding the objectives of both parties and the aim would be to achieve a result which leaves the dignity of all concerned in tact. We would argue that one can use persuasive techniques in order to progress and speed the process of persuasion, but manipulation must be avoided.

THINKING ABOUT PERSUASION

It is important to recognize that the process of persuasion takes place in the other person's mind and that our role as successful influencers is to help the other person towards making some sort of decision or taking positive action. In order to be able to achieve this we have to have a clear understanding as to what we want the other person to know or do.

When presenting a persuasive argument there are essentially two approaches which might be taken:

- An appeal to logic
- An appeal to emotion

It is quite common to see emotional arguments taken in advertising. For instance, when trying to persuade people to give to charity, a picture of starving children or suffering families is shown in order to evoke emotions. The aim is to encourage you to write out a cheque there and then. While emotional arguments can be very effective, the danger is that they persuade you in the short term, but in the long term such persuasion may not last. So in the example above, though you might give to charity there and then, based on the emotional argument, you are less likely to be influenced to give on a regular basis.

STORYBOARD THE IMPACT OF FEAR

Chris was driving along at about 160 km per hour when he saw the carnage of a car crash on the roadway. Several vehicles were involved, it looked as if there were fatalities.

After passing the accident he found that his speed seemed to slow naturally, now he was driving at about 120 km per hour.

This apparent change in his behaviour was probably a result of him seeing what had taken place and then having been suitably shocked to think along the lines of 'Oh how awful, they were probably driving too fast—it is danger-ous—I must start driving slower myself.'

He remained driving more slowly for about the next hour and then uncon-sciously he gradually crept back up to his original speed.

In the above example fear is a very powerful emotion, yet unfortunately it does not last. Over time it dissipates and to be effective needs to be continu-ously reinforced. Hence coercion using emotional arguments is not necessarily a good influencing strategy.

In contrast, however, the logical approach tends to emphasize the importance of doing something because it makes sense on a purely rational basis. If the intention in influencing is to bring about a lasting change, in other words the person is to remain influenced over a period of time, then a logical approach to persuasion is likely to be more successful. Having said that, a logical process delivered with strong emotional tones will probably better than a single dimen-sional approach.

THE 8 Ps OF PERSUASION

We have identified eight key stages of the persuasion process which can serve as a checklist that might be used as you progress through a persuasive discus-sion. The other application of the 'eight Ps of persuasion' is in serving as an aid to preparation for the actual meeting or indeed to act as a structure for pre-senting data.

You will see in Fig. 10.1 that we present the stage of persuasion through the model of 'the eight Ps' as a cycle of key parts; this is to suggest an approximate order of events in most persuasive discussions. It should be recognized, how-ever, that the actual order of the discussion may vary according to the nature of the meeting and often the preferences of the other person. So while you might prefer to deal with put offs or objections later on in the discussion, you may find that the person you are trying to persuade actually wants to raise

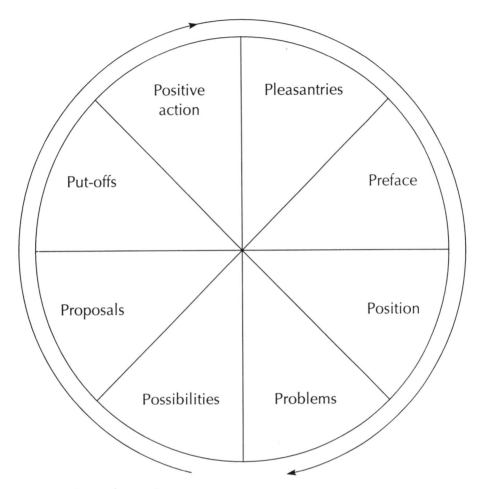

Figure 10.1 Stages of persuasion

objections at the very start; in this sense it is important not to be constrained by insistence that discussion follows this pattern.

The only stages that really are fixed in this model are the first and the last: pleasantries and positive action, respectively. It is important, when attempting to persuade, always to spend some time on the initial ice-breaking conversation at the start. Similarly it is also essential to ensure that there is some agreement on the action which will be taken by both parties after the meeting.

Below we work through the eight Ps in turn, explaining the key stages and where they fit in with the overall process.

Pleasantries

The pleasantries stage refers to the polite conversation which normally takes place at the early stage of the discussion. This is the warm-up dialogue which helps both parties to feel at ease and establishes a climate that is conducive for the main discussion to take place. Essentially this involves the competencies of impact and rapport.

Even where the person you are trying to persuade is known and a good relationship already exists, it will still be relevant to spend some time on pleasantries; it would be wrong to assume that because there is an existing relationship there is no need to invest time putting each other at ease.

Preface

This stage is the preface to the main discussion and it is here that there is an opportunity to raise or attract the attention level of the other person. Comments to preface the discussion could relate to, for instance:

- A relevant and interesting fact
- Some recent research
- Activities of competitors

This sort of preface need not be delivered in a grand and formal way, but could simply be dropped into the conversation in order to raise awareness of the relevance of the topic that is to be discussed.

Position

It is helpful early on the meeting to provide some sort of overview statement of the current position. Usually this summarizes the position as it currently stands as opposed to the preferred position if the other person has been influenced effectively. This is not as simple as you stating your position and assuming the other party will necessarily have the same picture of the current position.

Through an interactive discussion and with the effective use of questioning, listening, and summarizing skills, the aim is to arrive at a mutual understanding of the current situation.

It is this mutual understanding that forms the cornerstone of the remainder of the process.

Problems

If you are seeking to encourage someone to change or to accept your proposals it is useful to state some of the problems which currently exist, so that you create an acceptance that there is a need to do things differently. Problems may have been identified by yourself but it is even more powerful if the problems have been identified by either a third party or even by the person you are trying to persuade.

Once again the skills of questioning and listening are critical at this stage.

Possibilities

In presenting a range of possibilities, a particularly persuasive approach is to include the proposals that you intend to make but to add them to a range of other possibilities.

In fact you may have a range of desired outcomes and it can be beneficial to include as possibilities your second and third choice outcomes. If you do not achieve your ideal outcome, then it may be that there are other options which would be more acceptable to you than no action at all. Additionally it is worth stating that one possibility would be to do nothing at all; the thinking here is that you are showing, in what seems an objective way, that you have considered the full range options. You might, though, summarize what you feel the implications of doing nothing are; they may appear so unacceptable that some action is bound to be taken.

The order in which you state the possibilities is significant. There is a natural perceptual distortion which means that we tend to pay particular attention to the early part and the final part of a presentation or discussion, often referred to as primacy and recency effect. Thus if you state the possibility that you would like to see as the outcome first or last in your list of possibilities, then this is likely to make more of an impact on the person you are attempting to persuade.

Another useful technique is to place your first choice first on the list of possibilities and your second choice last on the list.

Remember, possibilities are not about a heavy sell, but primarily to enable you to show your breadth of thinking about the subject and to structure the other person's expectations in readiness for you suggestions. Consequently it is important that the other person acknowledges that this list of possibilities is complete.

Proposals

Having discussed a range of possibilities, it is necessary to make proposals regarding further action. Naturally one should have a clear idea in advance of the meeting regarding the proposals that might be made; the secret, however, is to remain flexible regarding specific proposals because the discussion may actually reveal that the other person is cautious about certain possibilities and enthusiastic about others.

When stated, proposals should be made clearly, concisely, and to the point. We should then pause for effect and to gain some feedback.

Put-offs

Put-offs refer to the objections which may inevitably be raised. By taking a methodical approach at the preparatory stage, possibly with the help of a perspective specification, it should be possible to identify some of the likely put-offs which will be raised. It is also helpful to consider at the preparation stage the style of the person you are trying to persuade. Some examples are provided below:

- Do they have a high need for security, safety, and adherence to rules? If so, consider how, if you are presenting what might appear as a high-risk strategy, you might reduce the risk.
- Do they have a driving, competitive, and forceful style? If so, consider how you can demonstrate that your proposals will lead to visible results and achievement?
- Are they ambitious and keen for personal kudos? If so, think about how you could, through your proposals, provide them with opportunities for recognition and raising their profile.

As you can see in the above examples, identifying the style and motives of the other person can help considerably in the identification of some of the potential objections.

Anticipating these objections may lead you either to pre-empting them though your presentation or simply holding on to your answers until the question arises. This latter point is of particular importance. In general terms, if you believe that an issue is going to be raised, then pre-empt it first and give a considered yet minimalized answer. If, on the other hand, you feel the matter is unlikely to be raised, do not raise the subject. The danger here is that we make issues of things that were previously non-issues.

Positive action

This is in many ways the most important but also the most neglected of the stages of the persuasion process. All to often good persuasive skills are demonstrated but there is a failure to agree what will happen next. How often have you attended a meeting and found that the various parties leave the meeting with different pictures of what has been agreed?

Often the failure to 'ask for the order' is influenced by a fear of being seen as over pushy or aggressive; however, this stage need not be conducted in a 'hard sell' style. It can be as straightforward as summarizing who has committed to do what or even putting a date in the diary for the next meeting.

Another common reason for failing to be successful with this stage is our fear of rejection. The only way we can manage this is by positive inner dialogues and by realising that saying 'No' is often a signal for saying 'I am not yet convinced'. In situations like this the secondary competence of *tenacity* becomes paramount.

Pause for thought

What does manipulation mean to you?

Which stages of the eight Ps of persuasion do you manage well?

Which areas could you improve?

INTEGRATING THE COMPETENCIES

In working through the eight Ps of persuasion, it is essential to approach the process as a dynamic and interactive interaction. The model can help in giving structure and in serving as a checklist as different stages are completed, but there is clearly a danger in allowing yourself to be constrained by the model. If the other person wants to raise a 'put-off' early on in the discussion, then you will have to deal with this as it arises, this requires the secondary competence of *adaptability.*

If the discussion is with one other person or even a small team, then it is likely to be interactive and comprise of a series of questions, answers, and comments from all sides. In a bigger group, if someone is attempting to persuade, then there is necessarily more formality and the eight Ps might provide a useful structure for a more formal discussion.

In Chapter 8 we considered questioning skills in the context of the diagnosis stage of the EDICT model. At the diagnosis stage questions aim to ensure a sound understanding of the other person's viewpoint and perspective.

Now, however, we will look at some specific types of question which can be used in the persuasive dialogue in order actively to influence the other person.

The rhetorical question

This is the sort of question that sounds like it is a question, but in actual fact an answer is not really expected. In a persuasive sense rhetorical questions are often asked in a leading way. The intention is to ask a question which leads the other person to answer in a particular way. The answer is either obvious or is leading the person being persuaded down a particular path which the questioner has determined. Examples of rhetorical or leading questions are listed below with comments in parentheses regarding where the questioner is trying to lead the person they are persuading.

> 'Do you believe quality is an important issue in your organization?' (Quality is important in most organizations, so the answer is likely to be 'Yes'; this question could be leading the respondent towards the acceptance of a proposed product or service which arguably will contribute to the improvement of quality in the business.)

'Are you interested in developing your own personal skills for the future?
(Most people are interested in personally improving themselves; this
question could be leading to a proposal of training or some sort of
change in working practice.)

'Would you be interested in reducing your overhead costs?'
(Most people would be; this suggests the person could be leading to the
offer of a service, product, or new working method.)

Rhetorical questions can be powerful if used with discretion. As with most
persuasive techniques, however, rhetorical questions can backfire if used in
the wrong context or in a very transparent way. The skill of the person trying to
persuade is to be able to integrate such skills into a repertoire of behaviours
and to apply judgement in the application of these skills.

The alternative closed question

The alternative closed question is where the person persuading offers the
other person a choice; however, the choice is in itself restricting.

A good example to highlight this approach is where the parent, in trying to
persuade the child to go to bed asks: 'Would you like to put on your blue or
green pyjamas?' The decision has, in fact, already been made; the child has no
choice but to get ready for bed. In a more subtle way we often see such
questions used as a way of pressing for some action on the part of the other
person. Another example of an alternative closed question is that used by the
manager who is concerned to secure a second meeting with a colleague who
is showing signs of resistance. She might say 'Would you prefer me to come
back for a further discussion tomorrow or would next week be better?'

The alternative closed question can be a very effective way of moving things
forward if there seems to be a lack of action and if the person you are trying to
persuade seems to be prevaricating. The important skill is to be able to judge
whether the other person is close to accepting a proposition and then to use
the alternative closed question. Such judgements can only realy be made after
considering all the verbal and non-verbal signals. If this is misjudged, and used
at too early a stage, then the other person may consider the technique manipulative and resent it.

Assumption statements

A similar approach which is often used effectively is to use the 'assumed close
or assumed statement'.

This is the verbal technique where a comment is made which implies that the
other person is going to take the preferred course of action. Using the example above of the manager who is trying to persuade a colleague to meet again

in the future, an assumed closed comment would be: 'When we meet again I would propose we ask some of your team into the meeting in order to help them to understand what we are discussing.' The real issue here is not so much one of involving the colleague's team members, but actually getting the colleague to attend a meeting. By moving one step ahead of the next move there is an implication that the meeting is bound to take place.

IMPRESSIONS MANAGEMENT

Managing the first impression

Impressions management is the concept that says that whether we like it or not, other people are going to form opinions of us, and that these opinions will in general terms be influenced by their perceptual processes.

In Chapter 6 we identified the importance of first impressions, or the primacy effect. This is a common perceptual distortion resulting from our strong tendency to make judgements based on an assessment made in the first four minutes. This can effect the success or otherwise of making impact and building rapport.

First impressions could prove to be accurate, or conversely could be erroneous. The key issue from an influencing point of view is to recognize the importance of making the impression that we want to make right from the start because it is very difficult to change the other person's perception once an impression has been formed. We use the term 'impressions management' to describe the way that one should recognize and attempt to influence the other person's impression.

Apart from the phenomenon of first impressions, there are a number of other ways in which impressions tend to be distorted and these provide further opportunities to influence others.

Another area of where perception is distorted, which is the flip side of first impressions, is known as the recency effect. Essentially the recency effect is the term used to describe the fact that last impressions are also of particular importance. In the same way that people naturally place an overemphasis on the first period in an interaction, so they tend to focus particularly on the most recent contact.

Using recency

One area in which we see the recency effect most clearly is that of performance review. If attempting to review the performance of a subordinate over a period of, say one year, the tendency is actually to review only the last few months. Of course, if one is attempting to influence someone, then there may be opportunities to use the recency effect in a positive way. For instance, when making a formal presentation, it is important to have a powerful conclusion.

Alternatively, if you are due shortly to meet a potential client who you are concerned to impress, you might send them, a few weeks before the meeting, a relevant article or paper which supports your main message. In doing this, when you do meet, the potential client is likely to recall the recent article and if this has made a positive impact, then recency effect is likely to work in your favour.

Stereotyping ourselves and others

Previously we identified that humans have a tendency to stereotype other people; we figuratively put people into boxes or label them and say that because he is x, he is also bound to have y qualities.

In order to try to make judgements about people, we try to make them fit with a stereotype or even a number of stereotypes based, for instance, on their gender, race, profession, social class, or age. The reason that we tend to stereotype others is that it essentially convenient and provides a quick and easy way of making judgements about others when do not have the time or inclination to get to know what the individual is really like. In terms of making accurate judgements about people, there are clearly dangers of stereotyping: firstly there is a distinct possibility of getting it wrong, and secondly if the person you are stereotyping becomes aware of it, they are quite likely to feel insulted. So from an influencing perspective stereotyping of other people is unlikely to be helpful. It is interesting, though, to note the extent to which humour is based on stereotypes.

But let us take a look at stereotyping from another perspective. Whether you like it or not, other people are stereotyping you all the time. They will form stereotypes based on minor amounts of information such as your name and your role. When they do meet you, the stereotyping process will continue, based on, for instance, your looks, dress, and the way you speak. They will even form stereotypes based on the accessory symbols you wear and surround yourself with.

Some people will, in a fairly obvious way, attempt to make a statement about themselves by adorning their bodies and surroundings with accessory symbols: who actually wears a Rolex watch in order to be able to tell the time? Such accessories are about making a statement regarding one's worth or values. And this does not only relate to material wealth. Consider, for instance, the sports person who wears a tie or scarf with the club colours or motif displayed. The message here could be 'I am sporty' or 'I am a team person' or even 'I am a member of an exclusive organization'. In this example it could also be used as a way of identifying with like-minded people.

In order to influence the stereotypes that others will form of you it is important to ask the question 'What is the stereotype which this person may have of me and do I want to reinforce it or do I want to shatter it?'

Pause for thought

Consider the stereotypes that other people are likely to hold of you. What generalizations are they likely to make based on your:

appearance	*age*
job	*culture*
speech	*background*
education	*interests*
family	*location*
car	*accessory symbols*

Now consider an influencing situation which you are likely to find your self in the near future.

How appropriate are the stereotypes that might be held of you?

Do they actually help you influence or do they hinder your influencing position?

Next consider how you might reinforce relevant stereotypes and how you might shatter inappropriate ones.

Halo or horns?

Another major perceptual distortion which lends itself to the approach we call impressions management is the 'halo' and 'horns' effect. Again there is a natural human tendency to put a figurative halo or set of horns over another person's head because of just one of their strengths or weaknesses, respectively.

An example of the halo effect would be recruiting someone for a job as marketing manager because they once played international sport; their sporting prowess actually has no relationship with their marketing skill but there is a false linkage made between the two issues.

Conversely, one negative factor could create the belief that everything this person will ever do is bound to result in failure. For instance, if assessing a member of your team for their suitability to work on a high-profile client contract, an assumption might be made that because they had some problems with one client in the past they are bound to have similar problems in the future and therefore they are ruled out.

From an impressions management perspective the important point is to recognize that the phenomenon can affect the qualities that other people will attribute to you. If you are able to identify the nature or source of the halo or horns, then you can encourage the halo effect and discourage the horns effect.

As long as this is done in such a way that there is no dishonest intent, which would suggest manipulation, then reinforcing positive halos can prove an effective influencing technique. Of course, you need the confidence to be able ultimately to live up to positive image others have of you, and if you actually feel that there is evidence of an entirely misplaced halo effect, then the best approach would be to explain the limits of your knowledge or expertise.

With the horns effect it is important from an influencing point of view to challenge and confront comments which might be unfounded because they are making a sweeping generalization about one's abilities based selective evidence. In the next chapter we will look at the subject of how to confront assertively.

THE TECHNIQUES OF PERSUASION

Having considered a number of ways that one can use perceptual distortion in order to manage the impressions that others form of us, we will now discuss some of the practical techniques which can help the process of persuasion. These techniques are drawn from our studies of the specific behaviours of successful and persuasive international figures who in many ways can serve as effective role models.

Build personal credibility slowly

It has been observed that some of the most persuasive figures and speakers are subtle in building their own credibility. They will tend to build up their own image gradually and steadily. Often they do this through low-key, almost passing references to their own relevant experience or expertise. They will not be afraid to discuss their own strengths and abilities but will do so without overselling themselves personally. So a manager, in building credibility with a customer, might start by referring to her current senior role and a little later would mention in passing some of the organizations she has worked for in her career, being careful to select those organizations from her portfolio which the customer is likely to relate to best. She might then at a later stage again mention her role in developing certain well-known products, and then later again refer to articles she has had published in relevant industry journals.

This approach is quite different from that taken by some people who naïvely believe that the best way to persuade people regarding their credibility is to declare all their strengths up front at the start of the interaction. This approach can be seen as rather too forceful and other people are prone to back off at this hard-sell approach.

Identification

Successful influencers are able to identify well with other people; they are able to give the impression to the other person that they are similar. They are very skilled in quickly picking up and building on relevant information regarding possible areas of common interest; they will not be afraid to discuss openly common interests and they will give the impression that because of the common interests there is a unique relationship. This process of identification tends to accelerate the process of building trust and the feeling that there is some common bond.

Clearly judgement needs to be applied when using this technique; it can, for instance, be a dangerous strategy to attempt to identify by referring to a common interest which you cannot support if the other person decides to probe with deeper discussion. But approaches to identification could be as simple as:

- Identifying the areas that you both have in common and be sure to make these similarities known.
- Asking about their children and talking about yours if they are of a similar age.
- Referring to people you both know personally.
- Showing similar experiences.

One particular method of identifying with the other person is through the use of *third-party references*. By referring to the work being carried out with a customer in the same industry as the potential client, a salesperson is able to demonstrate implicitly an understanding of the client's business as well as demonstrating the fact that he is valued by others.

One cautionary note: as we previously discussed, discussing one's family or using self-disclosure may be culturally unacceptable in some societies.

Painting pictures

Consider for a moment what goes on in your head when you think. Do you think in words, images, pictures, faces, or situations? Do you think in colour or black and white? Most people, when we ask this question, surprisingly have to think about it quite hard. Then the majority will say that they think in pictures or images; some even explain that when they think, they almost see a cinema screen with scenes being acted out in their mind. Only rarely do people say that when they think, they see text or numbers.

Bearing this in mind, there is a lot to be said for attempting to create pictures and images in the mind of the other person when trying to persuade them. It is particularly advantageous if you can create a picture of how things could be if your proposals were accepted. In this sense the use of metaphors and analogies can be very powerful. Consider the images conjured up by the following statements.

> 'Bringing about major culture change in the organization is difficult; it is rather like trying to turn a supertanker in the ocean—you have to accept it won't happen overnight but once you do get things moving it will be hard to stop.'

> 'He is so tenacious—he is like a terrier dog—constantly snapping at your heels to try and get information out of you. He is so persistent that eventually you give in and let him have his way.'

Some people seem to have a natural ability to paint pictures, which clearly gives them an advantage when it comes to influencing others. Another related verbal technique which increases impact is the use of *alliteration*, such as the title of this section 'painting pictures' which uses alliteration to aid recall as well as conjuring up a visual image.

Selective head nods

When two people have established a strong rapport, then it is common to see them subconsciously mimicking one another's non-verbal behaviour.

It is possible to use this information consciously and to encourage the other person to mimic oneself. In an influencing situation where you are attempting to gain agreement to a proposal if you selectively nod your head, frequently you will notice that the other person also starts nodding.

The reason that this may be an effective approach to gaining agreement is that studies into body language have shown that when a person is forced into using a particular non-verbal gesture, then the relevant thinking actually follows. So experiments where certain members of the audience in a presentation have been instructed to keep their arms folded have shown that their learning has been significantly reduced compared to those who were allowed to sit as they pleased. In a similar way if a person starts to mimic your selective head nods, then they are more likely to agree to your proposition than if they do not engage in such mimicry.

Repeat, repeat, repeat

The benefits of the use of repetition in persuading other people should not be underestimated. The benefit of repetition is that the process of using the same words ensures that key messages are reinforced. This is an approach that some politicians and public speakers are very strong in using. Repetition can also help in buying thinking time for the speaker.

One approach to repetition is to use certain words at the *end* of a sentence and then, after a suitable pause, to start the next sentence with the same words or expression. For example:

> 'The main reason that we should mobilise our forces is because of the external threat . . . The external threat is so powerful because . . .'

Emotional stimulation

It has been recognized in the field of sales and marketing for some time that one way of increasing the demand for your product or service is to appeal to the potential purchaser's emotions.

Some advertisers have capitalized on this in quite an aggressive way in recent campaigns. Consider the many advertisements for motor cars which tell a romantic story of boy meets girl, or the advertisements for up-market ice-cream which manage to create erotic connotations associated with their product. Such approaches have proved controversial, for instance, in the areas of cigarette sales where linking the product with sporty, macho, or romantic images has led to accusations of exploitation.

The learning point from the marketeers is that if we can appeal to the other person's emotions (particularly pleasure, joy, and happiness), then there is more chance of gaining interest in what we are proposing. Consequently if we can make our ideas sound like they are fun, exciting or interesting, then there is significantly more likelihood that they will be accepted than if we simply propose the facts in a dry manner.

Psychological relief

In some ways this is the opposite to the above. History is littered with examples from the world of advertising which capitalise on the fact that, if it is possible to generate fear in a person, then the way to really create demand is then to propose a way of relieving them of the fear. So, for instance, cosmetics are often sold on the basis that they will 'relieve' you of the potential implications of ageing. You might be encouraged to fit a fire alarm in your home after you have seen the frightening pictures of the family sleeping while their house is burning down. In a similar vein, consider the example in the following storyboard of an extract from a letter from a financial services organization selling its insurance products to the self-employed.

STORYBOARD   VICTIMS AND RESCUERS

Dear Mr X

Did you know that in this country 10% of men over the age of 40 suffer from long-term sickness of at least one year duration. Half of the breadwinners of the family are forced through sickness to retire early and the majority of these are left unable to provide adequately for their family. Furthermore with reductions in the amount of state aid available there is a serious danger of being left to face a future of poverty.

With our new family income protection policy, however, it is possible to provide for your family's future in the unfortunate event of . . .

The above example was not particularly subtle, yet we discovered subsequently that this kind of approach was producing a better than average response rate.

On a more discreet level, in an influencing context it is possible to sense when the person you are attempting to persuade is feeling under some pressure whereby you may be able to relieve them psychologically of the problem that is weighing heavily on their minds. For instance, you might be attempting to persuade your boss to allow you to take on more responsibility in your job role. Using this approach, you might spend some time making sure that they realized that there is a lot of extra administrative work building up and that it must be placing quite a pressure on him. Having built up the pressure psychologically, you would then relieve it by offering your assistance.

In this example your boss would feel only too pleased to delegate or hand over certain tasks to you in order to relieve the pressure on himself. Thus occasionally the tactical raising of the temperature can create a climate which is conducive to raising the demand for your assistance.

Appealing to status

It is well known in the area of sales that one sure way of creating demand from a potential customer is to make them feel important. If you can present your product or service in such a way that it suggests the customer's image will be enhanced in the eyes of other people, then they are much more likely to respond in a positive way.

Take, for instance, the salesperson who identifies a customer as a young, upwardly mobile professional and appeals to status by saying: 'This is a beautiful car. The thing about driving a BMW is that it really makes a statement to other people that you have arrived in life!' This may sound like a rather obvious, unsubtle approach; however, there is no doubt that some people are particularly motivated by recognition and status. On a more subtle level, a manager might delegate a task to her subordinate while implying that if it is carried out successfully, it will raise the profile of the subordinate among her superiors.

In terms of motivation theory, if the technique of offering psychological relief is appealing to our human need for security and safety, then the technique of appealing to status capitalizes on the human requirement for recognition and acceptance by others.

Clearly one needs to exercise some caution in appealing to the status of the other person; if the technique is overdone it can appear as flattery, which may work occasionally but if overused can seem transparent and manipulative.

Linked to this approach is the technique of persuading people by suggesting that what you have to offer is in high demand or is what other people want. If you are able to suggest that the demand is coming from a person or organization respected by the person you are attempting to persuade, then you are likely to increase still further the level of demand.

Have you ever had the experience of deciding to buy something and then when you come to order being informed that the product is in short supply because of high demand? This usually increases individual demand dramatically. Of course, some people have used this understanding of human psychology in a coercive way: take, for instance, the real estate agent who, when you place an offer on your dream property, informs you that there is another potential buyer in the race. This ploy might be used in order to encourage you to increase the level of your offer so that you can secure the property. Yet it can also easily backfire!

In influencing situations it is generally possible to use the same sort of approach to encourage others to accept your proposals. It could be, for instance, that you convince your boss of the need to upgrade the departmental computing facilities by referring to the fact that other successful managers in the organization have made similar changes. This might capitalize on the fact that your boss will be interested in having what others have, as well as the fact that others who have made the upgrade of senior status.

So far in this and the previous chapter we have been primarily considering the competencies of body language and persuasion. We identified in the EDICT model of influencing that there are two secondary competencies which feature in the *influence* step: focused feedback and verbal skills. We have given these competencies secondary status because although both are used, generally the significance is less.

FOCUSED FEEDBACK

Often when we are in an influencing situation, it is necessary to be able to let the person we are dealing with know how effectively they are operating and to inform them of the impact they are making on you or others.

Arguably feedback is one of the most powerful aspects of persuasion. This is about the ability to provide others with feedback in such a way that they are influenced to make a personal change in the way that they operate. If feedback is given in such a way that it is accepted and the other person, on reflection, decides to change the way they operate in the future, then such feedback might be considered effective.

> Focused feedback is the ability to provide feedback by being specific and descriptive and non-evaluative and by focusing on modifiable behaviours. Such feedback is given in a timely way and is balanced. It is for the benefit of the recipient, not the provider.

What is the use of providing some supposed feedback to someone if they are incapable of making the changes you would like to see—or, as is often the case, the feedback is provided months after the event it is meant to relate to? Feedback is sometimes given so that the person giving it feels better; this is particularly the case with feedback of a negative nature. This is not really focused feedback and probably does little actually to influence the other person.

It is interesting to note that feedback often has negative connotations. Consider the situation where the boss calls the subordinate on a Friday afternoon and says "Can you come and see me on Monday morning—I would like to give you some feedback.' Such a comment is guaranteed to spoil the weekend for the subordinate who will be preoccupied wondering 'What have I done wrong?' Similarly, consider the comment made by the business man or woman who says to a colleague staying at the same hotel 'I am going to go down to the reception desk and give them some real feedback'. The statements in these examples are clearly loaded and imply that there is likely to be a strongly negative flavour to the discussion. All too often the word feedback is used to signify a release of emotion on the part of the giver of the feedback, rather than being seen as the provision of useful information for the receiver.

We would do well, though, to remember the concept of feedback in an engineering sense. A feedback loop is a built-in mechanism in systems to provide information on performance so that changes can be made in order for the system to continue to operate effectively. In a human sense there is no reason why the same interpretation should not apply. Feedback need not always be associated with letting someone know where they have got it wrong; it is also extremely helpful to let them know when and how they managed to get it right so that they can continue to do so in the future.

In order to influence the behaviour of another person, there are a number of useful ground rules which will help to ensure the feedback is effective.

First of all feedback should be provided in a descriptive way; it should describe the behaviour which is observed. There is no need to make value judgements and personal comments such as 'You are hopeless' or 'You are great'. These sort of comments do little actually to inform the other person why you considered them to be hopeless or great. Without this specific knowledge it is difficult to reinforce strengths and to minimize weaknesses. So if, for instance, providing feedback to a colleague on their contribution to a meeting, a descriptive piece of feedback might be given as follows:

> 'I believe you showed real strengths in that meeting. First of all you were one of the early speakers which meant that people paid attention to your inputs throughout. Secondly you used some powerful examples to highlight your opinions. OK, you might have spent a little more time listening to Brian and some of the quiet members of the team but overall I have to admire your meeting skills.'

If we are to analyse this brief piece of feedback we notice that by saying "I believe" it is presented as just one person's opinion or interpretation rather than a definitive and omniscient judgement which could appear arrogant. Two specific strengths are described—the early contribution and the use of examples—and this tells the person what to do again in the future.

One area for improvement is presented but it is not laboured and it is descriptive, providing a specific example of what might be done differently next time, i.e. listening to all members of the team.

It is also important when providing feedback to others that it is given soon after the event to which it relates. It would be of little value, for example, giving the feedback regarding the meeting in the above illustration, several meetings later: the impact and relevance of the feedback would be lost.

The amount of judgement provided is a matter of fine assessment. Too much, and the other person will reach saturation point whereby they may appear to be listening but information is not being interpreted. When providing feedback on another person's behaviour, just two or three specific examples to back up a description of an observed behaviour are sufficient, and in an informal discussion it would be unrealistic to cover more than, say, three different behaviours.

When feedback is provided, it should be given with the implied message 'Take it or leave it' because it is simply not possible to force a person to accept feedback regarding such personal issues. One's own self-perception will always be distorted due to the psychological defence mechanisms we use to protect our ego. Providing feedback is a way of attempting to give a person the opportunity to develop a realistic image of themselves. If they receive similar feedback from a number of different people, then they are more likely to accept it as valid.

The other rule in giving feedback is to try to focus on behaviours which are modifiable. In an obvious example there is little to be gained from providing feedback to a presenter that they are 'Six inches too short in height to make an impact'. Advice regarding making an impact might better be directed at developing impact through voice projection and the content of the presentation.

Finally feedback should always be balanced. In the example above both strengths and weaknesses are identified. It is worth considering that in matters relating to personal and behavioural style, one person's weakness can always be related to their strengths. Feedback is more likely to be accepted if it identifies both strengths and weaknesses. Furthermore if it can be presented as a 'feedback sandwich' with strengths–weaknesses–strengths being covered in this order, as in the above example, then it is likely to be more palatable. You might at this stage be considering 'How can all weaknesses be related to strengths?' If so consider the list of strengths and potentially corresponding weaknesses shown in Table 10.1.

When considered in this way, it is not difficult to find strengths which are related to the weaknesses or areas for development. We are not saying that one must always try to say 'nice things' when giving feedback, but when discussing personality-related behaviours it is important to recognize the richness and complexity of human personality and to look for strengths as well as weaknesses.

If this proves difficult, then the positive note might simply relate to the behaviours or new approaches which the person commits to in the future.

In the workplace we are seeing a significant broadening in the use of feedback as an influencing skill. The successful influencers we have observed through

Strengths	Weaknesses
Competitive, strong willed, task oriented	Overbearing, domineering, autocratic
Influential, strong social skills, good at making impact	Superficial, lacking depth or substance
Reliable, neighbourly, steady	Unexciting, uncomfortable with change
Good with detail, procedures and rules	Non risk-taker, unadventurous
Reflective, thoughtful, pensive, intelligent, probing	Hesitant, withdrawn, introverted
Conceptual, strategic, visionary	Daydreamer, head in the clouds, not practical

Table 10.1

our research, however, consistently showed strong ability to provide feedback to others and to confront and provide such feedback in such a way that it was likely to help the other person recognize the need for the change.

VERBAL SKILLS

How often have we heard the expression: 'It's not what you say, it's the way that you say it'? Although we would argue that this is a somewhat simplistic way of looking at things, we do believe that the way that we use our voice can be significant in influencing others. Consequently we feel that this is an important secondary competence of influence.

Verbal skills are related to the way in which we as individuals use words, construct sentences, and use the range of our voice. Verbal skill can be seen to consist of a number of separate constitutent parts.

Diction

Diction is concerned with the clarity with which we say something. Generally speaking we found that successful influencers tended not necessarily to have an extended vocabulary yet their diction was almost always clear and precise. They appeared as if they were conscious of creating the words they were using by the movements of their mouths. In particular they would often emphasize specific words or syllables.

Vocabulary

Vocabulary does not necessarily appear to be a critical issue of influencing, yet influencers do appear to select their words with some care.

As previously discussed, successful influencers appear to use a higher number of power words or power statements than other less influential people.

Power words are any words that conjure up power, achievement, or success. Power statements are when the words are strung together to achieve a particular response. This may include alliteration or even rhythm—anything that makes the statement more memorable to others.

By contrast, the less effective influencers tended to use more hesitant words or expressions that are riddled with doubt and uncertainty, or they speak quietly, or in a monotone without any emphasis.

Speed of delivery

One of the most surprising findings was that successful influencers would be very flexible in their style and speed of delivery. Overall there was a tendency to talk slightly quicker than the average, and what was interesting was that as the number of words per minute increased, the other person heard less; yet they are still able to actually hear more than they would have heard if the person had been speaking at an average rate. It was ironic that when talking faster, the other person could actually hear more (try listening to the speed of commercial radio adverts), yet after a period of time this was likely to irritate the listener.

We also found that such individuals appeared to have a good control of their facility to slow their voice down. This latter aspect seemed to have a positive effect on their audience: when the voice slowed down (which was frequently accompanied by a reduction in volume, the listeners seemed to increase their level of attention.

Volume

In general terms the volume appeared to be just a little louder than was re-quired for the occasion. These individuals would use the full tone of their voice and when their voice did become louder they would often contrast this with a pause or quiet level of speaking.

Intonation

Those people whose voice was naturally deeper than average tended to find it easier to have others listen to them. By contrast, some higher voices are be-lieved to be better at portraying emotion or enthusiasm.

To summarize: the way in which we use our voice can do things that either enhance our message or alternatively detract from what we are trying to com-municate.

Pause for thought

When did you last give somebody some positive feedback?

What was the impact on them?

Do you always follow the above guidelines on giving feedback?

What aspect of your verbal skills in influencing can be improved?

Do you use power words or statements?

Do you need to speak louder in order to command attention?

Question time

IS IT REALLY POSSIBLE TO READ SOMEONE'S THOUGHTS BY STUDYING THEIR BODY LANGUAGE?

Of course it is never really possible to read another person's thoughts, but the really powerful messages regarding how a person feels come from non-verbal communication including tone of voice and body language. We encourage people to look for clusters of body language from, for instance, stance, facial expressions, eye contact etc. It is also significant if we identify that there are inconsistencies between the spoken word and the body language; the body language carries the real feeling.

WHEN DOES INFLUENCING BECOME MANIPULATION?

It is sometimes argued that the techniques of influencing are manipulative. The issue is the context in which techniques are used. If there is an intention to deceive the other person and there is some malicious intent, then indeed the techniques of influencing might be considered manipulative. This is, however, not an approach we advocate: apart from being inherently dishonest, manipulation does not work in the long term—people become wise to the fact they are being manipulated and seek to payback the manipulator.

HOW CAN I PRACTICALLY USE THE EIGHT Ps OF PERSUASION

The eight Ps of persuasion provide a useful framework for use in two ways. Firstly, when preparing for a formal influencing situation such as a presentation to a potential customer or client you can use the eight Ps to give you a structure. Secondly, when in a less formal influencing meeting the eight Ps provides a mental checklist which you can use to ensure that all the key issues have been explored. Although the first and last stages (pleasantries and positive action) tend to be fixed, the other stages are difficult to control in an informal discussion but we should be aware of the importance of dealing with these intervening stages.

193

IS IT ALWAYS POSSIBLE TO GIVE POSITIVE FEEDBACK TO OTHERS?

Unfortunately the word 'feedback' usually has negative connotations. Feedback should be given for the benefit of the receiver, not, as is often the case, as a release for the giver. Even if addressing the subject of a person's weakness, it is possible to identify some strengths or simply to discuss in a positive way how such weaknesses might be overcome in the future. While focused feedback is classified as a secondary competence because it is situational, it is one of the most powerful skills in an influencing context; if you are able to give someone effective feedback, then they will act upon it and you will therefore have influenced them.

Part 4

Confrontation

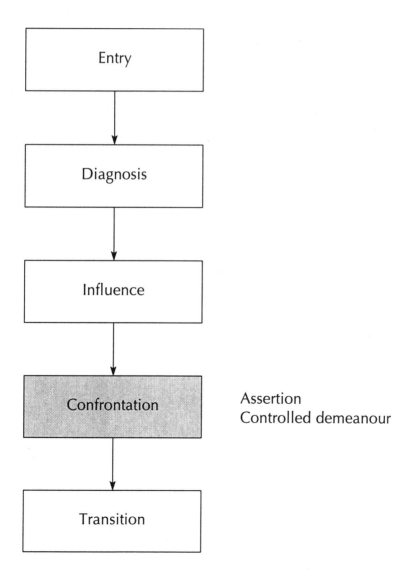

Entry

Diagnosis

Influence

Confrontation

Transition

Assertion
Controlled demeanour

11 Getting to win–win

Chapter objectives

- To explore the notion of assertiveness, primarily as a philosophy of personal responsibility.
- To explore a continuum of behaviour, ranging from passive or submissive, through assertiveness to aggressive, and to examine the consequences of each.
- To explain the steps of assertion and examine the basic techniques of assertion.
- To consider ways of confronting other people and demonstrate how to say 'No' effectively.
- To explore the subject of human emotion, in particular how we can control our own anger and manage situations where others become angry.

So far in the EDICT model we have looked at the first three steps: how to gain effective *entry*, how to use *diagnosis* to explore the situation, and how to *influence* other people.

We will now consider the subject of how to manage the confrontational situations which often occur during the influencing process.

The successful influencers we interviewed as part of our research consistently showed the ability to confront others in an assertive way and to remain calm, displaying controlled demeanour, often when all those around them strained under pressure. When we examined their behaviour under pressure, we discovered that there were some specific techniques which can be taught (and learnt) in a systematic way.

Our practical international experience with thousands of different individuals through the design and delivery of the Power of Personal Influence Programme has shown us that practising the skills and techniques of assertion can in fact result in significant behavioural change, and that such change can be accelerated if combined with mental practice and the use of cognitive techniques such as self-assertion statements.

To begin with we will discuss a range of behaviours positioned on what we will refer to as the assertiveness continuum.

THE ASSERTIVENESS CONTINUUM

What do you think of when you hear the term 'assertiveness'? When we ask this question to groups of managers we often hear comments such as:

'Getting your own way.'
'Being able to say what you think.'
'Standing up for your rights.'
'Staying cool under pressure.'
'The ability to deal with difficult situations.'

All of these definitions are, in part, correct. They refer to the subject of assertiveness, however, primarily from the point of view of the person being assertive. We consider assertiveness to be a philosophy, a way of thinking about oneself and about others which is manifested though our behaviour as well as the use of specific verbal techniques.

The assertive philosophy is about believing in the value of the individuals and also the value of other people. Assertiveness means respecting the rights of both parties in an influencing situation.

It is not about getting your own way every time, nor is it simply a series of techniques providing a way to manipulate others while appearing to be considerate.

Simply put,

Assertiveness is about saying the right things, in the right way at the right time.

Clearly it is easier to achieve one or two out of three in this definition, but getting three out of three is significantly more difficult. This is compounded by the fact that the times when we most need to remain assertive are those when there is a danger of emotion, in particular the emotion of anger, either our own or that of others, overtaking us.

For example, there are many situations where a person does or says something that we may find annoying or strongly disagree with, and we have to decide whether to confront them or not. You may have thought at some time after such an event 'I wish I had told them . . .' or 'I should have said . . .'. But do we actually confront them? Alternatively there may be situations where you do attempt to confront them but either you find that your message becomes confused and weakened, or the whole thing escalates and becomes emotional.

It is interesting, though, to note that everyone has a tendency to react in diffi-cult situations in a particular way across a range of behaviour which we will refer to as the 'assertiveness continuum'.

Figure 11.1 shows the assertiveness continuum as a line of behaviours, with aggressive behaviour at one end and passive behaviour at the other. The mid-point shows the types of behaviour we describe as assertive, and it is in fact the competence of assertion that we believe to be the most appropriate in the majority of influencing situations.

Assertion is the word which describes a range of skills that will tend to result in the following benefits:

- Being honest with yourself and others.
- Saying what you want, need, think, and feel (but not at the expense of others).
- Showing confidence and positive behaviour and being prepared to move towards a workable compromise which respects the rights and needs of both parties.

Before we try to understand the concept of assertiveness, first let us look in more detail at the behaviours at both ends of the continuum.

In order to illustrate the range of behaviours we will describe the extreme examples. It should be recognized that very few people actually operate at the

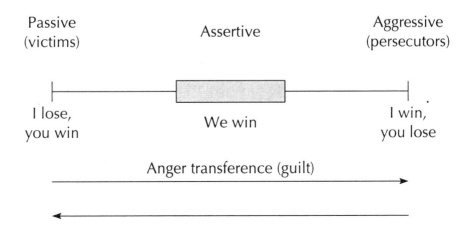

- Frustration
- Being used
- Low self-esteem

- Social isolation
- Others 'paying them back'
- Stress

| Passive (victims) | Assertive | Aggressive (persecutors) |

| I lose, you win | We win | I win, you lose |

Anger transference (guilt)

Figure 11.1   The assertiveness continuum

extremes all the time, and those that are will tend to suffer from social and possibly even serious psychological problems.

When we have described the passive and aggressive extremes and the assertive ideal, we will ask you to consider where you think you sit on the continuum in terms of your normal style for dealing with difficult situations.

Aggressive behaviour

Aggressive behaviour can best be described as an approach which works on the basis that 'I win and you lose'; the rights of the other person are not necessarily recognized and it is assumed that the way to achieve things is to take from others and force them into submission.

People who operate at this extreme of the continuum tend to have learned their predominant behaviours from a very early age. So the child who learned to get what he wanted at an early age by taking from other children would, if successful, learn that such aggressive approaches work. This would be likely to lead him or her to use such approaches throughout later life.

In extremes cases aggressive behaviour is seen in organizations where adult 'bullies' achieve things through the use of force, threats, harassment, coercion, fear, and the intimidation of others. Such people tend to be extremely competitive to the extent that they will always want to play win–lose games, this they will be prepared to do so against not only the competition but also other departments, or even their own colleagues. They do not mind if this is at the expense of their relationships with others.

Such aggressive behaviour can be identified by a range of verbal and non-verbal behaviour. Aggressive people are likely to be preoccupied with themselves and will tend to use very much a telling style in managing others. They will give feedback to others in a judgmental way and are less likely to give constructive advice regarding how things could be improved. They will use sarcasm and cutting one-line comments to put people down such as 'You would say that, wouldn't you . . .?' or 'Yes, but that's only your view' or 'What do you know . . .?' They will also use threats in order to force people to do things, so will tend to use phrases such as 'I'm warning you', 'If you don't do this, then . . .'.

Non-verbal behaviour of aggressive people might include frequent raising of the voice or even shouting, abrupt speech, and extreme sharp hand gestures such as finger pointing and fist clenching. Facially, aggressive people push their chins forward and tend to scowl and frown in a threatening or doubting way, particularly when listening to others presenting their case. They are likely to overemphasize staring at the other person and seek to adopt a dominant sitting or standing position, frequently invading the personal space of the other person.

In many ways these are the primitive behaviours associated with dominance and some of these characteristics are seen in the animal kingdom and in tribal behaviour.

Of course, some people are very successful using this style of behaviour and may find themselves rising to senior positions in organizations.

What do you think the consequences are of such behaviour?

These people tend ultimately to become socially isolated as those around them either consciously or unconsciously keep their distance or decide to combat the aggression with aggression. What is interesting about the response of some people when confronted with the overtly aggressive approach is that they may on the face of it seem to accept this behaviour, but covertly they may seek to 'pay the other person back'. This concept of payback is an important one because although it may be overt, often it is demonstrated in very subtle ways without the person on receiving end even knowing that it is happening. Consider the following storyboard, which is based on an actual meeting from a real organization.

STORYBOARD LONG-TERM PAYBACK

Sarah worked for a major public transport organization and had recently been promoted from a corporate personnel role to a senior management position, heading up one of the operating divisions.

Sarah had been told when she was promoted that the division seemed to be very set in its ways and that part of her role was to encourage a more forward-thinking approach among the managers.

She had recognized right from the start in her new role that there was a considerable amount of underlying tension between the various middle managers she was responsible for. Interestingly she had detected this, not from obvious displays of tension, but from the unnaturally high level of politeness.

In one of the management meetings she decided to turn the meeting over to an organizational development exercise. She decided on what was a potentially high-risk strategy in order to confront some of the blockages. Her approach was to explain that as part of the opening up of communications she wanted each of the ten managers in the room to think of one thing they disliked the most about the person sitting opposite them. She then asked them to stand up and point at this person and verbally tell them what it was they particularly disliked and why.

She felt that by using this type of approach she was likely to get to the real issues or underlying tension.

It was the response of the first manager to speak that was the most telling. He pointed across the room and said 'I remember in 1967 when we were trainees, you lost some of your technical equipment and you borrowed my toolkit. Although you promised to return everything, I never did get everything back, despite asking several times.'

This manager was recounting the story as though it had just happened, despite the fact he was remembering an action from many, many years before, when he was an apprentice.

The fascinating issue here was that the manager had not overtly confronted the aggressor before being pushed to do so through the unusual intervention of Sarah.

If this manager had borne a grudge for all these years, the question this raises is what had he done over this period in order to 'pay him back'?

Payback is the behaviour which we often see when someone feels that they have been dealt with in an aggressive manner by others; and the key point about payback is that it can, as in the case described above, take place over a protracted period of time, with the nature of the payback often being disproportionate to the original issue.

So in the above example, the manager who was aggrieved was likely, over a period of many years, to have paid back the aggressor several times over. And to make matters worse the nature of the payback may well have been through the use of manipulative or covert means; in other words the original aggressor may have been getting paid back· without even knowing it. Such payback might have taken the form of, for instance:

- Spreading rumours through the informal grapevine.
- Adversely influencing his staff.
- Creating situations where he might publicly lose face and credibility.
- Failing to co-operate with requests for help.
- Withholding critical information.

It should be noted that aggressive behaviour can be seen to be further classified as either aggressive manipulative, which is nearer to the centre, or aggressive hostile, which is nearer to the extreme.

In many ways aggressive manipulative behaviour is more difficult to deal with because it is not necessarily obvious to you or to other people that you are under fire from the aggressor. Such behaviour might be characterized by, for example:

- *Loaded questions* Questions which appear to be quite innocuous but which carry a hidden message that is in fact aggressive. For example:

'I find it interesting from a group working perspective that attention levels have dropped since you started your lecture.'

Supposed message—'Lets look at behaviour in groups.'

Real message—'You are boring.'

- *Backhanded compliments* Comments which appear to be encouraging but which carry a message which is far from complimentary. For example:

'I really like your hairstyle—it's much better.'

Supposed message—'You look good.'

Real message—'You used to look awful.'

Often people who operate at the aggressive extreme end of the continuum tend to live their life on the brink of abnormal behaviour. Their extreme competitive nature means they might compete with their own colleagues, staff, friends, and even children. Their behaviour is often driven by insecurity and anxiety and they tend to be possessed by a need constantly to impose themselves and their views on others. The consequence of this is that they are prone to the effects of chronic stress which results from such extreme behaviours.

It may seem from the outside that such people are successful in the obvious sense of getting what they want, because the personal effects of such behaviour are not always obviously seen by outsiders. Ultimately, however, extremely aggressive people are likely, if only privately, to feel lonely, isolated, and stressed. Increasingly they will question the validity of their own existence.

Passive behaviour

In contrast to the behaviour of aggressive people, passive behaviour describes the mindset which says: 'I lose and you win.'

People who operate at this extreme of the continuum always put the rights of others before their own rights. The assumption which people displaying strongly passive behaviour make is that other people are of more value.

Examples of passive behaviour would be:

- Agreeing to give their time to an activity that they are not really committed to.
- Allowing someone to say something about themselves which they feel is unjustified but not challenging them.

- Apologizing to others for taking up their time when they have something to say to them.
- Saying 'Yes' when they really want to say 'No'.
- Making up spurious or tangential excuses for not doing something rather than explaining the real reasons.
- Taking the blame for something which someone else was responsible for.
- Failing to intervene in a group discussion when a decision is being made about something with which they disagree.

It is not difficult to identify people who are at the passive extreme of the assertiveness continuum. They often fail to have their voice heard at meetings; if they dare to try to voice their opinion but other, stronger characters speak louder, then passive people will easily give up and their inner dialogue is likely to say 'Oh, she has a better point to make than me, I could never compete with her. Anyway my views are not that important.'

Verbally, passive people may use roundabout ways of saying anything that may make the other person disagree. Their fear is of offending others and of being drawn into any form of confrontation. As opposed to aggressive people who put other people down, passive people will overtly put themselves down with comments such as 'I do not know much about this but . . .', or in a group discussion, when it comes to their turn to speak they will say 'How could I possibly follow that—my question is going to seem really silly, but what I would like to say is . . .' as though to suggest that they are in no way as important as the other person.

Just as aggressive people will overtly evaluate other people negatively, passive people will negatively evaluate themselves. They will say, for example, 'I am no good at this . . .' or 'I really need to improve my ability to . . .'.

In a similar way, the non-verbal behaviour of passive people might be seen as the opposite of aggressive. They will back away and place themselves in sub-missive positions, often making themselves seem physically smaller. They will look away rather than making direct eye contact and their voice is likely to be hesitant, quiet, and apologetic in tone.

Clearly we are painting the picture of the extreme here, but such people do exist and as with the aggressive style, the passive style is often learned at a very early stage in life. So for young children, passive behaviour may be re-warded by others feeling sympathetic or sorry for them. They learn that the way to get what you want is to opt for the 'sympathy vote', to act helpless and hope that others will seek to save them. And yes, some people will save them and feel sorry for them—up to a point. Eventually, though, the sympathy may turn to pity and loss of respect. It is also worth noting that passive behaviour stems from insecurity and anxiety and leaves the person vulnerable to the predatory behaviour of aggressive individuals. So others, particularly those at the aggressive end of the continuum, will take advantage of their passive be-haviour in order to make sure the passive person does indeed 'lose'.

Interestingly there are some relationships which exist primarily to support one person's aggressive behaviour and the other person's passive behaviour; this has, for example, been observed in boss–subordinate relationships where the boss is primarily motivated by a desire to verbally 'kick the subordinate around', and the subordinate thrives on the fact that he or she is treated in this way because it satisfies a need for confirmation that 'I always lose and things are outside of my control.' While both parties may seem satisfied with this sort of relationship, the false sense of security that it leads to can ultimately result in the isolation of the two people from others.

Ultimately the consequence of passive behaviour is that people will feel used and their self-esteem will be particularly low. When asked how they feel about their lives, they will say they feel 'used'. This should not be a surprise because they are used by those who are happy to take advantage of them. Over long periods of time this can lead to intense frustration and even ill health.

The other danger here is that such passive behaviour will lead to a build up of emotion and anger which is kept hidden from others. Suppressed anger slowly builds into resentment until such a time as there is a spontaneous explo-sion—and then it is not uncommon to witness what we describe as 'anger transference'. This is where the person is no longer able to control his or her feelings and there is a cathartic dumping of emotions onto one person in one situation. Anger transference describes the transfer of anger onto one particu-lar target, usually an easy one and often a different target to the source of the anger; for that reason some psychologists refer to this concept as displace-ment because the anger or frustration is displaced to an innocent party. For example, the manager who, over time, feels a build up of pressure as result of being put upon in a work situation, may transfer his or her anger onto family in a domestic context. Alternatively, the business traveller who has put up with a difficult journey to the other side of the world, having missed trains and been delayed at airports, may on arrival at the destination hotel find that a room has not been booked. This might result in a dramatic explosion of emotion and anger all directed at the receptionist which is totally disproportionate to the given situation.

The skill of the receptionist in this case, of course, is to remain calm under pressure, and we will look at this competence of controlled demeanour later in the chapter. Often the consequence of anger transference is that the individ-ual ultimately feels guilty on a personal level particularly as the anger subsides and they return to their more natural style. As a result of this guilt or discom-fort, they may find themselves engaging in various psychological defence mechanisms like rationalization or atoning; these were described in more de-tail in Chapter 4.

Having discussed the two extremes of the assertiveness continuum, we will now look in detail at the competence of assertion which, in most influencing situations is the preferred option.

Assertive behaviour

In many situations where there is a conflict of interests it is all too easy to be drawn into an emotional and hostile confrontation. Assertive behaviour is about seeking win–win solutions where there is an outcome which both parties accept and believe in, even though both people may approach a situation from different perspectives.

With an assertive approach, however, it is possible to accept and understand the differences without allowing them to destroy the relationship. This clearly calls for a measure of self-control and discipline and we will look at some of the psychological aspects of how it is possible to control one's emotions. Our experience of teaching the skills of assertion, however, have also shown that it is possible to learn both the steps of assertion and the techniques of assertion. By learning the steps and techniques and practising them in real situations, and combining them with the appropriate metacognition, it is possible to bring about real and lasting changes in the ability to be assertive.

Let us now consider the recommended pattern, or steps of assertion when providing an assertive response to another person.

The steps of assertion

The first step is to *show the other person that we are listening and that we understand their point of view*. This does not necessarily mean that we agree with what they have said, more importantly it recognizes their right to say what they think, and acknowledges their need, albeit different from ours.

This step requires the skills of active listening which we discussed in Chapter 6; this means that listening is not enough in itself, we have to show that we are listening.

This is a particularly important step in assertion for those whose natural tendency would be to operate at the more aggressive end of assertiveness continuum; it is important for such people to resist the temptation to jump in straight away with their own views. When the other person is presenting an argument or point of view which you happen to disagree with, maintaining a controlled approach to active listening is admittedly difficult. The danger is that one resorts to a push approach (pushing your own views) rather than a pull approach (identifying their views and working with rather than against their arguments) to influencing.

Only once you have genuinely understood the other person's viewpoint you should move onto the second step of assertiveness. At this point you should *say what you think, need, feel, and want.* This does not mean that you are going to get this; however, it should be seen as your desired outcome.

It may be that due to the use of strong active listening skills you find out that your perspectives are not actually as different as you initially assumed: this can prevent a polarization of attitudes early on and can thus reduce the likelihood of becoming involved in the 'locking of horns' which is commonly associated with conflict situations.

People who are generally at the aggressive end of the continuum usually do not have a difficulty with this step; however, saying what you want and feel is especially important, and potentially more difficult, for those people who are more passively inclined.

Thirdly, having explained what you think and feel, it is then necessary to *say what you want to happen.* It may not be possible for you get this actually to happen; however, it is this third step that forms a basis from which you can seek a workable compromise.

Workable compromise is the key. This means seeking a solution which will satisfy the needs of both parties; it infers that both sides will need to give a little if a win–win is to be achieved. It may be possible for each party to con- cede something and to gain something else, or even better it may be possible to find a solution which neither person had previously considered and which simply results in a gain for everyone concerned.

In the absence of such an approach, one party will perceive themselves as winners with the others seeing themselves as losers, with all the resultant con- sequences.

So in summary the steps of assertion are:

1. Show listening and understanding.
2. Say what you think, feel, need, or want.
3. Say what you want to happen.
4. Search for a workable compromise.

To illustrate how the steps of assertion can work in practice we will take a real work-based example.

STORYBOARD THE STEPS OF ASSERTION

Paul is a team leader of a software engineering team in a high-technology engineering organization and one of his responsibilities is to manage the con- tract software engineers working in his area.

An inherent difficulty in this working relationship is the fact that the contract staff have little real loyalty to the organization; they are on a short, fixed-term contract, earning high rates of pay and then moving onto other organizations. In addition to this they are leading edge experts in their subject and have invaluable expertise which is vital to the success of the project.

Naturally this makes management of the contract engineers more problematic; it is not possible for Paul to rely purely on position power, he has to use his personal influencing skills in order to obtain their co-operation.

Consider the following exchange where Paul uses the steps of assertion in order to manage what might have been a difficult situation. You will notice from the comments against some of his statements that he also uses some of the techniques of assertion which we discuss in more detail later in the chapter.

It is Thursday afternoon, the project is under extreme pressure to deliver against a tight timescale, and Paul has to organize the staffing schedule for the weekend. Jayne is one of the contract engineers in the project team.

> *Jayne* Paul, I was wondering if I could take the day off tomorrow; something has come up which I need to deal with at home.
> *Paul* Ah, Jayne I was just working on the scheduling for the next two weeks and I needed to sort out the shifts for the team. Tell me what exactly is it that you are looking for? (*active listening*)
> *Jayne* Well I just need tomorrow off so I can sort out a few things.
> *Paul* I see . . . mm . . . mm . . . (*active listening*—using pauses, silence, and non-verbal prompts)
> *Jayne* Well if you must know I am having a few problems with my partner and we have agreed to take some time off to really sort ourselves out.
> *Paul* Oh, I see Jayne—I am sorry to hear that you are having a difficult time. I know it can be quite stressful—particularly when you have a busy job—I am sure you know best how to deal with the situation, but if there is anything I can do to help I would be only too pleased. (*active listening*—showing empathy)
> *Jayne* That's very kind of you Paul. The main thing I need is time, to be honest. Can I assume that it would be OK to take tomorrow off. (*broken reccord technique*—Jayne is using the broken record technique to assert her needs; we discuss this technique later on)
> *Paul* No, that will not be possible Jayne; however, I do believe we can come to an arrangement which is good for both of us. I feel that there is a need to draw on all of the team at this stage of the project—in fact to be frank I am under quite some pressure myself, Jayne. (*state what you feel*—Paul is making it clear how he feels about the situation; he has also taken an effective approach to saying no, which is to say the actual word 'no' and to say it up front and early in the discussion. He uses the word 'however' rather than 'but', being careful not to fuel the confrontation with emotionally provocative language. He is also using the technique of

self-disclosure in order to reveal his own circumstances which can help in building the strength of the relationship)

Jayne So you are saying I can't take time off to deal with the problem, Paul?

Paul No, I am not saying that, Jayne—what I am saying is that I want to have the whole team on site tomorrow. It may be possible to make a few hours of time available if we can find some way of getting cover for you. Is there any possibility that you could come in tomorrow for half a day?

Jayne Well I suppose I could, but I really must have the discussion to-morrow before the weekend because we are not together from Saturday on for a week and things are really coming to a head. Would it be possible for me to come in really early and then to leave by ten o'clock?

Paul I'm sure that would be OK if you could find someone from another team who is looking for some overtime who might be able to cover for you. (*workable compromise*—Paul is clearly seeking a workable compromise. He is looking to meet Jayne's needs without weakening his own position with regard to staffing cover over the weekend. He is also placing some responsibility onto Jayne to help resolve the problem)

Jayne Well I guess that is only fair, Paul. As a matter of fact I know that Systems Group have some people who feel a little underutilized—maybe I will have word with Kurt.

In the example above Paul follows the steps of assertion by showing Jayne that he is listening and understands her point of view before stating how he feels, what he wants and working towards a compromise which satisfies the needs of both himself and Jayne.

The true test of assertion is whether the dignity and esteem of both parties is left intact at the end of the day. Paul might have taken an aggressive approach by insisting that Jayne should simply work when he required it, without taking any notice of her own views or feelings. Equally, if he had taken a passive approach and simply accepted Jayne's demand for time off without questioning it, she may have taken advantage of his approach, and his role in managing the project would have been undermined.

We identified in the storyboard that as well as working through the steps of assertion, Paul used certain techniques of assertion. We will now look in more detail at a range of techniques that can be deployed, particularly in confrontational situations where you hold different views from the person you are attempting to influence.

THE TECHNIQUES OF ASSERTION

In Fig. 11.2 we identify nine techniques of assertion and we will discuss these below. One concern that some people raise when discussing the techniques

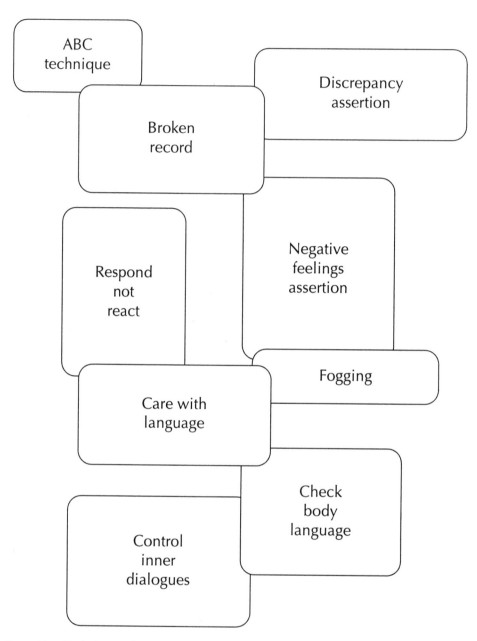

Figure 11.2 Techniques of assertion

of assertion is that it may be possible to define the techniques in theory, but in practice it is difficult to remember them all, and using them can seem rehearsed or artificial.

Well in part we would agree with this argument; it is evidently more difficult to use such techniques in the early stages of learning them. However, by learning and practising these techniques in a systematic way, and by persevering, we have seen managers significantly increase their repertoire of skills when faced with confrontational situations.

Incidentally we have just used one the most powerful techniques of assertion, which we refer to as fogging. This is where, when faced with an argument that you disagree with, you start by agreeing with the other person's point of view, but only in part. You then present your counter-argument. The trick with fogging is that you deflate the impact of the other person's argument by agreeing with them just when they are expecting you to disagree. This has the effect of 'fogging' or limiting the hostility of the interaction; by coming in at a later stage with your own views you are showing that you are not necessarily diametrically opposed in your respective positions, but that you have some areas of agreement and some issues to resolve.

When people are angry they do things which attract attention to themselves, e.g. raising their voice or banging the table. The use of fogging also lowers the temperature by recognizing and legitimizing the angry person's need to be noticed. Having been told 'It's OK to be angry . . .' this starts to dissipate the anger.

From a personal perspective, it is important when facing confrontational situations to control one's *inner dialogues*. We have discussed the concept of inner dialogues in some detail in Chapters 3 and 4.

In the context of confrontational situations it is important first of all to recognize the nature of our inner dialogues. Typically when faced with confrontational situations, inner dialogues tend to be negative. So in the storyboard it would not be unusual for Paul, on realizing the nature of Jayne's request to follow a line of inner dialogue such as:

> 'Oh—here we go again—the staff are always trying to find reason's for not pulling their weight.
> This project is turning out to be a nightmare in terms of administration.
> Jayne is using the sympathy line again—it's strange how everyone has a major personal problem when it comes to working hard.
> And what is more these contractors, they really do try it on—they know they can hold us to ransom.
> I know if I disallow her time off, she will resent it. It will only reflect in her work. And what is more she will tell other people that I am a tyrant.
> I can't seem to win in this job—I've got the customers shouting at me for delivery and the senior management pressing me to control the budget, and the staff who are uncontrollable.'

Notice how in this example of an inner dialogue Paul gradually convinces himself that he is in a situation he is unable to control; this belief in itself is likely to be the cause of significant personal stress. The other characteristic of negative inner dialogues is that they tend to escalate—so the situation appears worse and worse, the more the dialogue continues. Of course, the nature of such a dialogue is largely inaccurate and Paul would be better advised to engage in positive inner dialogues. So he might say:

> 'Jayne must be having a difficult time at the moment. I would like to help her but I must keep momentum going. Generally I have a lot of committed and talented staff—I am sure between us we can pull the project through what is proving to be a challenging time.'

So one of the key techniques in dealing with conflict is to be aware of our inner dialogues and to check whether they are rational. Another important point is to recognize the fact that we can control inner dialogues before, during, and after difficult events.

With regard to the external verbal dialogue it is important to *respond* and *not* simply to *react* on an emotional basis.

The danger with reacting emotionally rather than responding to the actual information provided by the other person is that we tend to make assumptions about their position and views. Often these assumptions are fuelled by misplaced inner dialogues and only serve to polarize positions.

In practice this may require us to count to ten, or one hundred, or one thousand—whatever it takes to give us time to give a measured response rather than a knee-jerk reflex action.

We mentioned in the storyboard that Paul was selective in his use of language: he used the word 'however', which is much less confrontational than 'but'. Taking *care with language* is often a matter of subtlety: consider, for instance the different impact of the following two statements, which are actually intended to convey the same message:

> 'I have called this meeting to discuss the problem I have with you.'
> 'There are a few issues I feel we could usefully discuss.'

The first example could be construed as quite personal and threatening, whereas the second example suggests much more of a joint problem-solving approach. They key point with the use of language in potentially confrontational situations is to think about how the words you select could be construed by the other person; often words and comments which seem quite innocuous to us can be interpreted by others in a very different way.

It is also important when confronting others to *check our body language*. Again there is a danger that facial expressions, gestures, our sitting position or stance, and tone of voice can be interpreted in ways that we did not intend. This becomes a hindrance if it polarizes positions and the skill is to be aware of the messages we are giving out through our body language and to check that they are consistent with our verbal communication. If verbal and non-verbal communication are in conflict, then the other person is intuitively likely to read along the non-verbal channel for the real meaning.

It is no good strictly adhering to the steps of assertion if we get too close and threaten the other person, or alternatively if we draw back and make ourselves insignificant.

Ken and Kate Back in their book *Assertiveness at Work* (1992) identify a number of different types of assertion, some of which are particularly relevant to the influencing situation. They use the term *discrepancy assertion* to describe the assertive technique whereby we point out the differences between what a person is saying and what they are doing; so in the storyboard Paul might use discrepancy assertion in the following way:

> 'Jayne, you said that would be prioritizing more time on Project A; however, I have noticed that you are still spending all of your time on Project B; I wonder how you feel about this?'

Equally, discrepancy assertion is the technique we would use describe the difference between two 'discrepant' messages we are receiving from the same person. So again in the storyboard example, Paul might say:

> 'Jayne, I am a little uncertain as to what you are saying here. First of all you said the problem was a domestic one and then you mentioned that it was really to do with your frustration with the job: could you clarify which is the real issue here?'

Discrepancy assertion is a particularly useful technique to use when the other person is becoming emotional; when they are in an emotional state it is likely that they will hurl lots of different problems at you, some of them genuine and some spurious. Discrepancy assertion helps you distinguish between the emotional and the real issues.

Negative feelings assertion is another technique that is particularly useful when you actually feel yourself becoming emotional. This is where you point out to the other person the effect their behaviour is having on you. So if Jayne is becoming hostile to Paul and he is finding it difficult to control the discussion, he might use negative feelings assertion in the following way:

> 'Jayne, I have to say that when you thump the desk and raise your voice in this way it makes it very difficult for me to concentrate. I do not feel this is helping our discussion. I understand that you may be very angry, and I can understand why; however, just standing there and shouting at me does not help us to move things forward.'

Negative feelings assertion is really a way of, in a figurative sense, holding a mirror up to the other person in order to show them the way they are behaving and to let them know the effect it is having on yourself or on others. Notice also in the above example of negative feelings assertion how Paul states what he feels while also showing some empathy for the way that Jayne may feel. The use of negative feelings assertion is also a way of expressing your feelings without being drawn into an emotional situation.

The *broken record* technique is a simple but effective way of asserting your views to the other person and is the approach of repeating, like a broken record, the key point which you want to be heard and understood by the other person.

This is, in fact, the approach taken by the young child who uses the broken technique to persuade his or her parents to buy an ice-cream; on the fourth or fifth time of asking, having previously had the request declined, the child ultimately wears the parents down until they concede. Often the same sort of approach can be used but in a more subtle way by saying the same thing but with slightly different words.

THE ABC TECHNIQUE

Finally we believe a powerful technique of assertion and one to be used invariably as a last resort when other techniques of assertion do not seem to be working, is the ABC technique for giving powerful feedback to others. The ABC technique works in the following way:

Action	We describe the situation or context of the other person's actions
Behaviour	We then go on to describe the behaviour which we observe
Consequence	Finally we explain the consequences of such behaviour, in other words the action we or others may take if the behaviour does not change.

So in the storyboard, if Jayne was failing to gain any co-operation from Paul despite several attempts to seek time off, she might use the ABC technique in the following way:

'We have been discussing the matter of time off for some time now *(action)* and you have on four separate occasions blocked my requests without making any alternative suggestions *(behaviour)*. If you continue to block any of my attempts to find a way around the problem, then I will have no choice other than to ask the Human Resource Department to transfer me on to another project *(consequence)*.'

The key issue with the ABC technique is that this is not about making threats to try and coerce the other person into doing what you want them to do. In an assertive sense it is about simply stating in a factual way what the consequences will be if the other person fails to change their behaviour, and it should be used as a last resort.

SAYING 'NO' EFFECTIVELY

Another key issue which is frequently the cause of a great deal of stress in people is the inability to say 'No' to others. This is particularly an issue for those who are more passive. They are likely to feel very guilty about saying 'No' to others for fear of offending them. Such people will often go to great trouble to say anything other than 'No' when responding to requests which are made of them. They will, in extreme cases, agree to do things and accept comments from others which they do not really agree with on a personal level.

We have found, when studying the behaviour of those successful influencers, that they tend to be capable of saying 'No' without feeling guilty and without fuelling a confrontation.

The way that they say 'No', however, tends to follow a certain pattern in order to be effective, i.e. for others to accept the 'No' for what it is rather than attempting to come back repeatedly with the same request, with the resultant feelings of guilt.

We summarize the rules for saying 'No' as follows:

1   *Say 'No' and say it early*

This means you should say the actual word 'No' rather than, as is often the case, using any other word. Frequently people will use words or expressions such as 'Maybe . . .', 'Possibly . . .', 'I am not sure . . .', 'Could I get back to you on that . . .?', rather than actually saying 'No' The danger here is that the other person will interpret such responses as meaning that there is an opportunity to come back and make the request again, hoping for a 'Yes'.

Because we tend to listen intently to the first things others say, special care needs to be taken to ensure that the actual word 'No' is said early in your response, rather than tagging it on almost as an afterthought

2   *Care with apologies*

When declining a request from another person it is necessary to be careful not to over-apologize. If you do so, it actually weakens the strength of your argument and implies that you should actually be saying 'Yes'. It also sends out a signal to the other person that if they were to come back at you with their request, you might eventually say 'Yes'.

3 Avoid excessive elaboration

In a similar way it is difficult for others to accept your point of view if you spend too much time elaborating on the reasons why you are unable to do something. This may be seen as excuse making and this is also often inter-preted as meaning that you could be persuaded if the person persists.

4 Offer alternatives

Ultimately it is helpful if, rather than only saying 'No', you are able to offer some alternatives that both parties would be satisfied with. This is about seek-ing a workable compromise and it may be possible to identify options whereby you meet the other person halfway or you identify an option or solu-tion which they had not considered.

Of all our findings this appeared to be the most significant in terms of making the other person accept the refusal.

MAINTAINING CONTROLLED DEMEANOUR

We said that the secondary competence in the confrontation stage of the EDICT model is that of *controlled demeanour*. This is about, in the influencing process, staying cool and calm when we are dealing with others who may be either emotional or even directly aggressive. As a skill it has two components: our ability to deal with other people's anger, as well as our ability to manage our own feelings. The reason that we have designated this as a secondary competence is not because it is any less important than the competence of assertion in dealing with conflict and confrontation, but because it does tend to be more situational. *Controlled demeanour* is required in particularly hostile situations and when emotions, particularly the emotion of anger, come into play.

> Controlled demeanour is he ability to stay controlled when faced with either personal or professional attacks. This means not reacting to provo-cation, but responding in a stable and disciplined manner. Rather than behaving aggressively or passively it is about behaving in an assertive way.

When facing hostility from others, our psychology is such that we are likely to naturally adopt a 'fight' or 'flight' response; in other words we will feel the urge to stand up for our rights and fight in order to protect ourselves, or we will make an instinctive decision that the best route to self-preservation is to es-cape and to avoid the fight. These instincts date back to our prehistoric roots and naturally our actual behaviour has been modified considerably as we have developed; however, it is still possible to observe behaviours which have their roots in the fight and flight response.

A critical skill in influencing is the ability to manage one's own emotion and to keep control; this means sticking to facts and responding to others rather than reacting.

Some people are in jobs where there is a particular need for controlled demeanour because they are in the firing line for attacks from the customer or client; think, for instance, of the hotel receptionist or the airport desk attendant or those in service or customer care. In this sort of role employees are taught how to deal with complaints in such a way that the emotion becomes diffused and the relationship with the customer is maintained. This is quite some skill because it often means not only taking control of one's own emotion but also managing the emotion of the other person. While it may not be possible actually to control the emotion of others, it is possible to use a number of techniques to help them control their own emotion.

The successful influencers who took part in our research displayed strong ability to remain calm when those around them were becoming flustered and emotional; furthermore they also showed an ability to have a calming and placating effect on others when they became emotional.

Internal control

Internally the ability to maintain controlled demeanour is about first of all recognizing the emotion we are starting to experience, and this means being aware of the physiological changes which are taking place and which indicate that such emotions are coming to the fore.

Clearly the signs will be different for each of us, but are likely to include changes such as a rise in temperature, increased heartbeat, and tensing of the muscles. Recognizing the signs, which are really the symptoms of the emotion, is the first step towards identifying the emotion.

Secondly and probably more important is accepting such emotions as our own. This is a critical point in controlled demeanour, because any emotion, particularly anger, is the result of our own thought processes. You may have heard people say things such as 'You made me angry' or 'She upset me': in a sense such statements are maligned. It is not really possible for one person actually to control the emotions of another. Yes, they might do or say something that has an impact on our thinking but ultimately our emotions come from our own thoughts, and therefore it is the individual who is responsible for their own emotions. Recognizing our own role in developing our emotions and subsequently claiming them as our own is the first step towards managing personal anger.

Then there are a number of options regarding how we deal with the emotion. There is no doubt that finding some way of expelling our anger or indeed managing it is a much preferred option to storing it up. All the evidence suggests that by simply storing up anger and hoping it will go away, it actually can turn into resentment and is likely to be expelled in an unmanaged way through, for instance, anger transference or long-term payback or other self-destructive acts

If in a particular situation we have time available to expel our anger through other activity, this can be a cathartic experience. Some people do this through physical activity or indeed some activity which is totally different to the anger-provoking situation. Also it is possible to channel one's energy, which may come from anger, into some other constructive pursuit. For instance, if you are upset by a disappointment with one customer, you might channel your energies into winning other customers.

History is littered with examples of people who have achieved great things due to being driven by anger on a broader scale. Take, for example, the case of Lee Iacocca, who turned Chrysler around driven by the anger he felt having been fired from Ford (Iacocca, 1989). His sole motive was to beat Ford in the marketplace and for Chrysler's part this was a very focused and constructive channelling of anger.

Another powerful approach to dealing with one's own anger is to use social support systems. These might include family, friends, or colleagues who can provide support by way of allowing you to express your feelings. Often simply explaining your feelings to an independent person can help; they need not provide you with a solution or advice, just a 'shoulder to cry on'.

If we are in an anger-provoking situation that is spontaneous, then we may not have the time available to indulge in some of the activities mentioned above. In such circumstances we need to rely on psychological techniques in order to manage such emotion and this means controlling one's inner dialogues. Often the knee-jerk reaction when becoming angry is to generate particularly negative inner dialogues that have little foundation on fact and tend to be based on emotional and sometimes irrational reactions. We need to be aware of our inner dialogues in such situations and to question whether they are well founded.

Some people have described the fact that they are capable of checking and controlling their inner dialogues and that by turning the negative dialogues into positive one's they actually manage their own emotion more effectively. This technique, which we described as the APT technique in Chapter 3 encourages you to become *aware* of negative inner dialogue, *pause*, and *thought select* a more appropriate thought. This seems to support the notion of some early religions that we should pray for our enemies. Clearly if we were to be able to do this it would be difficult to maintain our anger because the changed thinking would change the feeling.

The other psychological technique that can be effective is to put the anger-provoking situation into context. This could mean putting the situation into context with other more important issues: 'This really is not worth getting worked up about—there are more important things in life and this, after all is only a work situation.' Equally, if we can put a particular situation into a time context, this can reduce the immediate stress: 'Well, this may be a major problem right now, and currently I feel pretty angry, but I know that in a couple of weeks I will be able to look back and laugh at the situation.'

Where individuals regularly experience these difficulties of anxiety and anger, it is useful to write down all the things that you are currently worried or angry about and then to hide the list. After a week return to the list, you will probably be struck at how insignificant the issues that were causing your concern now appear. The use of this sort of technique is useful for getting things into perspective.

Another technique which can be powerful in managing our own anger, particularly where the source of the anger can be traced to a particular person, is to engage in 'alibi making'; this is where you consider the other person and internally you attempt to make an excuse for their behaviour. So, for instance, you might say to yourself 'I can understand that he may be acting like this—he may have had a bad day and I know he is under considerable pressure at the moment. I really must not take it personally.' Interestingly this is a technique used in behavioural therapy with children and is really about enabling individuals to change their thinking.

Managing the emotions of others

Clearly managing the anger of others is a significantly different matter to managing one's own anger. However, often the two matters have to be addressed at the same time. Frequently if someone else is angry and it is due to a personal confrontation with you, there is a distinct possibility that you will become angry too.

Managing the anger of the other person could simply mean allowing them to let off steam and vent their anger. This may call for some strong self-discipline because simply allowing someone to show their emotion, particularly when it is directed at you, can be difficult.

When someone else is angry the skills of active listening are particularly important. At a basic level this means shutting up and letting the other person speak; at a more advanced level this means showing empathy and understanding. Of course, we can show empathy without having to agree with the angry person's point of view.

It is important in the early stages to avoid being drawn into an argument. The fogging technique which we discussed above is particularly useful way diffusing some of the emotion. By actually agreeing in part with the other person's point of view, you provide them with what they want: attention. Furthermore you also show that their point of view is being listened to even if you do not agree with the total argument.

In a sense controlled demeanour is about remaining assertive in situations which might otherwise become very emotional; effectively all of the techniques of assertion are important and there is a need to apply judgement in how and when these are applied.

OTHER BEHAVIOURAL STYLES?

In this chapter we have discussed the philosophy of assertiveness as a behaviour and looked at the practical steps and techniques of assertion.

We believe that in most influencing situations it is preferable to adopt an assertive stance. There may, however, be some occasions where it is appropriate to adopt a more aggressive approach or indeed to take a passive position.

> **Pause for thought**
>
> *Consider from your own experience situations of conflict where you have taken firstly an aggressive approach.*
>
> *How does this compare with a passive approach?*
>
> *How appropriate, on reflection, do you feel it was to take the approach that you did?*
>
> *In what circumstances do you feel it is appropriate to take an aggressive approach or a passive approach?*

In reflecting on the above questions you may have identified that there are in fact some situations when a more aggressive or passive approach are appropriate. Clearly if someone is using an overtly aggressive approach in order to intimidate you, then the only way to deal with this effectively is to challenge them.

In organizations there are people who behave like the school bully; they take pleasure from putting certain people, often the easy target, down. Often they will use one-line put-downs such as 'What do you know?' 'Who are you to comment . . .?' Such aggressive approaches need to be met head on and overtly challenged; this does not necessarily mean shouting and becoming emotional, but it could mean a stronger than assertive approach.

It also may be appropriate to take a more aggressive stance if there is a situation where the health or safety of others is at stake. So often safety rules are enforced very powerfully where there is no question that the rules are correct and the transgressor is wrong.

There may also be occasions when it is actually preferable to adopt a passive approach. One thinks particularly of situations where, for instance, you may want to gather more information so that you can come back with a more assertive approach at a later date. Or you may decide to concede on an issue in order to provide psychological credits with another person. This is way of creating a situation where the other person owes you a favour which you may want to call in later on. In a negotiating context a common convention is to make low-cost concessions in order to persuade the other person to give you something that you really want. In an influencing context this could mean giving way on certain issues that you recognize on a personal level to have less value, so that you can actually gain useful concessions from the other person.

To summarize, although we are advocating on an overall basis that the use of assertiveness is probably most appropriate in 80 per cent of occasions, there will be other times when a more aggressive, passive, accommodating, or avoiding approach is more suitable. This requires a high level of personal judgement.

The real skill is in being able to make that judgement at the right time!

REFERENCES

Back, K. and Back, K. with Bates, T. (1982) *Assertiveness at Work*. McGraw-Hill, Maidenhead.

Iacocca, L. (1989) *Talking Straight*, Corgi, London.

QUESTION TIME

HOW DO WE BECOME PASSIVE OR AGGRESSIVE?

In essence we learnt this through a process of conditioning. In other words when we were young we tried a few things out and because they worked we tended to repeat our behaviour. This way we learnt that by either being either passive or aggressive we were likely to get what we wanted. In addition some conditioning was probably related to our gender or even culture.

In a similar way we have a built-in response that we use when we are anxious or frightened; this is sometimes known as the flight or fight response. As a result we tend to act either passively or aggressively.

IS ALL AGGRESSION THE SAME?

The cause may be the same; however, it may show itself as being either aggressive–manipulative or aggressive–hostile. Clearly manipulative behaviour tends to be covert or hidden, as with something like sarcasm, whereas with hostile behaviour the person tends to be more open and direct.

In many ways the aggressive–hostile is easier to deal with because at least you know where it is coming from!

WHAT IS THE BEST WAY TO DEAL WITH 'PUT-DOWNS'?

People who tend to use put-down statements are generally being aggressive manipulative. In principle they do not want to say anything direct but prefer to use sideways or ambiguous comments. The only real way of dealing with such individuals is to put them on the defensive by responding with a request for them to clarify exactly what they mean.

They are probably not going to want to do this, and although this may be difficult for you, it will give the other person a clear message that you are not going to accept that type of behaviour. What we are really saying is that you have to ask them to explain their hidden message publicly; however, take care to be assertive rather than aggressive.

222

HOW CAN YOU DEAL WITH DIFFERENCES THAT GET 'DEADLOCKED'?

Where this happens you could try recapping or summarizing; you may try giving some sort of low-cost concession or alternatively you could introduce constraints or adjourn. Whatever you do, you need to do something that allows each person to reflect on what has happened.

IS ASSERTIVENESS ALWAYS THE RIGHT CHOICE OF BEHAVIOUR?

On a percentage basis assertiveness is probably right in 80 per cent of cases; however, there are always situations where an alternative response is needed. This might be passive, accommodating avoiding or even aggressive, it is only when we find ourselves behaving consistently like this that we need to consider modifying our behaviour.

Part 5

Transition

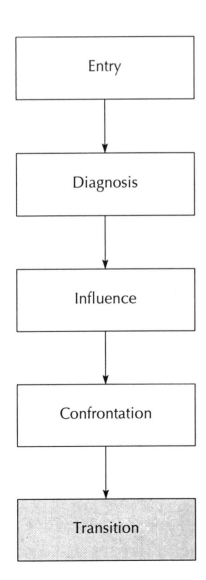

Change orientation
Adaptability
Tenacity

12 Making it happen

Chapter objectives

- To explore the notion of transition as the changing between two states.
- To discuss the secondary competencies of change orientation, adaptability and tenacity which are the critical skills of the *transition* step in the EDICT model of influencing.
- To consider the critical stages which people progress through in managing personal change.
- To discuss the practical issues associated with integrating the competencies of influencing into one's everyday behaviour.
- To review and summarize the key messages of the book.
- To examine specific skills to assist transferring the skills from this book back into your everyday environment.

We have now discussed the key steps of the EDICT model of influencing *entry, diagnosis, influence,* and *confrontation.*

In discussing these key steps we have considered two issues in tandem: the behavioural skills which are required and the cognitive thinking processes which need to be addressed at the same time if you intend to truly improve your ability to influence others.

In this final chapter we will focus in on two separate yet integrated areas. Firstly, we will explore the way individuals pass through clearly defined stages when they have made a commitment to do something different.

Secondly we shall apply the same principles to our own learning, in other words we will explore ways in which you can get the best from this book by planning your own transition to new and improved levels of influencing

EXPLORING ISSUES OF CHANGE

Why is it that some people seem better at managing change than others? Put simply, they have learnt to become more oriented to change; in part this

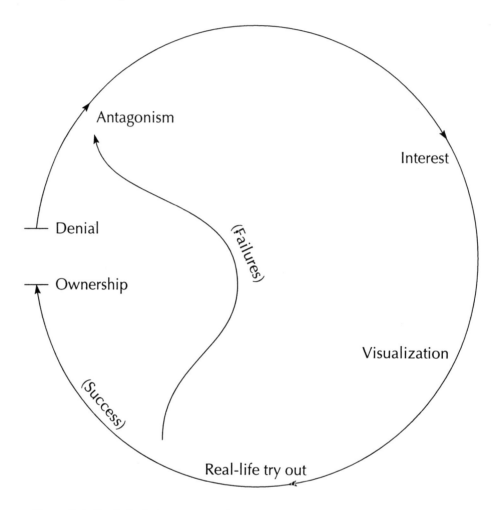

Figure 12.1 Psychological response to change

appears to be an attitude, and in part it is about our understanding and knowledge of the process of managing change.

> *Change orientation* is the ability of a person to understand the process of change and their positive willingness to accept that change is an ongoing and continuous process.

Successful influencers are distinguished by their ability to enjoy change and to accept or even welcome the need continuously to learn new skills, acquire new knowledge, and even adopt new attitudes. But it should be recognized that coping with change, including the consequence of having been influenced, on a psychological level is not a straightforward issue.

A model of the transition of change

There are a number of psychological steps which people tend to progress through as they move towards the acceptance of change. We will consider these steps in the form of a model of the response to change and then look at a worked example of someone resisting the change required in order to make good use of technology.

Figure 12.1 shows a model of the psychological response to change starting with denial. Let us look at this model in some detail so that we can identify the key stages which need to be addressed before real personal change can be effected.

Denial

This is often the initial reaction when someone is presented with an argument for change or new ideas which suggest personal change. This is when, if we are attempting to influence another person, we are greeted with comments such as 'Why change?', 'There is no need for change' and 'That may be fine for someone else but it is not relevant to me.'

Clearly for those with a higher change orientation this may be less of an issue; however, if we are attempting to influence those who are more inclined to resist change, then it is important to recognize the significance of the denial stage. When presenting an argument for personal change it may be appropriate to accept denial as a first reaction rather than to use a forceful pushing approach.

Antagonism

Quite often this reaction of denial will evolve into a kind of antagonism with comments such as 'Why should I do things differently anyway? I have always been quite successful doing things my way in the past', 'What is it with you people always interfering?' Sometimes the antagonism is directed against the idea or subject being discussed, and in more extreme cases it is channelled towards the person attempting to influence the change.

When attempting to influence someone to accept the need for personal change it can be reassuring to know that antagonism is a key stage in the journey towards acceptance and internalization of such change. A good strategy at this stage is to resist personal confrontation but to present arguments for change in as objective way as possible. So if one can provide some examples of others who have made such changes or data regarding the advantages, then this will clearly help.

Interest

It can be fascinating to notice the development from antagonism to the next stage of interest; this is when we are likely to receive hesitant and tentative questions. Often interest is shown without the person making an open declaration of interest or commitment. It would be typical to hear questions such as 'Tell me a little more about how this idea might work?' or 'What benefits do you gain from using this approach?'

At this point as the influencer needs to provide strong arguments in favour of change and again to provide examples and data that the other person can relate to. So if you were attempting to influence your boss to develop a more participative style of management you might at this stage provide some case studies of how other departments or organizations are being managed with some facts regarding the results they are achieving. At this point it is essential to start painting a mental picture of the possible results or outcomes which would be likely if a change was made.

Mental try-out (visualization)

Following interest, comes the stage of mental try-out. This is when the person will start to toy with the idea of change in their head. At the stage of mental try-out you are likely to hear comments such as 'I could see how this might work.' Often the terminology, as suggested in this example, reveals a mental visualisation process, so we hear phases such as 'I see' 'I feel' 'I sense'. This is a necessary precursor to real-life try-out.

Here the influencer needs to continue to build on the picture or vision regarding how things might look in the future if a transition is made. The more we can use language which appeals to one's powers of visualization the better: analogies and examples reinforced with emotive imagery and non-verbal communication will help. At this stage one would reinforce some of the logical arguments which may have been previously presented with more emotion. So, for example, as the other person starts to see how it could be in the future, the influencer might demonstrate enthusiasm and excitement regarding the possibilities—emotions which are likely to be infectious.

Real-life try out

Real-life try-out is where the change is actually effected. And the consequence of the real-life try-out will lead either to success, which will then result in ownership and personal acceptance of the change, or failure, at which point there is likely to be a regression back to the denial stage.

Presented below is a real example of taken from a series of exchanges between two people over the period of just-twenty four hours. During this time Rhian progresses through all five stages of the cycle from denying that computer technology has any place in her life to actually working with a laptop computer.

STORYBOARD   MANAGING PERSONAL CHANGE

Rhian is a successful lawyer working in a legal partnership specializing in family law. She followed a traditional training route into her profession. Martin, her husband, is a self-employed design consultant; he works in a 'new age' organization whereby he has an office at home and communicates through a computer network with a number of like-minded designers who are part of the same strategic alliance.

Martin and Rhian are spending the weekend at home. Martin is setting up an upgraded computer system including a networking facility because he believes this could be a useful way of advertising his services and gathering in useful information for his business.

Rhian is spending most of the time preparing for the forthcoming Christmas holiday. The following exchanges are taken from various discussion held over the period of the weekend.

> *Martin*: It's an amazing thing this Internet—hundreds of networks of computers all linked up around the world. Fifty million people able to communicate with each other all for the price of a local call. I've already managed to find out the movements of the NASA spaceships next week and I've found a great recipe for chile con carne from Mexico.
> *Rhian* I just cannot see the relevance of such a thing to running a business design group. (*denial*) It doesn't particularly help with our Christmas preparations either for that matter. Anyway we all seem to have managed up until now with letters and telephones as a perfectly adequate means of communication. (*antagonism*)
> *Martin* Well you can't deny that computers have helped me in my business; I would have been lost without them. Anyway they estimate that by the year 2005 everyone in the planet will be linked up by computer so I'm getting involved now. Don't you use computers in your business?
> *Rhian* Not really—well there are some computers which the secretaries use but, as for the lawyers, we don't need them. We tend to use our verbal and intellectual skills without needing to much help from the technology. (*more denial*)

Several hours later . . .

> *Martin* This new system really is excellent. I have just sent a whole file to a client using a the telephone line.
> *Rhian* Fine, but I have been dealing with all the Christmas cards, writing them out and trying to work out who we need to send them to. I could really do with some help you know. Anyway, I bet it's costing ten times as much using the phone line with your computer as it would sending the document through the post. All it is really is a toy for playing games

with. And that's the trouble—if the kids see you spending all day playing in front of the screen then they are bound to want to do the same—and that cannot be any good for their education. They will become totally anti-social. (*antagonism*)

Martin   Oh, you're just overreacting. I'll tell you what, why don't I produce labels for our Christmas cards using the database on the computer. I've got all the addresses of the people we need to send one to stored on disk.

Rhian   Well, that would help. It is such a chore having to spend the whole weekend on this job. If you really can produce the labels that would save time. How does the database work then? I didn't even know you kept that sort of information on computer. (*interest*)

Martin   Yes I use the database all the time. It's a kind of sophisticated filing system, except its a lot faster than working with hand-written notes and files.

Rhian   Do you think we would be able to use the same system at work for keeping notes on clients and changes in the law? I could see a database possibly being quite useful if it speeds things up because we have hundreds of hand-written notes and files at the moment. (*mental try-out*)

Martin   Let me show you how it works. We can use the Christmas cards exercise to help you learn it. You'll only take about half an hour to pick up the basics.

Rhian   OK—I'll give it a go . . . but half an hour only. (*real-life try-out*)

While this storyboard summarizes the essence of several conversations which took place over the period of twenty-four hours, it clearly demonstrates that in accepting change there are these key steps to progress through. As the person doing the influencing, it is noteworthy how little pushing Martin actually did. He took a very reactive stance but provided sufficient information to maintain Rhian's interest and then offered to help her through the real-life try-out stage. The key is to be aware that the initial stages of denial and antagonism are natural stages on the route towards acceptance.

(What actually happened with Rhian in the storyboard was she proceeded to purchase her own personal computer and became the partner with special responsibility for systems, having successfully introduced computers to the professional team at work.)

Helping others make the transition

In the above example the progression through the stages in the change process was relatively fast. To move from denial to real life try out in twenty-four hours is, to say the least, unusual. Often we see these stages over a period of months and through a series of meetings. A good example of this is the acceptance of compulsory early retirement by someone who has pursued a very

Recognizing the signs	*Possible responses*
Denial	*Denial*
'It's irrelevant to me.' 'We do not need it.' 'Not yet.' 'They tried it before and it failed.' 'Why me?'	Do not confront the denial head on—it may be better to allow them to go through the denial stage. Agree it may not be for them but keep presenting the advantages and use real evidence from your experience.
Antagonism	*Antagonism*
'You should try and get someone else to do it.' 'Why are you picking on me? 'Its unfair.' 'I've got better things to do.'	Again accept the antagonism for what it is—a necessary stage. Try to help them to keep the matter in perspective, emphasise objectivity, try a take it or leave it approach, occasionally try some 'thrust and parry' counter arguments.
Interest	*Interest*
'How would that work?' 'Tell me more.' 'Why do you suggest this approach?' 'What are the benefits—what about the problems?'	Fuel the interest, reveal a little information at a time, do not 'over-sell', give examples, draw parallels with people/situations/organizations they will respect. Prepare them for mental try-out: 'Could you see yourself . . .?'
Mental try-out	*Mental try-out*
'I could see how this might work . . .' 'If I was to do this then I could imagine that . . .' 'I can picture the situation . . .'	Help them with the process of visualisation, use imagery, pictures, hypothetical examples and metaphors. Describe real situations, use pictures, colours, stories and anecdotes. Suggest real-life try-out.
Real-life try-out	*Real-life try-out*
'Show me how . . .' 'What should I do . . .?' 'Maybe I'll give it a try . . .'	Offer moral support, give ongoing help, consider coaching, offer training, provide counselling.

Table 12.1

active professional career. The initial reaction is often to deny that retirement is imminent, then to display some antagonism towards the employer, and then to start to play with the options which become available such as a second career or increased leisure time. At this stage you will often hear the person talking about what they could do with their new-found freedom—in other words, mental try-out. This is the preamble to actually experimenting with a number of options and ultimate acceptance of a major life change.

It might be argued that helping others to make the transition and ensuring they do actually effect the desired change in a lasting sense is a key aspect of influencing. It is all too easy to reach a situation where the person you are influencing agrees to make a personal change, but there is always a danger this change will not take place on a permanent basis unless they are assisted through the various stages of managing change.

In summary, it may help to consider the questions and strategies shown in Table 12.1.

Applying the model to developing our own skills

You might consider where you are in this model with respect to any personal changes you are looking to effect. Take, for instance, your own approach to developing your own influencing skills. You might have passed through the denial stage when you were saying 'This influencing stuff is OK for other people but I am not sure it is really for me.' You could have reached the stage of interest, saying 'I think there could be something in this subject for me' or even progressed on to the stages of mental try-out or even real-life-try out where you have taken some of the techniques of influencing and started trying them out.

As the model Fig. 12.1 suggests, if your real-life try-out leads to some success, then this is likely to serve as positive reinforcement of the experience and provide motivation to continue to use such approaches again in the future. Of course the converse is true: if you have a negative experience this could inhibit you from using such approaches again in the future. For this reason we would recommend that you attempt to bring about personal change in a gradual, step-by-step way. It is advisable to start by trying out some of the new skills and techniques of influencing in low-risk environments and in situations where you are most likely to be successful. In this way, if you provide yourself with early successes, then you will be inspired to continue to persevere with your new skills.

So far we have explained that a key factor in making a personal transition is one's orientation to change. We have identified the fact that there are a number of stages to pass through in the personal change process and being aware of these stages can help both in terms of encouraging others to make the transition and in guiding oneself through the process, of personal change.

We said at the start of the chapter that our research identified two other secondary competencies as being important to transition. These are the competencies of *adaptability* and *tenacity*.

While it may be the case that some people have a natural strength in these competencies rather than others, it is possible, to explore how these skills can be developed, thus increasing the possibility of making change last.

Being adaptive and sticking to it

Adaptability is about being able and willing to use a flexible range of techniques and skills in different situations.

A critical ability here is being able to recognize when to use certain approaches and techniques and then being able to apply them with discretion.

Occasionally we have encountered individuals who are hopeful that by simply learning the skills of influencing and then practising them in a mechanistic way in every situation, they will develop the power of personal influence.

The fact is that the various people we need to influence in different situations are likely themselves to have a range of different styles, and we need to recognize their style and work with it rather than against it.

Take, for instance, the scenario where you are attempting to persuade a sales director to purchase your services. This person is extremely experienced in the school of life, he has a reputation for being a forceful character and achieving sales targets. The folklore of his organization says that on one occasion he was in London when he heard over the telephone that one of his sales team in the Middle East was having difficulty finalizing the last stages of a major contract with a key client. The story was that he personally got on a plane to the Middle East that day and met the client himself and had closed the deal within twenty-four hours. Now in attempting to actually influence this director to purchase your services, what approach do you feel would be appropriate? It might reasonably be assumed that this is the sort of person who will respond well to you asking for the order and taking a quite forceful approach.

Contrast this, then, with another director in the same organization who, by contrast, is recognized by many as an extremely diplomatic, polite, and politically correct character. He is known for his ability to make good decisions but only after due caution and consideration. He is described as a 'steady hand on the wheel'. Clearly if you were attempting to sell your services to this director, then a rather different approach might be appropriate. This might call for a less forceful approach and more time might be required. You are more likely to be successful by creating a situation where this director responds to your subtle suggestions and hints regarding your expertise rather than pushing yourself in a direct way.

Here the skill is to be adaptable enough to recognize first of all the need for different approaches, and then to use different tactics as appropriate.

Being adaptable means:

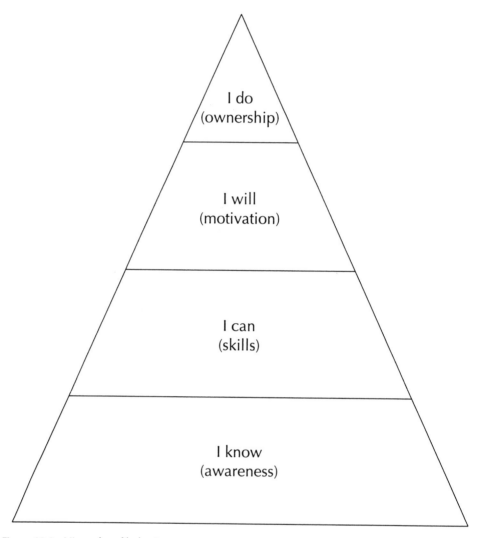

Figure 12.2 Hierarchy of behaviour

- Recognizing the different styles of those you are dealing with.
- Adapting your style of influence accordingly.
- Judging when to take an assertive, passive, or aggressive stance.
- Using terminology familiar to the person and organization you are dealing with.
- Recognizing changes in the mood of the other person and adapting one's own approach as appropriate.

It is these chameleon-like qualities—the ability quickly to adapt to the situation you are faced with—that are increasingly important. Those individuals who are unable to demonstrate this characteristic will find that they are increasingly experiencing problems in influencing others.

Finally we come to the characteristic of *tenacity*, which is one of the single most critical skills in effective influencing. Often it was sheer persistence on the part of the people we researched that allowed them to get what they wanted.

The example given of the sales director above is a real one. This is a director in an organization we have worked with and it is interesting to note how the consultant who eventually sold his services to him achieved a success. The sales director had clearly demonstrated a serious interest in our consultancy services; however, his approach regarding the lead up to his purchase decision was, for us, unusual. Having expressed his interest he left the onus on our consultant to follow up the lead. And then instead of responding to the consultant's calls straight away, he was unavailable for further discussion for some weeks. The consultant then proceeded to make fifteen telephone calls before pinning the sales director down to a meeting at which point the assignment was agreed. Maybe the sales director was testing a quality in the consultant which he particularly valued: tenacity. Even if this was not a deliberate tactic, then it was clearly critical for the consultant that he demonstrated real tenacity by saying 'I am going to just keep at it until I succeed.'

We have found that this quality of tenacity is critical to success in influencing others. Arguably this is not so much a practical skill as a state of mind or attitude, and in this sense it is less trainable. However, for those who have confessed a tendency to give up too easily, we have found that—as with many mental rather than physical skills—real impact can be gained by using self-assertion statements. So a self-assertion statement along the lines of "I enjoy the success which comes from persevering with my goals", if suitably imprinted and reinforced, can lead to a reappraisal of one's self concept as someone who quits easily.

Making motivation matter

Generally when we grow and develop, we pass through four key stages: these are shown in the form of a hierarchy in Fig. 12.2.

Firstly there is the stage of knowledge (*I know*); this is what we get as a result of what we learn, either by reading or being told by others. At this stage we are able to say 'I know about the steps of assertion.' Yet despite this knowledge, there is no guarantee that anything will change or be different.

Secondly we develop specific skills (*I can*). For example 'I now not only know about the steps of assertion, I can use the broken record technique.' However, again just because I can do something it does not mean I am actually going to do it.

Thirdly there is the stage of motivation (*I will*); this step presents the greatest challenge and it is during this point that the competence of tenacity becomes critical. Without such an ability we can be easily distracted or give up as other things overwhelm us.

It is only if we persevere at this level of motivation that we will eventually achieve the highest level of internalized behaviour (*I do*).

This simple yet powerful model suggests the importance of being aware of the stage that one has reached while at the same time recognizing the importance of motivation to the change process. This may apply to someone that we are trying to help through transition, yet is equally true in the development of our personal influencing skills.

Hierarchy of change

Another useful model which illustrates the need for all three secondary competencies in the step of transition is shown in Fig. 12.3. It can be seen that there a number of stages through which you are likely to pass in terms of the process of personal change. This model shows that in making any personal transition there are two key factors. Firstly your awareness of your own abilities, and secondly your actual skill or development level, which we describe as competence.

Before any personal change or transition you may be operating in the lower left box, i.e. in a state of *unconscious incompetence*. You may not even be aware of what you do not know or cannot do. So, for instance, before reading this book, you may not have even been aware that influencing was such a major subject and that there are a number of key concepts and skills to be learned and practised.

This stage of unconscious incompetence, or 'ignorance is bliss' is the normal precursor to the second stage of *conscious incompetence*, which is where you become aware of the sheer volume of knowledge and understanding that you need to acquire in order to become competent. This, incidentally, is the stage at which most people quit the transition process. It is often an easier option to say 'This is not really for me, I was happy as I was, I will leave these skills and abilities to the experts.'

If you do persevere, however, then you will gradually progress to the stage of *conscious competence* which is really about acquiring new skills but being very much aware, even over-conscious, as to how you are using them. When we have seen managers using some of the techniques of influencing for the first time it is noticeable how they will say things like 'This feels awkward' or 'I am very self conscious and feel a little embarrassed.' This is quite understandable, particularly with the subject of influencing, which entails the use of interpersonal skills.

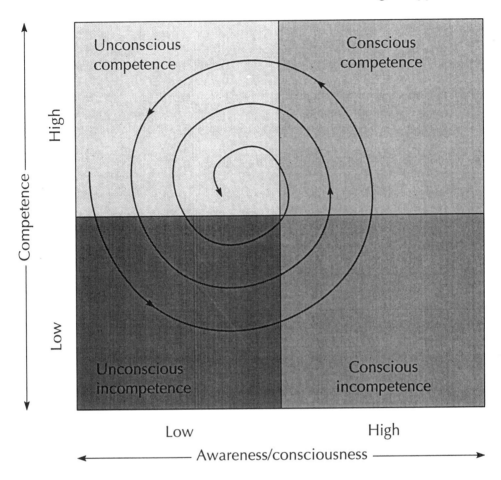

Figure 12.3 Stages of transition

Ultimately though, if you continue to practise the appropriate skills, then you will make the transition through to the stage of *unconscious competence*. This is the point at which you have incorporated the skills into your normal reper- toire of behaviours and are able to influence effectively without even being conscious at every stage of precisely how you are doing it.

A good analogy here is that of learning to drive. The young child might assume that driving a car is easy because she has seen her mother doing it and she made it look easy. Clearly those at the stage of unconscious incompetence do make it look easy. When the adolescent then starts to take driving lessons she realizes the moment she sits behind the steering wheel that it is not such an easy matter. There are a number of issues of sensory motor co-ordination and judgement which come into play. She may learn a number of the skills of driving in a discrete way and the learn to co-ordinate these skills, e.g. learning procedures such as 'Mirror, signal, manoeuvre'. The real transition, though, is likely to take place after she has passed her driving test: eventually she will be using skills without even being aware of it.

The comforting aspect of this model of transition is that one should recognize that the uncomfortable feelings which come from the stage of conscious incompetence and even conscious competence are necessary as one progresses towards unconscious competence.

Understanding the psychology of change and the stages in transition are also important from the point of view of helping others to cope with change and make the transition.

On a cautionary note it should be recognized that if you are to truly make changes in your behaviour, there are a number of people who know you as you were, and they have a vested interest in you staying the same. For you to make changes in your behaviour through the use of influencing skills may come as a surprise to them and they may attempt to resist such change. In this sense the ability to persist with your personal plan for change is critical. Consider the case of Andrew in the storyboard below.

STORYBOARD   THE PASSIVE MANAGER

Andrew is 42 years old, and who holds a senior managerial marketing role in an organization which is an international world leader in the manufacture of kitchen products. His educational background is impressive. He gained his first degree in electrical engineering and a master's in business administration. In addition to this he has attended numerous internal and external training courses. However, he readily admits that most of these were of a technical nature.

He attended a management training programme and his personal goals were to become more assertive, to feel more comfortable in confrontation situations and to learn to say 'No' without feeling guilty.

In many ways Andrew was a model participant. He quickly became involved in all exercises, participated in all group discussions, and his level of involvement and enthusiasm was high. It was clearly discernible how his performance improved during the course of the programme. This was particularly noticeable in the sphere of assertion. Originally he could have been described as timid, yet by the end of the programme he appeared comfortable in telling others what he thought, felt, and needed.

Three years have now elapsed since Andrew attended the programme. During that time the authors have stayed in contact both by telephone and through informal meetings.

Our first meeting was over dinner about three months after completing the programme and we were amazed at the way in which Andrew's behaviour appeared to have regressed to the way it was at the start of the training. Indeed during the course of the meeting we particularly observed that Andrew's conversation was self-deprecating and his style was apologetic.

In addition to this, he behaved in a manner that was at the least passive, at the worst submissive. This was evidenced by the example of how he dealt with payment for the meal. The restaurant was one of the poorest we have experienced and the service was non-existent; Andrew himself, in his conversation with us commented that this was totally unacceptable. When the bill arrived, however, Andrew enthusiastically proceeded to offer his credit card for payment and gave the waiters a healthy tip in cash.

When we challenged him as to why his behavioural change had not been maintained, he was, as might have been expected, suitably apologetic. He provided the following explanation:

> 'Yes I know what I am supposed to do but somehow it just doesn't seem to work like that. It's not that easy, I felt uncomfortable. I found myself behaving in a way that wasn't really me. I felt false; the first time somebody challenged me I simply crumbled. It was easier to stay the way that I was.'

What he seemed to be saying was, I know what to do, I have the skills to do it, yet somehow my thought processes have not caught up with this new image of me. What's more, because my head still doesn't believe it, at the first sign of resistance, it is easier to give up.

We probed some of these issues with him:

> *Authors* When were you first aware that you would have difficulties in using your newly acquired behaviour?
>
> *Andrew* On my way home, I found myself thinking of particular situations and people and I could not see myself being assertive. Somehow it was different from being on the course.
>
> *Authors* In what way different?
>
> *Andrew* Well I didn't know the people, consequently I had no preconceived ideas as to what they would say or do.
>
> *Authors* OK, but I understand that you actually tried to practice the new behaviours. Can you remember what was going through your head at the time?
>
> *Andrew* Not precisely, but I suspect that I was having a negative conversation with myself. I say this because I have a tendency to be like that.
>
> *Authors* What about your self-image, can you see yourself as being assertive?
>
> *Andrew* No, that's precisely the point. I have always been a com-

promiser and fairly passive in my behaviour. I find if I can't see myself
behaving in a certain way then it's hard to try to behave like that.

It was this last answer that seemed to hold the key. What Andrew appeared to
be saying was that his ability to effect personal change was directly linked to
his ability to conceive or visualize himself in the 'transformed' state. In this
sense in order to bring about lasting changes you may need to question your
own self-image at the same time as working at a practical level on the actual
skills and techniques.

SOME THOUGHTS ON CONTINUING SELF-DEVELOPMENT

In this penultimate section we wish to consider three key issues: how to stay
committed to your goals; how to take the initiative; and how to handle mistakes that may happen.

Let us first consider the issue of commitment.

Pause for thought

Reflect on the points below and ask yourself the following questions:

How much do I want to improve my influencing skills?

Specify when you anticipate success will be achieved?

*Write an objective which focuses on one aspect of your influencing skill
that is both specific and measurable.*

You may wish to continue the process of objective setting in order to ensure
you bring about real personal change. Remember to have both long- and
short-term objectives; also when setting objectives, do try to take an aerial
view of your life. Commit yourself not to give up too easily and finally commit
to start making the improvements from this moment onwards.

Secondly, let us think about how you might take the initiative to help you
achieve your goals

Pause for thought

*Consider the following issues in respect of you improving your influencing
skills:*

Who can I contact and ask, that can help me with my development?

Am I really prepared to take risks?

Is there at least one area or competency that I feel strongly about in re-spect of trying to improve my personal skills?

What else can I learn about the subject?

Remember initiative requires taking action. Plan to do something but start now. Do not necessarily go for 100 per cent improvement, settle for 1 per cent for the next 100 days.

Finally, let us consider the issue of how to handle mistakes.

Pause for thought

Think about the following issues in relationship to how you handle mis-takes:

Consider what is the worst thing that could go wrong if you try using these new skills?

Do you make space to allow yourself to reflect of success as well as fail-ure?

When you make a mistake that others get to know about, do you let others know when you put things right?

Making mistakes is a normal part of learning, particularly when one is attempt-ing to make change in a behavioural sense. However, what separates successful people from other, less successful people is their ability to handle mistakes positively. In many ways this is about whether we look at such events as being either problems or opportunities.

When something does not go exactly according to plan, talk to other people about it and try immediately to give yourself a positive experience. Develop personal philosophies that help you cope with such circumstances, e.g. 'Win-ners never quit, quitters never win' or 'If you don't succeed at first try, try and try again.'

In anticipation of the fact that it will not be easy making personal behavioural changes, you might initially try your new skills out in low-risk situations; by this we mean situations where if it does not work exactly as planned, all is not lost.

AND FINALLY

One of the key messages throughout this book, and indeed one of its distin-guishing features, has been the emphasis on the importance of addressing influencing on two levels: the physical and the cognitive.

We have explored a number of practical and cognitive techniques throughout the five steps of the EDICT model.

At the *entry* stage we identified the importance of preparing for the influencing situation, if this is possible.

Preparation should involve trying to anticipate the situation from the other person's point of view, and though preparation can be time consuming, this should be seen as an investment that is likely to pay dividends at a later stage.

Of course, preparation is not possible in all influencing situations; however, even where there is little time to prepare physically it is still beneficial to proceed through some process of mental preparation. This latter point should not be underestimated.

Vital to one's success in any influencing situation is the ability to make an 'impact' in the first few minutes of the interaction. It is critical to consider your verbal, non-verbal, and physical presentation because you do not get a second chance to make a good first impression.

It is also important to spend some time early in the interaction building 'rapport'. This means being able to establish trust quickly and being able to put the other person at ease. But rapport should not simply be positioned at the start of the discussion and then forgotten. Rapport is an ongoing process and there is a need to keep checking throughout the influencing process that the other person is with you.

The *diagnosis* step is to do with diagnosing the viewpoint of the other person. One of the common pitfalls in any influencing situation is that of using a push approach where one attempts to force one's views on the other person without really understanding their position. The key competencies here are listening and questioning.

Listening should be viewed as an active skill whereby you use relevant verbal and non-verbal techniques to help the other person express him or herself. A range of questioning skills should be used with judgement to draw the other person out, keep them on track, and clarify understanding.

The *influence* step is where a high awareness of the non-verbal communication of the other person is called for. But the competence associated with 'body language' is not just about reading and interpreting the body language of the other person, it is also about checking one's own body language to ensure that we are giving out messages which are consistent with what is being said verbally and what is intended.

There are a number of specific skills and techniques associated with this step and we grouped these under the competence of persuasion. Indeed persuasion also means having a structure, or at the very least a checklist regarding the stages of persuasion, which usually are proceeded through in order for the other person to be convinced.

In certain situations it may be necessary to provide the person we are attempting to influence with focused feedback regarding the way they are behaving and the effect it is having. There are also a number of verbal skills which are helpful at this stage.

Many influencing situations, and arguably the most difficult ones, involve some form of *confrontation* and in this step it is important to understand that there are a range of options regarding how confrontation is handled.

Usually a more assertive approach is appropriate because 'assertion' means seeking a 'win–win' solution where the rights of both parties are respected. There may, however, be situations where a more passive or even aggressive approach is called for; the key issue is to be aware of your own normal style and to be aware of which approach you are using.

When managing emotions in confrontation situations, the key competence is that of controlled demeanour—the skill of remaining calm internally when others are becoming flustered and also managing others effectively when they are emotional.

Finally in this chapter we have explored the step of *transition* and have seen that this is a dual step that relates to influencing other people as well as helping with the development of our personal influencing skills. In particular we have recognized the importance of the secondary competencies of change orientation, adaptability, and tenacity. It is interesting to note that of all the competencies, these are the ones that are most linked to our personality. Nevertheless we have seen that it is possible to develop these behaviours and thought processes.

Ultimately in life it is not what you know that matters, but what you do. Consequently, as we conclude this chapter, we hope that you will now take the time and make the necessary commitment to put the ideas that you have learnt into practice; we wish you success as you develop the power of personal influence.

Question time

WHAT IS THE BEST WAY TO HANDLE ANTAGONISM?

There is no simple answer, experience suggests that antagonism needs to be confronted in an assertive, persuasive style. Just remembering that it is a normal, natural process should help you reframe the situation and develop the correct mindset.

CAN THE SECONDARY COMPETENCIES OF TRANSITION REALLY BE LEARNT?

In reality such things as adaptability and tenacity are learnt, albeit early in our lives. However, we feel that although these traits may be formed early on in our lives, such characteristics can be improved through diligence and discipline. In part this may require us to ensure that our self-image is consistent with the behaviour that we are trying to develop. Self-assertion statements can help in this way.

WHAT ARE THE COMMON BARRIERS TO EFFECTIVE CHANGE OR LEARNING?

These include such things as denial, poor listening skills, inability to receive feedback, and failure to plan transfer of new knowledge or skills. Equally there is the issue of others resisting changes we may attempt to make in our behaviour.

WHAT ABOUT LEARNING STYLES?

Of course each of us learns differently; it has been suggested that there are four predominant styles: activist, reflector, theorist, and pragmatist. If we are able to identify the way we learnt, we should seek to exploit opportunities that are consistent with our personal style. For example, if I learn best by reflecting and taking time to consider material, then ideally I should choose training that suits my personal style rather than something that will cause me unnecessary stress.

246

HOW IMPORTANT IS ACTION PLANNING?

Critical: without this change will not happen. Take time to think through the way that you can actually apply your newly acquired knowledge and skills.

Appendix 1
Transfer of learning—research findings summary

The analysis below shows a comparison between three groups of managers who had attended the 'Power of Personal Influence' programme and who were tracked at regular intervals after the training.

The control group were provided with classic skills training which used lectures and role plays to practise the techniques of influencing.

The experimental groups were introduced to the thinking techniques associated with effective influencers and practised these as well as the external skills of influencing; the open group knew they were contributing to the research from the start whereas the blind group did not.

Participants answering 'Yes' to the question 'Are you regularly using the skills that you acquired?'

| | Control group traditional skills training | | Experimental group: combining traditional and cognitive skills training | | | |
| | | | Aware of the fact they were involved in research | | Unaware of the fact they were involved in research | |
Months after training	% answering 'Yes'	% loss of learning	% answering 'Yes'	% loss of learning	% answering 'Yes'	% loss of learning
3	71	29	92	8	80	20
6	49	51	76	24	60	40
9	35	65	56	44	45	55
12	20	80	32	68	35	65

Comparative analysis of reasons for non-transference at 12 months

This shows the reasons given by 34 members of the open experimental group and 13 members of the blind experimental group when they were asked to identify possible reasons for their failure to transfer their learning into permanent changes in behaviour. Managers were asked to tick the reasons which applied to themselves; the first figure shown in each column shows the total number of managers ticking against the column and the second figure shows the number of managers ticking this reason as a percentage of the total surveyed in the open or blind categories.

Reason	Open group	Blind group
Intellectual acceptance, but not really believing it would work for me	18 (53%)	3 (23%)
Negative influence of other people on my attempts	6 (18%)	2 (16%)
Changing behaviour is difficult due to time pressures at work	6 (18%)	3 (23%)
Did not see real opportunities to try things out	6 (18%)	2 (16%)
Reduction or loss of personal motivation	12 (35%)	2 (16%)
Unable to see myself behaving in the way that is needed	9 (27%)	1 (8%)
There was little or no chance to practise the new skills	6 (18%)	1 (8%)
Forgot or did not remember to practise the new skills	8 (24%)	2 (16%)
Fell back into old habits or ways of doing things, or lazy	12 (35%)	4 (31%)
Failed to exploit opportunities for feedback	15 (44%)	5 (39%)
Lack of confidence	—	—
Other reasons	3 (10%)	2 (16%)
	34	13

Appendix 2
Exercise—the EDICT inventory

PURPOSE

To enable you to profile yourself against the primary competencies required for effective influencing and to identify particular areas to focus on for personal development.

INSTRUCTIONS

Work through the 28 questions posed, considering your approach to influencing in one particular context, either work-related or non-work based. This is a forced-choice questionnaire which means you must select an option for each question that you believe best describes you.

1. In the first few minutes of an interaction with a new group of people do you . . .

   A   Find yourself taking a 'back seat' in the discussion?   [ ]

   B   Wait to be brought into the discussion by someone else?   [ ]

   C   Try to find an opportunity to get into the discussion?   [ ]

   D   Explain your position and role early on?   [ ]

2. In a meeting with people you do not know very well, how quickly do you get into discussing the key issues?

   A   Straight away   [ ]

   B   After introduction of the agenda   [ ]

   C   After some initial polite and neutral discussion   [ ]

   D   After a few minutes of 'small talk'   [ ]

3. In influencing situations do you feel you have a clear understanding of what actually motivates and drives the other person?

    A Frequently uncertain of motives   [ ]

    B Sometimes I know what they want but I am not sure why   [ ]

    C Eventually I manage to work it out   [ ]

    D Usually have a clear understanding   [ ]

4. Do you ever find that you lose track of what someone is saying?

    A Often   [ ]

    B Sometimes   [ ]

    C Not very often   [ ]

    D Never   [ ]

5. How easy do you find it to maintain eye contact with others?

    A Conscious of using eye contact to enhance communication   [ ]

    B No problem, it seems to happen naturally   [ ]

    C Sometimes unsure how much eye contact to make   [ ]

    D Feel awkward and uncomfortable   [ ]

6. How do you feel about telling others about your achievements?

    A Prefer not to be seen as 'showing off'   [ ]

    B Only to people I know well   [ ]

    C Sometimes mention achievements   [ ]

    D Often mention my achievements with pride   [ ]

7. If others make requests of you which you are not really committed to, how easy do you find it to decline such requests?

    A I always decline the request and explain why   [ ]

    B Sometimes I explain my position   [ ]

    C Sometimes I give in and regret it later   [ ]

    D I usually go along with the request   [ ]

8. When you first meet someone, do you make a point of using their name?

    A Very rarely   [ ]

    B Not very often   [ ]

    C Frequently   [ ]

    D Occasionally   [ ]

9. How often do you start a discussion by talking about a subject which is not relevant to the agenda?

    A Usually   [ ]

    B Sometimes   [ ]

    C Not very often   [ ]

    D Never   [ ]

10. When you are in an influencing role do you feel the other person is holding back information?

    A Frequently   [ ]

    B Sometimes   [ ]

    C Not normally   [ ]

    D Never   [ ]

11. Do you find it difficult to stay on track in discussions?

    A Frequently   [ ]

    B Sometimes   [ ]

    C Seldom   [ ]

    D Never really a problem   [ ]

12. Do you use facial expressions to convey your feelings?

    A Consciously to emphasize points   [ ]

    B Aware of sometimes doing so   [ ]

    C Not conscious of doing so   [ ]

    D Have been described as 'straight faced' [ ]

13. How often do the objections presented by others take you by surprise?

    A   Never   [ ]

    B   Not too often   [ ]

    C   Sometimes   [ ]

    D   Often   [ ]

14. Do you find yourself making up excuses as to why you are unable to do something?

    A   Never   [ ]

    B   Not too often   [ ]

    C   Sometimes   [ ]

    D   Often   [ ]

15. Do you openly discuss/mention your expertise and relevant experience in discussion with others?

    A   Never   [ ]

    B   Not too often   [ ]

    C   Sometimes   [ ]

    D   Often   [ ]

16. How much do you know about the social and family interests of your business associates/customers/clients?

    A   Quite a lot   [ ]

    B   Some knowledge   [ ]

    C   Little knowledge   [ ]

    D   No real knowledge   [ ]

17. Do you ever leave an influencing situation wishing you had found out more information?

    A   Never   [ ]

    B   Not too often   [ ]

    C   Sometimes   [ ]

    D   Often   [ ]

18. Do you ever agree with the other person without fully understanding what is being said?

    A Frequently   [ ]

    B Sometimes   [ ]

    C Rarely   [ ]

    D Never   [ ]

19. Have others said you talk with your hands?

    A Never   [ ]

    B Rarely   [ ]

    C Sometimes   [ ]

    D Frequently   [ ]

20. Do you nod your head up and down when attempting to infuence others?

    A Yes, I do this consciously   [ ]

    B I believe I do, but not consciously   [ ]

    C Not sure   [ ]

    D No   [ ]

21. When influencing others do you explain your feelings and emotions?

    A Frequently   [ ]

    B Sometimes   [ ]

    C Rarely   [ ]

    D Never   [ ]

22. Do you find yourself mispronouncing names or titles?

    A Frequently   [ ]

    B Sometimes   [ ]

    C Rarely   [ ]

    D Never   [ ]

23. I enjoy small talk and use it to 'break the ice' . . .

   A Very rarely   [ ]

   B Not usually   [ ]

   C Sometimes   [ ]

   D Frequently   [ ]

24. How often does the other person appear confused by your questions?

   A Very rarely   [ ]

   B Not usually   [ ]

   C Sometimes   [ ]

   D Frequently   [ ]

25. Do you ever find that you are talking at the same time as another person?

   A Frequently   [ ]

   B Sometimes   [ ]

   C Rarely   [ ]

   D Never   [ ]

26. Do you try to interpret the body language of other people?

   A Frequently   [ ]

   B Sometimes   [ ]

   C Rarely   [ ]

   D Never   [ ]

27. To what extent do you use logical arguments or emotional arguments when attempting to influence others?

   A Logical   [ ]

   B Emotional   [ ]

   C Not sure   [ ]

   D Logical and emotional   [ ]

28. Do you ever find yourself feeling guilty about turning down the requests that other people make of you?

    A   Frequently   [ ]

    B   Sometimes   [ ]

    C   Rarely   [ ]

    D   Never   [ ]

SCORING AND INTERPRETATION BRIEF

Questions are grouped according to the primary competence they are assessing. Check your answer against each question and circle the score in the relevant column. Then add up the totals for each competence. You can then transfer your score for each competence onto the following bar chart for a visual representation of your influencing skills.

Question	A	B	C	D		
1	0	1	2	3		
8	0	1	2	3		
15	0	1	2	3		
22	0	1	2	3		
Total	+	+	+	=		Impact

Question	A	B	C	D		
2	0	1	2	3		
9	3	2	1	0		
16	3	2	1	0		
23	0	1	2	3		
Total	+	+	+	=		Rapport

Question	A	B	C	D		
3	0	1	2	3		
10	0	1	2	3		
17	3	2	1	0		
24	3	2	1	0		
Total	+	+	+	=		Questioning

Question	A	B	C	D		
4	0	1	2	3		
11	0	1	2	3		
18	0	1	2	3		
25	0	1	2	3		
Total	+	+	+	=		Listening

Question	A	B	C	D		
5	3	2	1	0		
12	3	2	1	0		
19	0	1	2	3		
26	3	2	1	0		
Total	+	+	+	=		Body language

Question	A	B	C	D		
6	0	1	2	3		
13	3	2	1	0		
20	3	2	1	0		
27	3	2	1	0		
Total	+	+	+	=		Persuasion

Question	A	B	C	D		
7	3	2	1	0		
14	3	2	1	0		
21	3	2	1	0		
28	0	1	2	3		
Total	+	+	+	=		Assertion

OVERVIEW OF SCORING ON THE EDICT INVENTORY

Impact	0	1	2	3	4	5	6	7	8	9	10	11	12
Rapport	0	1	2	3	4	5	6	7	8	9	10	11	12
Questioning	0	1	2	3	4	5	6	7	8	9	10	11	12
Listening	0	1	2	3	4	5	6	7	8	9	10	11	12
Body language	0	1	2	3	4	5	6	7	8	9	10	11	12
Persuasion	0	1	2	3	4	5	6	7	8	9	10	11	12
Assertion	0	1	2	3	4	5	6	7	8	9	10	11	12

Appendix 3
Exercise—managing internal change

PURPOSE

To enable you to explore and understand a number of issues related to the subject of thought processes, and to identify ways in which such processes can be improved.

INSTRUCTIONS

Consider the following six key questions about how you think. Use the completed exercise to consider any changes you wish to bring about in your thinking.

1. How much of my self-talk is positive?

| −5 | −4 | −3 | −2 | −1 | +1 | +2 | +3 | +4 | +5 |

Negative   Positive

What is my evidence for this rating?

2. Who have been, or who are the significant 'experts' in my life?

	Positive	Negative
1		
2		
3		
4		
5		

3. What general beliefs do I hold about myself?

Positive	Negative

How or where did I learn these beliefs?

Positive	Negative

4. Specific beliefs related to personal influencing

		Strongly disagree			Strongly agree
(a)	I am always prepared when I need to influence somebody	1	2	3	4
(b)	I nearly always create a good first impression with most people I meet				
(c)	I am quickly able to build trust and closeness with others through social interaction	1	2	3	4
(d)	I am a good listener	1	2	3	4
(e)	I enjoy asking probing questions to get to understand issues	1	2	3	4
(f)	I regularly provide feedback to others about their performance	1	2	3	4
(g)	I am consciously aware of using my body language to reinforce what I say	1	2	3	4
(h)	I am persuasive and influential in most situations	1	2	3	4
(i)	I find it easy to confront others by saying what I want, need, or feel about an issue	1	2	3	4

(j)   I stay calm when others get angry and I   1   2   3   4
        seldom show my annoyance to others

5. How clearly do I see things?

1	2	3	4	5	6	7	8	9	10

Always distorting events   Very clearly

6. How badly do I want to change?

1	2	3	4	5	6	7	8	9	10

Not committed   Highly committed

ACTION PLAN

Bibliography

Alder, H. (1991) Seeing is being: the natural way to success, *Management Decisions*, **29**(1), 25–30.

Alder, H. (1992) A model for personal success, *Management Decisions*, **30**(3), 26–31.

Alder, H. (1994) *Neurolinguistic Programming*, Piatkus, London.

Alder, H. and Whitlam, P. J. (1992) Imagery: its application to training. Paper presented to the 11th International Training and Development Conference, Brussels.

Back, K. and Back, K. with Bates, T. (1992) *Assertiveness at Work*, McGraw-Hill, Maidenhead.

Berne, E. (1968) *The Games People Play*, Penguin, London.

Buzan, T. (1986) *Use Your Memory*, BBC Publications, London.

Calvert, R., *et al.* (1990) *First Find Your Hilltop*, Hutchinson Business, London.

Dubrin, A. J. (1992) *Your Own Worst Enemy*, Amacom, USA.

Fisher, R., Ury, W. and Patton, B. (1982) *Getting to Yes*, Century, London.

Gallwey, W. T. (1976) *The Inner Game of Tennis*, Random House, London.

Hale, R. (1993) *Target Setting*, Kogan Page, London.

Hale, R. (1994) Using the outdoors to develop the competencies of tomorrow. Paper presented to the Strategic Planning Society, London.

Hale, R. with Whitlam, P. J. (1995) *Target Setting and Goal Achievement*, Kogan Page, London.

Handy, C. (1994) *The Empty Raincoat*, Hutchinson, London.

Helius, P. (1984) Developing managers for social change, *Journal of Management Development*, **3**(1).

Heller, R. (1992) *The Superchiefs*, Mercury, London.

261

Honey, P. (1992) *Problem People . . . and how to manage them,* IPM, London.

Honey, P. and Mumford, A. (1983) *The Manual of Learning Styles,* Peter Honey, Maidenhead.

Kamp, D. (1991) *Neuro-Linguistic Programming,* Training & Development.

Kirkpatrick, J. (1967) *Evaluation of Training,* McGraw-Hill, Maidenhead.

Kleinke, C. L. (1990) *Coping with Life Challenges,* Brookes Cole, California.

Kushel, G. (1991) *Effective Thinking for Uncommon Success,* Amacom, USA.

Naisbitt, J. (1994) *Global Paradox,* Nicholas Brealey, London.

Nelson-Jones, R. (1989) *Effective Thinking Skills,* Cassell, London.

Nicklaus, J. (1976) *Golf My Way,* Penguin, Harmondsworth, Middx.

Pease, A. (1981) *Body Language,* Sheldon, London.

Reber, A. S. (1985) *Dictionary of Psychology,* Penguin Reference, Harmondsworth, Middx.

Shone, R. (1984) *Creative Visualisation,* Thorsons, London.

Ury, W. (1991) *Getting Past No,* Century, London.

Wittig, A. F. and Belkin, G. S. (1990) *Introduction to Psychology,* McGraw-Hill, New York.

Index